The Death o~

Walter Johannes Stein

The Death
of Merlin

Arthurian Myth and Alchemy

Floris Books

First published as articles (details at end of book).
First published in volume form in German under the title
Der Tod Merlins. by Philosophisch-Anthroposophischer
Verlag am Goetheanum, Dornach 1984.
This abridged and amended selection
first published in English in 1989 by Floris Books.

Reprinted as a paperback in 1990.

British Library CIP Data available

ISBN 0–86315–113–2

Printed in Great Britain
by Billing & Sons, Worcester

Contents

Foreword

Walter Johannes Stein [1891–1957] was one of the most interesting personalities whom I have known. As a young man he was brought into close contact with the person and work of Rudolf Steiner and throughout his lifetime his strong intellectual faculty was united with the practice of a deep mystical meditation. This gave him a unique intuitive awareness and understanding of the spiritual realities behind the world of phenomena. In addition he possessed an almost encyclopaedic knowledge of many subjects from mathematics, physics and economics to history, art and medicine, all of which he was able to correlate against the background of his intuitive perception.

These words were written by A. P. Shepherd in his preface to *The British — their Psychology and Destiny*, a study rich in aspects of folk-psychology published after Stein's death.

On the Continent less was heard of Stein after he left Germany in 1933 not on account of distance but of growing conflicts within the Anthroposophical Society following Rudolf Steiner's death.

Nevertheless, beyond Stein's death, memory of him lived on as a stimulus to his pupils and friends as well as to those who had known his book on the Grail.★ They remembered him as an outstanding pupil of Rudolf Steiner. Even today, especially in the third generation of this century, individuals in many places are strongly stimulated not only by Stein's works but perhaps even more by the whole life of this pioneer. Their interest lives in the budding potential of his writings and deeds, as if these came from a still productive and ever-striving spirit.

Thus it would appear to be a propitious time to recall this pupil of Rudolf Steiner by means of a selection of partly unpublished works.

★ *The Ninth Century.*

The most important biographical source in English is Stein's 'Memoirs' which form Chapter 1 of this book. He had published them under the title 'Reminiscences of Life' in the periodical *The Present Age* which he founded himself. The memoirs end with an assessment of the changed situation within the Anthroposophical Society after the death of Rudolf Steiner in 1925.*

The year 1924 forms the watershed of Stein's whole biography with regard to both his age, thirty-three, and his development. In this year his inner cognitive endeavours culminate in that 'devotion to the concrete ideas of anthroposophy' which Rudolf Steiner called 'study'. Stein experienced the breakthrough into supersensory experience for which he had been training his faculties very strictly and methodically for many years, as the 'Memoirs' tell. As guide and interpreter of this unusual sphere Rudolf Steiner stood beside his disciple. This is attested by several meditative verses as well as a letter to Stein from Rudolf Steiner, all dating from 1924. Steiner wrote warmly but objectively: 'The fact that you have come to these things [the experiences described] is a good result of the vital way in which you have devoted yourself to concrete ideas of the spiritual world.'

Geographically Stein's life's journey ran roughly from East to West, with three main stages, Vienna, Stuttgart and London. Here a remarkable polarity can be discerned although it does not appear in every detail of the biography.

When the twenty-two year old student of mathematics and physics met Rudolf Steiner for the first time in Vienna in 1913, the latter gave him guidelines for his philosophical studies with special regard to Berkeley and Locke: 'Read the philosophical works of Berkeley who denied the existence of matter,' Steiner said to Stein, 'and of Locke who based everything upon the senses. Then write a theory of cognition for spiritual knowledge, avoiding both these one-sided points of view.'

* Additionally there is a recently published biography by Johannes Tautz, *W. J. Stein, eine Biographie*, which closes a vital gap and provides the foundation which has been lacking up till now for a complete appraisal of Stein and his life work.

What Steiner meant here by 'spiritual knowledge' he explained as follows: 'In the human being are all nine hierarchies, and if we know how, we can research and find the three levels of consciousness and the corresponding three theories of cognition which the first, second and third hierarchies each develop in the human being. That is what you should write, and make it a subject of your thesis.'

Whereas in Vienna under Rudolf Steiner's guidance Stein developed his cognitive powers to penetrate celestial heights, in Stuttgart — according to the accounts of pupils who are still living — the doctor of philosophy became an enthusiastic teacher of German history. Now the work of the individual soul came to the fore, even though in the background something quite different was happening: secondary school courses, the setting up of a Rudolf Steiner archive, and so on. Then finally in London followed a further metamorphosis,* for in addition to continuing with his lecturing Stein became a professional economist and a paramedical practitioner. We form the impression that the dominant feature of this twenty-year phase of Stein's life is his bringing into the earth spiritual impulses kindled by anthroposophy.

It was Daniel Nicol Dunlop (1865–1935), 'this sensitive anthroposophist who sets his sights on far off aims,' as Rudolf Steiner described him, who in June 1933 brought Stein to England after his thirteen years of teaching. Dunlop was General Secretary of the English Anthroposophical Society until his death. He was president of the British Electrical and Allied Manufacturers' Association and of the World Power Conference.† But it was for only two years that this fatherly friend, some twenty-five years older than Stein, could show him the way to set roots in British soil.

Shortly after Dunlop's death Stein was able to fulfil his friend's long-cherished wish for an independent cultural

* This thought comes from Herbert Hahn who composed a beautiful and informative memorial study on the occasion of Stein's death in 1957.

† The World Power Conference met for the first time in 1924 with the aim of bringing together economists and scientists from different countries for constructive co-operation. The Conference developed into a permanent institution, headquarters in London, with forty member countries. In 1933 Dunlop asked Stein to come to Britain to take up a post in research for the World Power Conference.

journal. In the first number of *The Present Age* (December 1935) Stein wrote a notable tribute to Dunlop.

In a letter of 1935 he gives the following picture of Dunlop:

> Mr Dunlop was quiet. He liked to let his plans mature in stillness, to wait long, and at the right psychological and practical moment to put into effect as much as seemed to him possible. I had the good fortune to be 'educated' by him, and he taught me more by his example than by words, more by his goodness than by insistence, more by the ability to wait than by pushing ahead. He would wait and suddenly everything was there, and the others carried out what he had been planning for so long. . . If you did something with Mr Dunlop you felt freer than if you were doing it all on your own.

Following Dunlop's wish Stein took up various studies in economics, geography, geology and other fields and brought together the results in a special number of his periodical under the title 'The Earth as a Basis of World Economy'. His many writers included non-anthroposophists. The comprehensive subject range and the quality of the contributions, and their practical application made this a model periodical. Contributions came from authors like Rom Landau, Jules Sauerwein, Graf Polzer-Hoditz, but most of the articles were by Stein himself.

The Present Age appeared for four years until the outbreak of the Second World War by which time Stein had acquired British nationality. In another respect also 1939 brought a change in Stein's life, for in that year his lifelong friend, Eugen Kolisko, died. Kolisko's path of life also had led through the same places as his own — Vienna, Stuttgart, London — in a clear East-West direction and even further West with a journey across the United States. As a result of this journey Kolisko wrote three articles entitled 'America — Past, Present, Future'. They appeared shortly before his death in the periodical *Modern Mystic* in which Stein also published some notable articles.

Despite these events Stein's bond with his friends remaining on the Continent did not cease. It became more inward.

He wrote of it later:

> It is quite wrong to imagine the 'I' separated from
> other 'I's. The 'I's are interwoven. A great part of one's
> own 'I' is in others and much of others is in oneself.
> At last one realizes that each one of us does not have
> an 'I' which belongs to him alone, but which simply
> distinguishes him from others. As soon as he
> experiences that concretely he can only say: 'Christ in
> the cosmos' and 'I am' are one and the same thing.
> Aware of the differences we are cognizant; aware of the
> union we love. *

During and after the War Stein made many connections
in government circles in Britain, as well as with the Dutch
and Belgian royal families. His biography records the import
of these many connections and about the economic initiatives
towards a threefold social order that arose out of them. The
initiatives however were doomed to still-birth because of the
War.

Herbert Hahn tells about a visit to his old friend in
London:

> When we were able in our long and sincere
> conversations to go deeply into inner problems and
> into questions affecting our time it was with great joy
> that I was able to perceive a further intimate
> transformation not easily put into words. To give an
> indication we might say: what had been more
> Martian in his youth had now turned into a delicately
> flowing Mercurial element. Mildness had become a
> foremost feature of his being.

At an anthroposophical science course in The Hague
Rudolf Steiner described Stein in the following way:

> Dr Stein from his youth onwards has grown into the
> anthroposophical way of thinking and research as a
> matter of course because he had an inner predisposition
> for it. He is an acute thinker and courageously speaks
> about anthroposophy in a manner that reveals his own
> person. I said to him 'because you can master so
> much and can work at it with such mobility of

* Letter from Stein to friends in Germany, in *W. J. Stein/Rudolf Steiner. Doku-
mentation eines wegweisenden Zusammenwirkens,* Dornach 1985.

thought, you will in the future stand faced with
difficult personal tasks of cognition. But you will be
able in addition to all this to give to your listeners
the best of all: the whole of your own humanity.'

In the last eighteen years of his life Stein produced hardly
anything for publication. All the power of 'the whole of his
own humanity' seemed to be poured into the spoken word.
Stein became a rhetorician in the sense of the seven liberal
arts. The range of the subjects of his lectures — there were
up to three hundred in a year — was impressive. Those who
are still alive today speak particularly of his spiritual power
to enkindle his listeners, and at the same time of the calm
professional way in which his being radiated forth. Let us
call another witness to this lecturing activity — the basso
continuo as it were of his third life phase: George Adams,
who often had difficulties with Stein in spiritual matters,
wrote to him in 1949: 'But I value you all the more in my
heart because I see again and again how many people you
help through the way you speak so calmly and matter-of-
factly and yet so lovingly of the most profound facts of
spiritual life. Few of us have that calling.'

At Christmas 1951 Stein sat down once more to write his
memoirs because 'it is a long time ago since I was born on
February 6, 1891 in Vienna, Austria, and I do not know
how long Providence will allow my pilgrimage on earth to
continue.' He only managed five handwritten pages. About
six years later on July 7, 1957 his pilgrimage came to its
temporal end.

In recent years saga and myth motifs have appeared more
and more in literature and in films, and most noticeably in
those concerned with the Grail. But very few of the modern
productions penetrate to the earnestness and depth of those
motifs. Two tendencies can be seen in the way this subject
is treated. The presentation inclines either towards a senti-
mental romanticism or to a trivial sensationalism with a
cynical background. Midway between we may find a type
tailored for juveniles. For some it is 'the terrible war for the

Grail that no one can win,'* for others it is 'the embodiment of what Hitchcock has called the MacGuffin of a detective novel: the mysterious object, the metaphysical Easter egg for which everyone is searching.'†

These facts are symptomatic of three things: first, an inclination towards such material appeals more to a picture-consciousness than to the thinking mind. Such a consciousness held principal importance for an earlier mankind. Secondly, a preference for material from the King Arthur and the Grail sagas, whose unity is called here the Grail stream. Thirdly, the widespread incomprehension of the deeper content of these saga pictures.

From this follow three questions which we can formulate thus: first, what kind of picture-consciousness would correspond with the needs of *modern man* who has meantime reached an intellectual consciousness? Secondly, what can the pictures of the Grail saga give to those who are seeking a *new* picture-consciousness? Thirdly, what does the deeper content of the traditional saga-pictures consist in? Perhaps this book can give some answer to these questions.

The chapters vary in style, partly because they were written over a period of eighteen years, but also because Stein's readers were very varied, sometimes a smaller group with a thorough basic knowledge of anthroposophy, at other times the world-wide readership of *The Present Age*. Different again is the style of the lecture, Chapter 14. Here we can sense much more the speaker's clear warm individuality.

Two or more studies dealing with the same or similar subjects have been deliberately placed beside each other. While some repetition is unavoidable, the different viewpoints present the subject in lively movement. Perhaps today Stein might have said this or that differently, but his own particular mobility in illuminating a subject cannot be displaced either by later research in a particular field, or by subsequent conditions. Stein has the ability to surrender all individual standpoints, to acknowledge the validity of opinions and conclusions each reached from its own stand-

---

* Jacket blurb from *Parsival, or a Knight's Tale*, by Richard Monaco.
† *Der Spiegel*, October 26, 1981.

point, while the thinking that flows through it all is independent. This inner mobility of thought was achieved only by the perseverance and earnestness with which Stein worked at his thinking in preparation for his dissertations. In this connection it would not have been without reason that Rudolf Steiner, when asked what would remain of his work after a thousand years, told Stein: 'The Philosophy of Freedom, for in it everything else is to be found. If you can realize the act of freedom described in it you can find the whole concept of anthroposophy.'*

As long as Rudolf Steiner was still living, Stein went to him with questions. Once he sent him a list with no less than sixty questions on it. Rudolf Steiner loved to be asked, and indeed a question was a prerequisite for him to act or to give advice. Here we see for instance the importance of Marie Steiner's question whether a spiritual movement should not be started in Europe in contradistinction to the Anglo-Saxon Indian Theosophical stream. The fundamental significance of this question is highlighted by the following words of Rudolf Steiner: 'Therewith the possibility was given to me to work in the way that I had in mind. The question was put to me, and I could, according to the spiritual laws, begin to give an answer to such a question.'†
Many of the answers given personally to Stein came to effect in decisive points of his writings and articles. The questions did not arise from sheer curiosity but from the whole seeking human being. Therefore the answers could be absorbed by the whole human being. In this ability to ask is shown Stein's inner connection to the Grail stream. May this book make a contribution to a deeper understanding of this stream which is of such importance for today.

Basel, April 1989   T. H. Meyer

* W. J. Stein/Rudolf Steiner. See footnote on p. 11.
† Quoted by Johanna Mücke, Die Menschenschule, Vol. 16, No. 3, 1942.

1. Memoirs

The great educationalist Rudolf Steiner has indicated an important method of history teaching which avoids the tedious learning of dates by heart. To illustrate the method he used to call two boys out of the class and make them stand one behind the other. He said to the boy behind, 'Put your hands on the shoulders of your comrade who is in front of you.' Then turning to the class he said, 'You see these two. Imagine that the one in front is your playmate, but the boy behind is not; he is the father of the one in front. Now you will understand that the two of them, if they are true to their parts, will be seeing the world in quite different ways, for they belong to different generations. And if I now got a third boy to stand behind these two, you would have father, son, and grandfather, and they together would represent an entire century, for there are three generations in every century.' Then Dr Steiner let the children find how many boys would have to stand in a row in order that their memories — each of them playing his true part — might reach back to Charlemagne. Thus he made clear to the children that we are living thirty-three generations after Charlemagne.

When the children had got used to looking at the course of time and history in this way, he made them do another exercise. The children must keep to their parts; each one must really represent the time and point of view corresponding to the place he had taken. He now bade them describe various aspects of everyday life. For example, he would ask, 'What do you do when you go on a journey?' The boy in front would reply, 'I go by aeroplane or zeppelin'; the second boy, 'I go by train'; the third, 'I have to take the mail-coach.' And then of course there were still slower journeys. With the help of such exercises Dr Steiner contrived to give the children a living idea of time. After a while he went on to something different. He no longer made the boys stand one behind the other, but he let the same child take a jump backward — once, twice, three times — each backward jump to represent a generation. The child was to imagine how the whole picture of the world would change every time he jumped a generation back, or after every three jumps when a whole century had elapsed. Dr Steiner expected the history-teacher to bring this movement to and fro among the centuries and generations to perfection and to be able without embarrassment or hesitation to follow the course of history in this way. And I may recommend this as a valuable exercise to my readers too. I can imagine it developing into a new drawing-room game, as entertaining as it would be instructive.

In this article I shall apply the exercise to my own life, illustrating what the world looked like from the standpoint of the generation I myself belong to, and of the generations that went before and will come after it. This may result in a perspective of some value to 'the Present Age'. The reader need not take my story in any other way than as a stimulus to look back upon his own life in like manner. He will thereby be led to quite other aspects, of greater value perhaps than what I myself can give. Those of my readers who are a little older will perhaps comprise three generations as they look backward, and the youngest may be able to reveal something of the future we are to expect.

I was born on February 6, 1891, at half past five in the morning (as I may mention for the benefit of astrologers), in Vienna. I know the hour from a note in the handwriting of my father which is still in my possession. It is the beginning of a little note-book in which my daily weight was conscientiously recorded. Twenty-nine years later, when my own daughter was born, it did not occur to me to draw up such a table, for to regard the human being from the point of view of weight seems to me unnecessarily materialistic; five pounds of human being conveys nothing to my mind. My father, however, who had grown up amid the materialistic teachings of the nineteenth century, devoted his spare time to the study of natural science, if not of foreign languages (he was a lawyer by profession). He had no use for such ideas as were afterwards to occupy myself, his son, who early reached the conviction that a human being lives not only once but many times, going through repeated lives on

16

earth. Yet a few hours before his death, which was in 1908, my father said to me, 'I should like to be reborn to witness the advances in technical invention and in science. Men will be travelling before long by air as easily as we do by express train.'

The reader will see again from this remark how quickly the world changes from one generation to the next, for while the father still spoke of air-travel as of a future dream of mankind, the son already flies quite as a matter of course, if, for example, he has to lecture in Holland and is speaking on one evening in London and on the next at the Hague or Amsterdam.

I had a brother five years older than myself, who was in every respect like my father and followed in his footsteps in his profession too. My brother was killed as an artillery officer in the First World War, on March 22, 1915, in the Austrian army. Although he died so young, he played a great part in my life. He was an interesting man, whose tendency was to live very fully with the life of his time. My birth was in every respect a disappointment to him. He had been led to expect a very special event, so he imagined it would be a box of chocolates. When it was not, he guessed a new toy, but when it proved to be a little brother, and one too small and helpless for him to play with, he was definitely disappointed, and I much regret having been the cause of this. However, he consoled himself when he discovered that the little brother grew up pretty quickly and became better and better to play with, and thus he soon became an ideal playmate and protector of his younger brother.

The five years that separated us were, to begin with, an immense distance, which, however, grew ever smaller, a piece of arithmetic I leave to the reader to solve. By the time the War broke out we were more or less of an age. Nevertheless, the worlds in which we lived and moved remained very different throughout our lives. Even as a little boy I was mostly interested in technical and mechanical problems. The Dome of St Peter's at Rome interested me not for its beauty, but for the 'catenary' or chain-line used in its construction. I early learned what the line was. A chain suspended between two points makes the same form downward as the dome of St. Peter's does upward. My brother on the other hand was more of an aesthete. Beauty began for him in the midst of everyday utilitarian things, as in the meticulous choice of a suit of clothes or a tie, in his carefully manicured hands, in his impeccable manners — things which the younger brother only gradually learned to value.

Thoroughly modern as he was, my brother had a strong feeling for chivalry; in style and deportment there was something of the medieval knight about him. Gifted by nature, he was an excellent tennis player, rider, and fencer, a good shot with a pistol, and first-class skier and skater. The other games which are customary in this country had scarcely yet been exported to the Continent at the time I am now speaking of. Continental boys at most know football; golf for example was not accessible — not at any rate to the circles in which we moved. Of course my brother also had a number of duels, the results of which were plainly visible in the scars on his face, but the causes — for my tender years — were not told me, so I have nothing to relate on this point. Fighting in every form was his life-element. It was at Przemysl that he met his end. He was in command of a battery. When the fortress fell to the besieging Russians he did not want to be taken prisoner, and having sent away his soldiers he preferred to blow himself up with his guns. Before he did so he completed his diary, put down the date and the hour, signed it, and addressed it to us, his relatives. His closing words were these: 'Thus ends the war for me — the war which others feared and which I have loved.' So he was rather like a knight of the age of chivalry, in whose courageous deeds the joy of overcoming and of learning to command himself were visible. No wonder such a man had enjoyed defending others and waging intellectual battles at the Bar. He was an excellent speaker. Moreover, stimulated by his father, he had learned to speak English fluently, so that already as an undergraduate, at summer vacation schools at Oxford, he was able to lecture in English. He was particularly fond of England.

A lover of life, he danced excellently, was popular with

women, and loved to combine grace with wit and intellect. His ballroom conversation was often profound, as well as being humorous, merry, and topical. Myself, the younger brother, never accompanied him there, for I belonged to the generation whose youth was cut short. At the age when others go to dances and like entertainments, we went out to the war. I never loved nor could have loved war for fighting's sake; nevertheless, as I shall still relate in detail, this war became my friend. It led me out into nature and instructed me in things I should never have learned without it. But I am rushing too far ahead; I should really have continued from my birth.

Like the great majority of people, I can but darkly remember my birth and all that immediately followed. In my earliest memory-picture I see myself standing in the middle of a road on a wooded height, a little insecure on my little legs, faced with the task of crossing the road alone and unaided. The woman who is looking after me has hidden behind the trunk of a tree, and I know for certain that she is there and that she is not my mother. The lady is obviously making an experiment to see how independent the little man has become. I think I should recognize the place if I saw it; I imagine it to be on one of the wooded hills at Baden near Vienna.

Simple as the incident is, it is of great importance in the totality of my life, for at this moment I first became aware of the fact that I was an *I*. The feeling of having to direct my little body alone and unaided across the road gave me this experience in consciousness. I can remember distinctly how different my experience of space was from that of a grown-up person. I did not feel my self in my little body at all, but spread out all around it, and where I felt my self to be was not only not in the body, it was not even near it. I should not be describing this experience did I not know that it represents a process which everyone has undergone in one form or another. The attentive reader will, no doubt, be able to discover the parallel event in his own life — the moment when he first discovered his 'I'. I had the distinct experience of being spread out over the whole surrounding scene. My self included the whole width of the road and, too, the neighbouring trees, including the one behind which my governess was hiding. I still remember the inner feeling of delight it gave me to know that she imagined she was hidden from me, while actually my self was spread out over the space in which she was. She and the tree were within my experience of self, and though the little body down there felt something like fear at being left alone, the true self rejoiced in this fear and in the feeling, 'I am an I,' which went with it. Thenceforward, the dual nature of the Ego-experience stood before my soul.

I cannot emphasize too strongly that the things I am here describing have nothing to do with anything abnormal or pathological. I say that everyone has such experiences, only most people overlook them. They can be recalled by dint of earnest effort. My purpose in relating these things is to help others along the path of recognition and self-knowledge. Biography is only interesting in so far as it is universally human.

From this time onward, then, I knew that every human being is there twice, once in the sphere he senses all around him, the sphere which he embraces with his spatial feeling, and once again within his body. It was many years before I was able philosophically to understand this duel nature of the lower and the higher self in man. Indeed it was not until I was twenty-one years old. Only then did I begin to understand the experiences in consciousness, arising out of the human organization as a whole, which underlie this duel quality of self-experience.

To put it briefly, the reason is that we experience the world and ourselves with several senses, not only with one. In the act of sight, as is well-known, each of our eyes has a different picture. But the two pictures are stereoscopically superimposed and we see the object only once, unless we happen to be squinting. Now the bringing of the two into one is a very complex process. It is as though the right hand were to take hold of the left hand, and by so doing awaken to the experience 'I am an I'. So does the visual picture of the right eye take hold of the visual picture of the left. The superimposing of the two pictures not only results in the familiar principle of stereoscopic vision (judgment of relative distances away from us). More than that: it is primarily responsible for our feeling ourselves at a distance from the world of objects at all; that is to say, for our experience of our self as a separate self. We experience ourselves at the point where the visual rays from the two eyes meet and cross, that is to say, outside our body. But this is only one of the points at which we thus experience the self outside the body. If we take all possible points of the sphere in which the visual axes may meet and cross, we find what the little child experiences directly, namely the sphere of the self enveloping the body at varying distances. It is not a pathological matter but a genuine piece of psychology.

It is our bodily warmth on the other hand which gives us the experience of a self attached to the body. By virtue of the difference in temperature between our body and the other world we experience ourselves once again as distinct from the outer world — as an *I*. In a manner of speaking, the lower self is this ego that lives in the warm blood, while the higher self abides in the aforesaid idealized eye-picture which can reach out to the farthest star. I remember clearly that as a child, when I lay between waking and sleeping and remained conscious while all my inner life was already in the attitude of sleep, I could see my self go out of me; I felt it enveloping me as if it were a second and much smaller starry firmament. Needless to say, it was only at a much later age that I was able thus precisely to analyse and examine the ever-expanding experiences of this consciousness by night, and in the ordinary waking consciousness to submit them to the test of scientific thought. Here once again I affirm that every human being has such experiences, which he can raise into consciousness if he looks for them with enough courage and perseverance. Many children see themselves at night surrounded by animals which puff themselves out until they burst — an experience which is generally accompanied by fear and is not in any way abnormal. Such a phenomenon, when understood, is found to belong to the same realm of experience as the extra-corporeal self above referred to, with the exception that in this form of the phenomenon the emotions (pictured in animal forms) to some extent take the place of the higher self (starry firmament). In ancient star-maps, covered with pictures of animals, we see the relics of such experiences. To understand the transition from the one kind of consciousness to the other, one should not only read but feel and experience Giordano Bruno's book, *On the Expulsion of the Beast from the Starry Heavens*. Children are living in the same world in which philosophers go wandering when they conceive their deepest works. It would be well if we had a greater number of true biographies of children, and I regret that I can only offer my own.

Such experiences of my childhood afterwards made it possible for me to penetrate into the ideas of ancient times about the soul. I could understand, for example, in the light of such experiences, the passage in which Plutarch says, 'In addition to the part of the soul which is submerged in the earthly body, the human being has another and purer part, hovering outside him like a star above his head. This is rightly called his Daimon or Genius; it is the Genius which guides him and which he willingly follows through his life.' This star that illumines our path is ever carried and protected by the Angel-being who guards us throughout life. It is a phenomenon known to every occultist, but differently named by diverse times and peoples. What the Greeks called the *Daimonion* and the Romans *Genius*, the Christian Church called *Angel*. In most of the great religions the knowledge of the star has been preserved, and it is even called a star. This is the origin of Zarathustra's name, for *Zoroaster*, or Zerdutch as it is in Persian, means 'living and radiant star'. Zarathustra was so called because the star which is there in every human being was present in his case in a unique and high degree.

The star is the focus of activity towards which the forces of the surrounding sphere are tending, and from whence we constantly enspirit our corporeal nature. In the vision of the three Wise Men of the East who seek for the new-born Child and at length see the star stand still above a hut or tabernacle, we have a simple description of what is always there when a human being is born into the world. Whenever and wherever on the earth a child is born, the star of the higher self comes to rest over the tabernacle of the body. It is the power of the soul itself, which is body-free and does not ever become organically bound. In the Jesus Child, of course, the star was visible in a unique radiance.

The moment in which the human being experiences himself for the first time as an *I* is as a rule the moment to which memory reaches back. So it was at any rate in my case, as above related. My first memory of my mother belongs evidently to a much later time. We were travelling by train and had got out at a small station. I think it must have been one of the surburban railways of Vienna. It was dark and I was sleeping in my mother's lap. The train rushed into the station and we had to get in. My head was in my mother's lap and she was obliged to awaken me. She did it so tenderly and gently that her lovingness rather than the actual fact of being awakened entered my consciousness. It was the picture of 'the woman full of love, who is awakening me' that remained before the little child's soul as 'mother', and this became a lasting memory-picture for the rest of life.

My father I remember as a man of active, happy temperament, teaching me to be thankful for the gift of life. I see him walking beside me through one of the numerous parks or gardens of Vienna; I do not know if it was the Stadtpark or Rathauspark or the Volksgarten, or some other one. It was at the close of a hot summer's day, and a cool evening breeze suddenly came upon us. My father stopped and took a deep breath and I imitated him. He raised his finger as if to admonish me, and though he said nothing there was an entire lesson in his gesture. This is not my first memory of my father, but it is the one that generally comes to me when I think of him. Reverence for the divine in all life and in all nature was what he conveyed to me.

As to my brother, my first important impression seems to be of myself biting him in the arm. We had probably been quarrelling. All I know now is that the thing I had done gave me an awful shock, and that I vowed to myself there and then, come what might, I should never again be unkind to him in future. I think this is the first promise I ever made to myself, and I may say I kept it faithfully until his death during the War.

I am relating all these experiences of my childhood not because they seem important to me as my own experiences;

23

I do not think my own life any more important to relate than that of any other person. I relate them because they are typical experiences such as every human being undergoes, though every one in a different way. Being of universal human significance, they may serve as illustrations. My own childhood belongs to the epoch when nineteenth-century materialism was drawing to its close, and the first indications were already there of the awakening spiritual epoch into which we are now going forward. Such a life as mine, by way of an example, may therefore throw light upon this epoch, and the choice of my own life is justified inasmuch as one can speak of oneself with far less reserve than of others. The birth of what we are here describing as the 'Present Age' may therefore be characterized by means of an individual biography.

My education was on Christian lines; I grew up in the ideas of Christianity. I remember a nursery governess who was with us for a few years and who assigned to us children the parts we were to play in little fancy-dress tableaux or plays. I recall among others the fairy-tale of the 'Frog King', where the princess loses her golden ball in the well. Another picture, too, made a deep impression on me. I was supposed to be a little boy lying asleep in the grass. Signposts of green paper had been spread about to indicate the grass. A dangerous snake — we had cut it out in cardboard with much care and painted it in dreadful colours — was creeping near the boy. Behind him, however, there stood a white angel with a golden star above her head, who with outstretched hand and wings protected the little boy. In many situations in after life, the picture which had imprinted itself so deeply in my childlike soul did me the service it had been meant to illustrate. I was perhaps seven years old when this picture was impressed upon me in a simple nursery game, and it was fully fourteen years before I understood what it represented. That is another experience, to understand which is of universal import. The things we see in pictures in our childhood are in later life transformed into real powers — into the power to walk truly on the path of life. An hour or two spent in a happy children's game — the meaning of it is far more than this. How many people are aware of such things today, and give their children what they really need?

My father was a Hungarian, born in Hungary. He had come to Vienna as a young undergraduate and was afterwards naturalized as an Austrian citizen. Vienna at that time looked very different from what it does today. Where the Ringstrasse now encompasses the inner city like a belt, there were open fields, an immense parade-ground for the military. Important buildings, such as the Parliament House and the Rathaus or Town Hall, were not yet there. When my father told me these things as a child, I got the picture in my mind that cities too are living, growing beings, which perhaps too will die when their time comes — beings, at any rate, with a history all their own.

My father did not speak the Vienna dialect, but a correct and scholarly German. My mother, on the other hand, had the light and pleasant intonation of the Viennese in her whole way of speaking. We children therefore learned a mixture of the two. My father was deeply interested in languages and was an authorized interpreter in German, English, French, Italian, and Hungarian, all of which he spoke uniformly well. He also had an adequate knowledge of Latin and Greek and enough Spanish to be able now and then to hold a brief where a knowledge of Spanish was needed. Once in Italy I heard him speak in the vernacular with a coachman who, being a little tipsy, was driving us into the sea instead of along the straight road. My father spoke with such exactitude that the good man became quite sobered, and asked with some surprise where he had learned to swear so well in the native tongue. I have no doubt he had got it all from books during his studies! When he came home of an evening I often found him quite early on his sofa or even in bed, surrounded by huge tomes — the well-known dictionaries of Sachs-Villatte, Muret-Sanders, and others, piled on the floor within reach of his hand. So he lay there, learning more languages. He was also interested in languages generally, studied the etymological derivations of words, and was especially glad when he got back to Sanskrit. Travelling by train one day he fell into conversation with a man unknown to him. Conversation presently turned upon the French language, and the stranger remarked that the derivation of the word *fregolité* was unknown to him. The word means something like nimbleness or sleight of hand. My father said, 'You will not find it by the pure study of languages. If you have never heard of the great quick-change artist Fregoli, who could change characters on the stage with amazing rapidity, you also cannot know the derivation of *fregolité* from the proper name Fregoli.' '*Herzlichen Dank*,' said the stranger. 'That is the only word that had stumped me in the whole French language. I am the editor of the big Sachs-Villatte dictionary.'

My father occupied himself in this way with the general theory of language, and it was of no little importance for me to find in his extensive library such books as that of Lazarus Geiger, *Human Language and Reason*. Though he died too early to have any essential influence on the direction of my thought in scientific and philosophic matters, my father did all he could to give my brother and me the best possible education. He used to say, 'When I die you will inherit nothing, but on our travels you will have seen many important parts of the world, and with the best teachers to inspire you, you will have learned to derive true benefit from what you see.' And so it was when in 1908 he died. We had been to a first-class school, we had the best tutors at home in music and other subjects, and we travelled every holiday. Father himself nearly always spent his holidays in England and I can still recall his laughter when he told us how his telegram, 'Splendid passage, hotel splendid,' misled his office staff at home to re-address his letters, 'Splendid Passage Hotel Splendid London.' He loved both the country and the language, and there was probably no English poet or historian of significance who was not represented on his shelves.

I will pass over my earliest years at school — elementary school, that is to say — and come to things of more general interest, for my purpose in writing is to characterize the time in which we lived. Though our religion was Protestant, and religion lessons were given to me by the pastor of the evangelical congregation, I went to a Catholic school where the teachers were without exception Benedictine monks of the famous *Schotten* or Scots Foundation. The *Schottengymna-*

sium (*Gymnasium* is a classical or grammar school) is a venerable institution with very ancient traditions. It is conducted by the 'Scottish' monks, whose predecessors came to Vienna long ago from the Regensburg monastery, and had originally come to Regensburg from Scotland. Monks though they were, the instruction they gave was broad-minded and tolerant. I had occasion to hear both the Protestant pastor and the Benedictine monks speaking of Luther and his time. The difference was that the pastor was telling us the history of princes and the Benedictine monk the history of the larger world. Protestantism in effect had been supported by the princes of small German States; Roman Catholicism by the Emperor.

The teaching of history in the *Schottengymnasium* was on large lines and very stimulating. In spite of individual differences the men who gave it had this in common: they tried to give not only a sound description of historic facts, but a sufficiency of detail for truly living pictures to emerge. Emperors, scholars, popes, or reformers — we were enabled to see the characters of history as men of flesh and blood before us; we learned to know the way they lived and moved, their spiritual heritage, their characters as individuals. One of our two history teachers, I admit, seemed to feel that as a scholar he must make some apology whenever he was about to give a vivid description of some human being in this way. He used to say he was about to tell us, not history (*Geschichte*), but a 'little history' or story — *G'schichterl*, as the diminutive is in the Austrian dialect. Nevertheless his history lessons worked upon us so deeply that one day I felt inspired to go down into the tomb of Heinrich Jasomirgott, founder of the *Schotten* Church, who lies buried in the crypt beneath. As a memento for all time I took a leaf from the wreath on his tomb, and in a mood of infinite reverence brought it up with me to the light of day. In my childlike soul I felt eternal thankfulness to the man to whom we owed what we were learning. This prince's name is derived from the saying, '*Ja, so mir Gott helfen wolle*' — 'Yes, so help me God' — whence he was called, *Jasomirgott*. The very name had a strange and mysterious sound in our ears. How often must he have uttered it and how profoundly have believed in it!

Not that I learned very much history at this time of my life, but I did receive very deep impressions of a historical kind. My teachers did not think me a very talented child, and they were right, no doubt, for I was one of those who awaken late in life and undergo later what others go through at a much earlier stage. Nevertheless my examination essay, which was on a historical subject, bore witness to more knowledge than my history teacher had thought possible — as he himself subsequently told my mother. It was a rather special subject which he gave us for this essay. We were to show how the spirit of ancient Greece appears again and is carried further in the modern German people. In five hours I wrote about eighty pages on this subject. 'Germany, the Greece of Modern Time,' was the title — undoubtedly a subject to call forth rather unusual trains of thought. It reflects the inspiration of a distinguished man who had had a certain influence on the spirit of the *Schottengymnasium*, an influence which was still working there, though we no longer saw the man, for we belonged to a later generation. I refer to Karl Julius Schröer. He became famous as editor of the complete works of Goethe, and in his later life, like the librarian of the *Schotten* Foundation, Vincent Knauer, he had been Rudolf Steiner's teacher.

Reading Karl Julius Schröer's history of German literature,* we find him perpetually returning to this theme that German literature is a continuation of the Greek. He says, among other things: 'When we compare Germany as a whole with ancient Greece and the modern German states with those of Greece, we find a great likeness between Austria and Macedonia. We see the fair task of Austria thus illustrated: it is to scatter throughout the East the seed of Western culture.' Or, to quote another passage: 'Our literature is our Olympus. There live our immortal gods and heroes, the high ideals of our dreaming folkspirit; and, most important of all, in this realm the Germans, split up as they are into countless little nations, become one great people, equal to the

* *Geschichte der deutschen Literatur.*

28

greatest.' 'In literature and art the German people, divided as they are in politics, have found the soil wherein they grow conscious of their unity and live a great and noble life in common. But the modern German nation is not as isolated as were the Greeks of ancient time; rather does it live one life in common with the other nations of Europe and is building upon a common edifice with them.'

There are many other sayings of this kind, the most important of which I reprinted in my new edition of Schröer's edition of Goethe's *Faust* at the twenty-fifth anniversary of Schröer's death. Schröer had the cultural, not the political life, in view when he said these things. It was in the former field that he saw the essential task of the German people, and he saw it in connection with all European nations. He only took his prototypes from the age of classical antiquity.

The continued influence of Schröer's ideas in the *Schottengymnasium* was largely due to a man whom I knew well by sight, though he was no longer my teacher. His name was Hugo Mareta, and he still taught my brother. His whole life was devoted to German literature and he loved Goethe especially. On one occasion another teacher had Goethe's bust removed from the top form room, thinking, no doubt, that Goethe's life was not a very good example for young people. The aged Mareta, with great bodily exertion, carried the heavy bust again into the classroom, thus giving public expression to the difference of outlook which was to have been kept hidden from the pupils. This time the bust remained, and one may gather that the Goethean spirit continued to work there for a while. At any rate, it was still living when I went through the form five years later.

The life of the *Schottengymnasium* undoubtedly spread its influence into many countries. After the War, when the old Austria-Hungary was dismembered, Austrians especially were scattered far and wide. In the small fragment that remained there was no more room for many who had been brought up to play their part in a far larger country. Many of my friends from school — nearly all of them, indeed — were led by destiny abroad. My friend, Eugen Kolisko, who has now also come to England, was beside me at the *Gymnasium* for many a year. His elder brother and mine had also been friends at the same school; it was they who told us of the Battle of the Bust.

Austria has experienced many tragic destinies and this does not yet seem to be at an end. But the exposed international position of the country and its rather chaotic internal conditions — including, as it did, no less than thirteen different nations — made Austria a fitting school for outstanding individualities, who with the natural kindliness and fluidity of the Austrian temperament developed a rather world-wide range of vision, tending to lead them far afield. Such was the case for example, with Rudolf Steiner, and so it was with Karl Julius Schröer, who — in the spirit, at least — looked out over wide regions of the earth. Schröer's was a strange destiny, though I can only briefly touch upon it here. He was a professor at the Technical College of Vienna. His subject, however, was not a technical one; it was German literature. The Technical College at the time still included rhetoric among its normal subjects; rhetoric was deemed essential to a liberal education. This chair was held by Schröer, and he had to lecture under this title. But the rather medieval subject had no particular importance for engineering students, nor was German literature among the things they would be examined on. It came at length to this, that in Schröer's lectures only two students were present, one of whom after a time remained away. The one who was left was Rudolf Steiner. One might say that Austria had prolonged a medieval institution in order that a great individuality — one of her greatest sons, indeed, namely Rudolf Steiner — might have a great man as his teacher. In spite of the dwindling audience, therefore, it was not for nothing; it was for the benefit of one individual case, provided for, it is true, not by the wisdom of the educational authorities, but by destiny alone — the cosmic Ministry of Education. Schröer's influence, however, did extend to wider circles; he wrote important books, and his lectures in other quarters were well attended. His spirit continued to work, and at long last it indirectly reached all those who were destined at a much later time to meet Rudolf Steiner.

Vienna has always been a place for great individualities as teachers. They could prosper there because Austria was alive to the spiritual fertility of exceptional, even eccentric people. Dr Steiner valued this quality of his home country; he remarked on one occasion that Austria was the country where pedantry was always mitigated by *Schlamperei* — an untranslatable Austrian word, meaning a rather amiable lack of efficiency, 'go-as-you-please,' letting things take their course.

Another exceptional person was Gustav von Escherich, who introduced me to mathematical science. He never would believe that women could understand anything of mathematics. At the beginning of the term he would stand at his desk, counting the girl students with his finger, one by one. 'Ladies,' he said, 'what are you thinking of? There are no such professions for you. You should study something else, not mathematics.' Thereupon he gave one or two extremely stiff lectures. The third lecture would suddenly be easy, and he was highly pleased if by that time he had frightened off the great majority of his feminine audience. An excellent teacher of mathematics, he began lecturing at 7 o'clock in the morning, which gave me the opportunity of attending his lectures while I was still at the *Gymnasium* — long before I was really qualified to attend university lectures. Lessons at school did not begin till 8 o'clock. As I came regularly to his lectures I attracted the old gentleman's attention, and he occasionally called me to the board to work out some problem. I owe very much to his friendship.

One of my tutors at home was a lecturer from the Technical College. He often took me with him to the engineering laboratories, where one of his tasks was to examine the strength of materials — rails, for example, that had been the cause of railway accidents. My visits to his laboratory were of no little importance in the development of my world-outlook, for it was there that my materialism was first shaken. My tutor was making researches into the influence of the form of materials upon their strength. For the first time I learned that a material can even be made stronger by taking away some of the matter. A rectangular plate of glass, for example, will under certain conditions carry more weight if two semicircles have been cut out of it on either side. Such experiments brought me to the conviction that it is form and not matter which supports us, and from which we receive the sense-impressions we sum up as 'the material world'. It was a little after this that I learned through Vincent Knauer the significance of the terms *form* and *matter* in Aristotelian philosophy, and I became increasingly alive to the universal import of these two ideas.

I had thus come to an essential turning-point in the development of my world-outlook. And at this moment — when applied science itself, engineering in effect, was responsible for planting in my mind the first seeds of doubt in the materialistic world-conception — my father died. He died of diabetes. He had been following with scientific interest the courage of his fatal illness, being, of course, well aware of what was in store for him. The modern treatment, insulin, was not yet available. My father was treated by the greatest living authority on diabetes and he had many conversations on medical and scientific subjects with the distinguished professor and his assistants.

Medicine had always greatly interested my father. He subscribed to a number of medical journals, and as a boy I sometimes read an article in one or other of them. He had a not inconsiderable medical library. I often read a few pages in Hyrtl's *Anatomie* and marvelled at the contents of this book, extending as it did far beyond pure anatomy. We had a family doctor who had been with us for a long time and who never left me when I was a boy without saying, 'Do not forget, you are going to be a doctor.' I have not become a doctor, yet I have become acquainted pretty closely with most aspects of medicine.

The first doctor I can remember was the originator of psychoanalysis. I refer to Dr Breuer. He was called to our house because I was dangerously ill and the illness could not be diagnosed. Dr Breuer, having examined me, said, 'The boy needs meat. Give him ham. If he does not go off altogether, a meat diet will make him better.' I thought this a splendid idea and I preferred to get better; whether it was the ham that did it, I do not know. I call Breuer and not Freud the originator of psychoanalysis because his was the first classical instance of psychoanalytic treatment. It was a girl who could not bring herself to drink water from a glass until at length she remembered what she had quite forgotten; her nausea was due to a nasty animal which she had once seen drinking out of a glass. Dr Breuer, to whom in a way I owe my life, was an impressive and very sympathetic personality.

On the occasion when my father lay dying, other medical authorities were in the house, but they were unable to arrest his death, even with infusions of salt water. The latter only succeeded in awakening him from coma and that only for a brief interval. He called then for his wife and children. We were on the other side of the door and heard him call, but the doctors did not let us in, and when at last they did, he had lost consciousness again. My father at the end seemed to be sleeping peacefully and I could hear his regular breathing. The family, who had been without food all day long, went into the adjoining room to take a meal while I remained on watch beside my father. I suddenly became aware that he had stopped breathing. I hurried into the adjoining room, where there was also a doctor among the members of our family. It was not the doctor who was treating him, but a distant cousin. He came to the bedside and saw at once that death had taken place, but did not want to forestall the doctor whose patient my father was and whose return we were expecting any moment. Rather to help us get over the painful minutes of waiting, he said that a cylinder of oxygen should be obtained from the chemist's. I rushed downstairs — our flat was several flights up and there was no lift — obtained the oxygen and tore upstairs again as fast as my legs would carry me, and I arrived all breathless with my cylinder of oxygen at the very moment when the doctor, who had returned in the meantime, was informing us that our father was dead. My mother was weeping. My brother, in despairing grief, fell on his knees beside the bed and began to address his dead father, asking him why he did not respond, and other exclamations of that kind. Myself, on the other hand, what with bodily exhaustion and being out of breath, I was unable to feel anything at all. I stood before my dead father, whom I had loved so deeply, and yet, in spite of the fact that I was fully aware of our loss and of its meaning, I was not only incapable of tears, I could not bring forth any feeling at all. With absolute composure I stood there before my dead father and surveyed the scene.

At this moment it became clear to me that the human being can uplift himself in mind and spirit into a world that abides eternally in silence, far beyond the surging waves of pain and passion. The experience I had had as a little child in the middle of the road in the Wienerwald, where I had recognized 'I am an I' and had taken my first independent step in life, was now repeated and carried further. Once again I knew, 'I am an I,' and with this I I am rooted in the world of reality wherein my father too is living now, compared to which the events of our daily life are but a medley of dreams, an ebb and flow of surging movement.

I stood for a long time motionless and in silence. The cylinder of oxygen lay on the ground where I had dropped it. At last I said to my brother, 'Pull yourself together now. Why are you so in despair?' The doctor, however, drew me aside, saying, 'Let him be! It is only once that one's father dies!'

After this experience I knew that every human being lives in a threefold way. First, we live on earth in our earthly body. Then we express our life and being in a second way, namely, in all our passions, our pains, and joys, our hopes, and fears — in the world of soul. And thirdly, we reach out into a spiritual world, a world beyond all personal emotions, through our membership of which we with our true being are rooted in the objective spirit. The three succeeding years, 1909, 1910, 1911, wherein my schooldays came to an end and I had to take leave of the *Schottengymnasium*, were constantly occupied with thoughts about this threefold nature of man, and in this way I became prepared for my ultimate meeting with Rudolf Steiner and his teaching.

Having successfully passed the school-leaving examination, or *Matura*, as it is called in Austria, I followed up my father's principle — travel as the best means of education — and went on a journey through Germany. The thoughts I had given voice to in my examination essay accompanied me on my way through German country. From Salzburg I first went to Munich, thence to Stuttgart, Mainz, and Cologne, and back again to Stuttgart. I remember walking up the hill to the Uhlandshöhe, whence the beautiful garden city, for that is what Stuttgart is, stretches out before one, filling the entire valley and the steep terraces of the surrounding hills, covered with crimson roses and ramblers. A king who loved roses and who used to sign his name in Arabian characters had once transplanted these roses from the ramparts of Granada to Stuttgart. To me it was like a city from the *Arabian Nights*, and I wandered through it as in a dream. There is a little castle there, too, with the surrounding gardens laid out in Arabian style. The clean and tidy country with the red-tiled cottages to the left and right of the railway line, where even factory workers have their little gardens or plots of land to cultivate in their spare time, seemed to me like a country of good fortune as it lay there bathed in the red of roses. I went along the road where Napoleon's artillery had climbed and which is called to this day Kanonenweg.* Here the great army had passed on its long march, which did not end till they came to Vienna. I reached number 44, a building known at that time as the Restaurant Uhlandshöhe. It was a kind of café, and there was a flight of steps leading up to it. Standing upon those steps, an inexpressible feeling inspired me, but I could not tell then what it was. Yet all of a sudden I knew that my journey was at an end. I must return. So I went down to the railway station and took the next train home to Vienna.

That was in 1911. In fact, I had come there about seven years too soon. Seven years later I was standing on the self-same steps, being just about to leave, when a message was brought to me asking me to stay. Rudolf Steiner had agreed to my becoming a teacher in the Waldorf School. For the building at that time was no longer the Restaurant Uhlandshöhe; it was the Waldorf School of Stuttgart. Seven years had to elapse before the pupil of the *Schottengymnasium* became the teacher of the *Freie Waldorfschule*.

It was in that very year, after my return from Stuttgart, that I first met Rudolf Steiner in my native city of Vienna. It happened thus. One day on my mother's desk I caught sight of Rudolf Steiner's *Occult Science, an Outline*. Opening

* The present Haussmannstrasse. *Ed.*

the book at random, I read a few sentences of the chapter on cosmic evolution, wherein a pristine condition of the universe, preceding even the primeval nebula of Kant and Laplace, is described, as a condition wherein there was not yet anything of solid, liquid, or even gaseous matter. It was a condition preceding these three states of matter. Rudolf Steiner describes it as a condition of pure 'warmth' or 'heat'. Now for a man brought up in contemporary physics it was scarcely possible to think of heat in any other way than as a state of motion in the ultimate particles of solid, liquid, or gaseous matter. To a physicist it seemed impossible to regard heat as a quality having an independent existence of its own. I threw down the book on the table and said to my mother, 'This man must be asleep to the whole trend of modern physics.' Wishing to follow up my statement, I opened the book once more, and the words I lighted on were these: 'The author of this book can well imagine that anyone who reads what he has to say on heat or warmth will conclude that he is ignorant of the first elements of modern physics. Nevertheless the author has written as he has done precisely because he is well acquainted with these things and has indeed made a special study of the mechanical theory of heat. Fully to justify what is here said from the point of view of modern physics would, however, require the writing of many volumes, and that is not possible at the present moment.'

Reading these words, I said to myself: 'Then it is a question of finding out what these unwritten volumes would contain.' In that moment I knew I must encounter Rudolf Steiner. But first I wanted to have read as much as possible of his works. From that day onward, therefore, I spent ten hours a day reading his books and lectures till the opportunity should come for me to meet him. As I read on and on, I went through three distinct stages in my judgment of Rudolf Steiner. The first was when I had read a certain number of books and lecture-cycles. 'All that he says,' I said to myself, 'is in itself consistent, but I am well aware from mathematics that a system of thought need not represent any reality just because it is logical and free of contradictions.'

In the second phase of my investigation, I began to compare Dr Steiner's teaching with other philosophies, religions, and mystical systems. I found his work contained the key to all, and that all other systems were to his as parts are to the whole. 'Still it may be,' I said to myself, 'that these spiritual world-conceptions do not represent any reality at all. I must, however, admit that the system Dr Steiner puts before us is not only consistent in itself; it contains the key to all the others.'

In the third phase I began to study the relation of Dr Steiner's teaching to natural science — that is, in all the branches of science that were accessible to me. Where he diverged from the orthodox teaching I found he did so for good reasons. He was indeed further advanced than the official science and his system did, in fact, represent a reality, namely, the reality of nature.

When I had got thus far a lecture was announced to be given by Rudolf Steiner in Vienna, and I resolved to attend it. Dr Steiner gave a magnificent lecture on the trichotomy or threefold being of man. He explained how thinking, feeling, and will can be developed by an inner training of the soul into spiritual powers of cognition. Thinking is then transformed from shadow-like and abstract into a living picture-thought, Imagination, spiritual vision. Out of our feeling, when feeling is made selfless, grows the faculty of receiving divine Inspiration. Willing at last, when we direct it to the transformation of our own character and being, gives birth to what may truly be described as Intuition; that is the form of knowledge wherein we become at one with the universe and out of this at-one-ment form and guide our own *I* or Ego, until the harmony of inner life and outer universe produces insight which is no longer subject to error. I said to myself as I listened to this lecture: 'This man Rudolf Steiner is actually giving instructions for the development of a threefold faculty of clairvoyance. Now in his books he tells us that he teaches nothing he has not himself discovered. Therefore he must himself possess these faculties; he must be clairvoyant. If that is so, he will also be able to read my thoughts; he will be able to read what I am now thinking. I can therefore ask him questions by merely thinking them and he will be able to answer me in the course of his lecture.'

This I now did. I asked and asked again, and every time he answered. Being, however, brought up in a critical and scientific school, I said to myself: 'Why should it be any more than an illusion? The questions I am asking are ones that arise in a logical way from the content of his lecture. He, on the other hand, is developing his subject logically. He is not answering me at all; there is no need to conclude that he is aware of my questions. I am but imagining that it is so because that is what I really wish.'

However, after the lecture there was an opportunity to send up written questions. I wrote on a sheet of paper, 'Which came first, human language or human reason?' Rudolf Steiner read my question in its turn and answered, but he did not do so from the point of view I had had in mind. My question was inspired by a book I had been reading, Lazarus Geiger's *Human Language and Reason*. I wanted to know in what way and in what mutual relation language and reason had developed in the long history of mankind on earth; he, however, was answering from the point of view not of the history of mankind, but of the individual child's development. I was bitterly disappointed; he evidently had not understood my question. Rudolf Steiner put down my paper and was silent for a few moments. Thereupon he picked it up once more and said: 'What I have just been saying is only one point of view; there is another aspect which the writer of the question had in mind.' And he went on to tell how in the evolution of mankind language and reason had evolved by means of one another.

When question-time was over I went up to him and said: 'I am aware who you are and I would like to become your pupil.' Rudolf Steiner said, 'I take it you know English?' 'No,' I said. Nevertheless he continued: 'Read the philosophical works of Berkeley, who denied the existence of matter, and of Locke, who based everything upon the senses. Then write a theory of cognition for spiritual knowledge, avoiding both of these one-sided points of view. Do it as I have done: learn to know the fullness of the world through Aristotle, and the act of cognition itself through the philosophy of Fichte.'

So I became Rudolf Steiner's pupil, and the remainder of my life has been lived in the sign of this discipleship.

Quite early in my life, in the winter of 1900 to 1901 I had an encounter which, however personal in character, I will relate, for it is typical of an experience which occurs in the life of every human being and to understand which is important both for teachers and parents, and indeed for all of us. I had been suffering from a prolonged and obstinate cold, and my father, who in any case, as I have told, believed in travelling for education's sake, resolved to send me with my mother to the Italian Riviera, hoping for my quick recovery in the warm climate of Ospedaletti near San Remo. Nor was he disappointed; I was better very soon. But he decided then to let us stay throughout the winter.

The altogether different nature of the south made an unforgettable impression on me, child of nine or ten as I then was. Palm-trees were growing in the garden in front of our hotel, and in Bordighera near by there was a regular palm forest, while aloes grew on either side of the road. At sunrise and at sunset the loveliest colours were to be seen far away out over the sea, and in the distance the heights of Corsica were visible.

Rudolf Steiner once said that every one of us at the age of nine or ten has an encounter with some other human being whose picture remains indelibly written in our soul, never to be forgotten for the rest of life. Through this encounter we experience for the first time the indwelling soul of another human being. Thus it was Dante met with Beatrice, Goethe with Gretchen. Such experiences are indeed deep-rooted in the destiny of human souls. Beatrice became Dante's guide, although he scarcely ever met her after. Gretchen was changed for Goethe's inner vision into the being who could lead him up and on to the 'eternal feminine,' which signifies in Goethe's terminology 'consciousness' as against the universe, the 'eternal masculine'.

It was in Ospedaletti that I had my experience of this kind, whereof I have since convinced myself that every human being has it in one way or another. There was a young German-American girl about six years older than myself, to whom I looked up with untold reverence and tenderness. It was my first love, utterly childlike, ethereal, remote from the world; and yet perhaps for this very reason it worked all the more deeply in my soul, giving rise to an experience which never vanished. For the unfolding of my inner life the most important aspect of it was that the perceiving of another soul went hand-in-hand with the perceiving, for the first time truly, of the world of nature. Not until then did I begin to see the beauty of the sunrise and the sunset, the wind and clouds, the rocks and trees. It was this meeting with great nature which worked on in such a lasting way in the boy's soul and which had found its awakening through the encounter with a simple and lovely girl. All that took place between us was that I went with her on all her ways while we were there, and that she gave me as a parting gift a box of candies — a brightly coloured box which was among my treasures for many a long year. Seemingly insignificant as it may be, it was this encounter which led me to that awakening whereby the human being learns to know himself as a living soul, and nature as a being filled with spirit. Anyone who can read in the original Italian the beautiful words of Brunetto Latini, Dante's teacher, about his meeting with the goddess Natura will feel something of the breath of wonder which was wafted then into my childlike soul.

I believe every human being will discover this experience somewhere between the ninth and tenth year of his life, and if he examines himself closely will find how fruitful its aftereffects have been, though I admit that some have told me they can only remember having had such an experience while reading a book or in some other purely inward way. In my case I know that the experience found its continuation after my meeting with Rudolf Steiner, who showed me how to regard nature in an ever deeper and more spiritual way. Again and again in later times I thought about this question, entering into it more and more deeply in the successive periods of my life, and as I did so I realized increasingly that the way into the inner life of nature is only possible by entering the secrets of the human soul. It is not science *about* nature, but the perfection of our own human faculty of love, which leads us by and by to pierce through the veil of nature. It was Rudolf Steiner who encouraged me to work out such thoughts more fully and to develop them at length into a theory of knowledge for spiritual cognition, showing that it is not intellect but love which penetrates into the cosmic secrets.

In my doctoral dissertation I went into the subject thoroughly, also in its historical foundations. A few remarks must here suffice. Whenever we are thinking we forget ourselves, the thinker, altogether. We live in utterly selfless devotion to the object of which we are thinking at the given moment. This devotion does not rise into our consciousness, but it is there. All that comes into our consciousness is the result of our thinking, namely the resulting act of knowledge. But we can render conscious — in the way Rudolf Steiner has shown in his *Philosophy of Spiritual Activity* — this otherwise unconscious element in thought. We can bring into the field of consciousness the love and devotion which live as a rule unnoticed in the act of knowledge. When we do so we discover that all knowledge really rests on love, and moreover that all truly selfless love is knowledge. In the Bible, full as it is of deep wisdom, we read that Adam *knew* his wife, which proves that the writer, whoever he may have been, was aware of the inner connection between love and knowledge. In my doctoral dissertation, which was eventually accepted by the University of Vienna, I showed how the human being can develop his power of devotion stage by stage and can thus advance to higher forms of knowledge, to which the everyday consciousness cannot rise — not for lack of cleverness, but for lack of sufficient consciousness in the faculty of love.

For the benefit of students I may here remark that love, which in its least degree we are wont to call interest, is also the great secret of remembering what we have learned. What we love we do not forget. If a student learns without love, without real interest, only in order to pass his examinations, he may be sure he will forget as soon as the examinations are over, or perhaps before. People who complain of a bad memory should therefore try to improve their faculty of love; to understand and love what they desire to remember.

Love, as Rudolf Steiner said on one occasion, is the experiencing of the other being, consciously within our own. The same may be said of memory. Memory is to harbour inwardly what to begin with came to us from without. There is no memory without love. Intellect only reaches to the surface-pictures of memory; whoever wished to go farther, and to discover the hidden forces which are at work *beneath* the power of memory, must first equip himself with the strong force of love.

Questions like these reach up into the highest realms of philosophy – philosophy, in whose name after all the word *phileo*, I love, occurs. Yet they are already presaged in the experiences of our early youth, experiences seemingly unimportant but in fact of deep significance for all our life. Educators, parents, and in the last resort everyone for himself, should learn to understand their meaning.

After my meeting with Rudolf Steiner, of which I told above, I did not yet become a member of the Anthroposophical Society. I must, however, say a few words here about the said Society and my relation to it. Long ago Rudolf Steiner had given a course of lectures on mysticism in the Theosophical Library at Berlin. He told how mysticism represents only the other aspect of the scientific aspirations of humanity in modern time. As a result of these lectures, which were widely appreciated, Rudolf Steiner was appointed General Secretary of the German Section of the Theosophical Society. He accepted the position under certain stipulations, though he never actually became a member of that Society. Later on, when strong differences of opinion arose in the Theosophical Society as a result of the ideas entertained by leading members about the Christ, Rudolf Steiner and his followers were excluded. All this had taken place before my meeting with Dr Steiner. At the time of our first encounter there were indeed large numbers of erstwhile theosophists in his entourage, but he had nothing more to do with the Society as such. Neither, however (as he himself soon told me), was he a member of the Anthroposophical Society which had been founded by Dr Carl Unger, Marie von Sivers, and Michael Bauer. Dr Steiner never was a member of this Society, and he attached some importance to his non-membership. But he respected everyone's liberty of action; he allowed the Society to be founded, and indeed worked in it as lecturer and teacher. The name Anthroposophy too was due to him; he had used it in the title of his lectures even long before this time.

For my part, at the time when I first came into touch with him my interest in Rudolf Steiner himself knew no bounds, but I had no desire at all to become a member of the Anthroposophical Society. I did, however, want to be present at dramatic presentations which were being given in the summer months at Munich. I therefore went to Munich and found my way to the house where Dr Steiner lived. But I could not get past the staff of those who were looking after him. I was received by a Countess Kalckreuth, a lady whom I afterwards learned to know and to esteem. On that occasion she was rather difficult. She asked me what I wanted. I wanted to see the mystery plays. Are you a member? No. Then you cannot witness the Plays. Yes, but I have already spoken to Dr Steiner; I have even become his pupil. Maybe, but these presentations are for members only. I was about to go away in despair, but in that very moment the door opened and Dr Steiner appeared on the scene. He came up to me immediately, held out his hand, and said 'So there you are!' I told him of my unhappy position. I wanted to see the plays, but did not want to become a member; still less so after what had taken place. Dr Steiner looked questioningly at the Countess, but she remained unmoved. At length he said, 'I will have a membership card made out for Herr Stein. It shall not, however, become valid until the moment he goes in through the theatre entrance, and it shall lose its validity in the moment when he leaves the building. That surely will meet the case, Countess?' Of course it would; everything would that he said, but I could not comprehend why he submitted to these formalities. Armed, then, with such a card, I attended the performances. It would lead me far too far afield if I attempted here to describe what I saw. The plays, of course, have long ago been printed and everyone can buy them. Rudolf Steiner wrote four mystery plays and was engaged on a fifth at the time of his death. He wanted to show in these plays how a number of souls pass through repeated lives on earth and undergo destinies which are not to be explained out of one life alone. He wanted to show how karma works.

Deeply impressed by what I saw and heard, I went up to Dr Steiner when the performances were over. 'Well, Herr Stein,' said he, 'did you have a good time?' 'I know now what an ass I was,' was my reply, 'and I have no desire any more to leave the Society.' So I remained therein. In the year 1923 Dr Steiner newly founded the Anthroposophical Society and became himself the President, nominating a number of other persons in conjunction with whom he would lead it. But I shall come to that later. To begin with, I became a member of the Society. Marie von Sivers (afterwards Frau Dr Steiner) received me at that time in the kindest way, placed lecture-manuscripts at my disposal, and at his request answered the written questions which I addressed from time to time to Dr Steiner.

I was working very intently through Dr Steiner's introductions to the scientific writings of Goethe. I was especially concerned with Goethe's theory of colour, and was at pains to understand modern physics in the light of Dr Steiner's teaching. In this he constantly helped me. I owe very much, during that early period of my anthroposophical studies, to Dr Ernst Blümel of Vienna. Blümel, an excellent mathematician, was able to relieve me of many of my scientific scruples. Other anthroposophical friends, too, I learned to know at that time, among them Dr Karl Schubert, and I was soon convinced that the Society was a collection of highly original types, not to say eccentrics. They seemed to have nothing in common save their love for Dr Steiner, who accepted every one of them for what he was. I remember at that time, too, the distinguished French author, Edouard Schuré, who after a period of estrangement lived to confess once again his warm devotion to Rudolf Steiner. Being a new member, to begin with I saw very little of the life of the Society beyond the lectures and demonstrations; I had no knowledge of what went on in its leadership.

My mother at that time left Vienna and went to Switzerland for a long period. She wanted to help in the great new building, the headquarters of the Society which was being erected near Basle and was subsequently named the Goetheanum. Seventeen nations were represented among the members of the Anthroposophical Society who were engaged in this work together when the First World War broke out. I myself was visiting my mother at that moment and was attending Dr Steiner's lectures. My brother had accompanied us to the station. He was rather sad that his office work kept him back in Vienna, for at heart he was already an anthroposophist. None of us knew as he waved good-bye to us that it was good-bye for ever in this life; for shortly after this, as I have told, he was killed at the front.

I have a vivid recollection of the tension of those days, the anxiously awaited news from day to day before the actual outbreak of the War. Before the Goetheanum there stood Rudolf Steiner: my mother and I went up to him. We held in our hand the news that the Austrian frontier had been closed, and further news from thence was not to be expected. I said to Dr Steiner, 'Herr Doctor, I must go now; the mobilization order cannot reach me here. My brother has already been called up in the preliminary partial mobilization. What shall I do now?' Dr. Steiner took my hand in both his hands and said, 'Follow the voice of your heart, for it is there that you will hear your destiny.' So then I went into the war.

At the station at Basle I had an hour to wait, and wrote Dr Steiner a long letter full of love and thanks. I described what I felt: feelings arising in my soul which were not mine, something that took possession of my soul which was not I myself, and which was leading me into this war. At his lecture in the evening Dr Steiner read out the letter. The shorthand report must still be in existence. 'What is described in this letter,' he said, 'shows how at great historic moments the Spirit of the Nation one belongs to, and the Spirit of the Time, take hold of the human soul and live and move therein. Here in this letter a human being speaks of it.' These words I read many years after in the shorthand report in the archives at Dornach. My mother also wrote to me about it to the front.

I crossed the Swiss frontier into Austria and went on to Vienna. On the table in my room I found a farewell letter from my brother, a revolver, a pair of riding breeches, and full equipment left for me as a parting gift. I never set eyes on him again. There were still twenty-four hours before mobilization. I was in the Café Pucher in the Kohlmarkt when it came. I recall how for lack of vehicles I had to shoulder my own trunk all the way to the Southern Station. My regiment, Feldkanonen-Regiment 25, was stationed at Wiener Neustadt, a place of vivid memories for me. It was here that Rudolf Steiner had spent a considerable portion of his youth. Here, too, I was during my year of military service and for a few subsequent periods of training. Almost every day I rode on horseback along the same road along which he as a little boy had walked the long way to school. Here in our officers' training course we went out for our first rides. Here I drank countless times from the open spring, the *Sauerbrunn* with its lovely mineral waters, from which Rudolf Steiner as a boy had daily drawn the water in a large earthenware jug for his parents' supper-table. Every tree and stone and path are familiar to me. More beautiful flowers grow in this valley then elsewhere, rarer birds sing, the wind blows differently — nature tells her secrets. Even the stars glisten more brightly. Readers will say there is no such thing; it is a mere matter of individual feeling. But it is not so. Look in a book on the flora and fauna of the borderland country of Austria and Burgenland, and you will find that the valley of Sauerbrunn, along the railway line from Wiener Neustadt to Katzelsdorf and Neudörfl and on to Oedenburg, does in fact abound in plants and animals which occur nowhere in the district save in this valley. In this God-given nature Rudolf Steiner had spent a portion of his childhood; here too my friends and I had often come on our excursions, and here I was stationed at the outbreak of the War. We mobilized in this district, and then passed in triumphal march through Vienna. From every bridge and archway the people plied us with chocolate and bread and coloured ribands.

It was at Jaroslaw in Galicia that we left the train, and from thence we marched. Eighteen months in rain and snow and swamp, without roof, without protection, without hope that it would ever again be otherwise. Eighteen months of the World War; yet lovely months in spite of cold and snow and rain, swamp fever, cholera and dysentery, typhoid and war. A year and a half of nature! Should I without the war ever have had the patience to lie entrenched in the ground, watching the plants grow before me on a level with my very eyes? Or to watch the hares digging their holes in the sand? Through all the seasons, through all the hours of day and night, sunrise and sunset, we were there in the immense forests of Russia. What did it matter that we also fired, that there were days of battle, many of us were killed or taken ill, and so we ourselves might be tomorrow or the day after? What did it matter? We had nature about us as never before in life, the greatest imaginable subject for meditation. While I lay there in slime or sand I read Locke and Berkeley — in translation only at that time. I filled my mind with the two English philosophers, seeking the middle way between the two extremes of thought. I noted words from the original: 'notion' for *Begriff*, 'idea' for *Vorstellung*. So I plodded through. And between riding, fighting, and fevering, time and again I wrote the notes for my dissertation.

On all hands my comrades were laughing at me. I was the one who would not drink a single drop. That was the only condition Rudolf Steiner had made: not another drop of alcohol, nor have I ever taken any since. My captain wanted to force me; I declined to obey him. He poured alcohol into my coffee; the water was infected with cholera. I was resolved to die if need be, but I would not drink again. Was it really a matter of such importance? Probably not, but it was the exercise I had undertaken and I was determined to carry it through to the end. So then I read and wrote. My copy of Rudolf Steiner's *Theosophy* twice went up and down the front. Everyone who had read it inscribed his name. Twice it came back into my hands. Hundreds had read it: the chapters on the life after death and the eternal being of the human soul. On the third occasion the book did not return into my hands; it was buried with one of our comrades who was killed soon after he had read it. Somewhere on the eastern front it may be unearthed one day — the book which worked so powerfully in the souls of all who read it. Rudolf Steiner had said to me: 'Whoever writes an occult book takes on himself the obligation to help everyone who reads even a single line of it, throughout his future lives.' If this was so, he would have much to do! The last words of one of my comrades who had read it were about this book; a few hours later we buried him beneath the snow. What a power war is! Meanwhile I read and read; riding across country, in the midst of battle, in the long days of waiting, I read and wrote — mountains full of paper.

One day the order came through the telephone from General Headquarters: 'All officers who have been in the firing line continuously for the past eighteen months are to retire at once.' It was like a dream. Two hours later I was on the way in a peasant's cart through woods of oak and birch and across the marshes. I had not realized how far away we were. While the cart swayed and rattled and the thunder of the cannon could still be heard in the distance I had time to think of the past months. We passed by the place where I had been left behind with two of the guns to cover our retreat. The brigadier had said, 'Hold this position until six o'clock to-morrow morning. We are not reckoning on your return.' Here again was the place where we had been in battle all night long. Machine-gun bullets came on us like hailstones, while we could do nothing with our big guns in the forest. Here was the place where we had been so hungry — three days without bread, water, or sleep — and where a mule from the Russian army strayed into our lines, rice-soup still warm in the field kitchen it was dragging. All these and other recollections went through my mind. And then the march into Przemysl, the watch-fires burning at the entrance-gates, and every one of us — officers and men alike — having a hot potato thrown into his cap as we rode into the fortress. And how we ate them! That was the great retreat. Here were the crosses we had erected over the graves of our dead comrades. It was like a journey back through one's own life, as in a dream. And then at last came Vienna. Yes, this was Vienna, the city where I had been born, which I had thought never to see again.

There was a telegram from Rudolf Steiner: 'Am in Berlin for three days longer; can discuss dissertation with you if you can come.' How I hastened to the Ministry of War! I wonder if they will hang me after the event if I now relate what happened. I asked for a few days' leave of absence. Leave of absence, and to go abroad, in the middle of the war? Are you mad? Yes, I admitted it, I was, but I must see Rudolf Steiner. No, impossible. So there I stood. There was no higher authority to whom I might appeal. At that moment a little private on orderly duty passed by, carrying a mountain-load of papers. He stopped before me, seeing my look of despair. 'What's up?' said he. I showed him my form of application which had been refused. 'I absolutely must go on this journey, but the general . . .' 'Put it here,' said the little soldier. And he laid my application on the very top of his pile of papers. A few minutes later he came out again. My application form was signed, signed by the very officer who had only just refused me. I do not know to this day what exactly happened, but an hour later I was on my way to Berlin.

So I saw Rudolf Steiner again, and it turned out an important meeting. Count Ludwig Polzer-Hoditz was hurrying away as I came up to Dr Steiner's door. I had known him for a long time, and we were close friends. At this moment he was deathly pale. I asked him what was the matter. 'I am to get an important document across the frontier,' was his reply, 'a letter to the Emperor Karl of Austria.' 'Give it to me,' said I. 'No, no; at least I must first ask the Doctor.' So I came into the room. It was in July 1917.

During the war Rudolf Steiner had repeatedly been asked by leading persons: 'What should be done in Europe at this juncture so as to do justice to the forces prevailing in the depths of history and to bring reason and order into the chaotic developments of our time?' On this occasion it was Count Polzer-Hoditz who had asked him, and the question from this quarter was of some importance inasmuch as the Count's brother was Secretary to the Austrian Emperor *(Kabinettschef)*, and in that capacity one of the Emperor's closest advisers. Now Dr Steiner had drawn up a memorandum indicating the line of action he recommended, and the need was to get this across the frontier and into the hands of the Emperor. I was prepared to act as messenger. Dr Steiner, however, insisted that I should know what I was carrying, and read the memorandum out to me before handing it over. In Vienna I was simply to post it in a letter-box. Through this event I heard for the first time Dr Steiner's ideas of what should be done in Middle Europe.

I wondered how I should dispose of the paper on my way across the frontier. 'Put it in your suit-case on the very top,' said Dr Steiner. So there it lay when I reached the customs. The customs officer picked it up, put it on one side, and proceeded to rummage through all my other things; there-upon he carefully put the paper on the top again, closed the suit-case and marked it as passed in the customary way. The content of this memorandum has since been published in the memoirs of Count Arthur Polzer-Hoditz.*

That the memorandum did not reach the Emperor in time was not at any rate my fault. The *Kabinettschef*, so long as he remained in office, did not dare pass it on. It was not until the day of his resignation that he put it into the Emper-or's hands. So it remained without effect.

Dr Steiner's fundamental idea, developed in this memor-andum, was that individuals and political minorities should be given an absolute right of free choice in all matters con-cerning the education of children, languages to be used in schools, the kind of schools, and so on. The same principle as in matters of religious freedom should prevail in all edu-cational and cultural affairs, including all that had to do with nationality. For Austria especially this was of great importance, as the question of the languages to be used in schools was a perpetual bone of contention. Dr Steiner, for example, wanted the Italians in Trieste, which at that time belonged to the Austro-Hungarian monarchy, to be given an Italian university. For the political domain he wanted the frontiers of states to remain as frontiers only for police and military purposes. Individuals, however, should have the right of declaring themselves extra-territorial. A Frenchman in the Rhineland or a German in Alsace would therefore be able freely to declare his membership of the one or the other state. And he would freely decide whether to send his children to a French or a German school. This kind of

---

* Unfortunately, in the English edition of this book (*The Emperor Karl*, London 1930) the Appendix containing Dr Steiner's Memorandum has been omitted.

arrangement is indeed sure to come in time. After a few decades have passed no one will understand how it was possible for human beings to live in our time, compelled by their habitation to confess allegiance to one state or another. The Thirty Years War was fought to make it clear to modern humanity that religion is a matter of free individual confession, and that it cannot depend on the entry of a cavalry patrol into my village whether or not I shall remain thereafter for my whole life long a Protestant or be obliged suddenly to become a Catholic, while the next day perhaps other riders will appear on the scene, and I shall have to change again and declare something else to be the one and only truth. In religious matters, mankind today understands this; in political, we are not yet so far advanced. Yet by the end of the present century we shall at long last be making this discovery; we shall awaken to the full use of individual liberty in these matters. Membership of one or another nationality will then be a matter of free choice and confession on the part of every individual. Dr Steiner was a hundred years or more ahead of his time; in his memorandum all these and other things were contained.

The third thing Dr Steiner proposed was to remove all economic matters from politics. Agricultural and industrial associations and also the representatives of consumers (not only producers and distributors) should constitute a separate body, a kind of economic parliament. The latter should enter into communication with the corresponding bodies in other countries. One economy should deal directly with another over the heads of political governments.

Thus Dr Steiner sketched out the idea of a threefold social order:
1. A cultural parliament.
2. The political parliament.
3. The economic parliament.
Fourthly, there was to be a Senate, in a certain manner supervising all the three. Thus he envisaged the structure of the new Austria. In the cultural parliament distinguished artists, scholars, and other prominent individualities should come together and take counsel about educational and kindred matters. In the political parliament public security and

hygiene, the defence of the realm and police matters in the widest sense should be dealt with. Criminal law should come within the sphere of the cultural body, being essentially a matter of education. Civil law, however, should be the province of judges belonging to the political or civic realm within the threefold order. Economic and industrial matters were to be dealt with on purely economic grounds; finance and currency should come within the sphere of the supreme economic body.

I can only sketch the idea at this moment. During the following years I was among those who worked out these ideas in great detail, and I did so notably at the time when D. N. Dunlop called me to England to help in developing the economic aspect of such a programme.

For the moment this much may suffice. The programme was intended in a very realistic and scientific sense, and if carried out would have led not only to a thoroughgoing transformation of Austria but would soon have extended to the rest of Europe. It is indeed to this day the only true social programme, and the realities of life are fighting for it by the rather violent and ruthless weapon of the world crisis, which will not give way until at least a certain number of countries have made the above three principles their own. This idea of a threefold state was indeed implicit in the three watchwords of the French Revolution: liberty, equality, fraternity. Liberty is needed in the cultural member of the body social, equality in the political, while fraternity arises of its own accord where economic life is severed from the politics of armed power. The three demands of the French Revolution, mutually inconsistent in the totalitarian state of Louis XV (for liberty is inconsistent with equality) are realizable if the social life is 'membered,' so that each of the three members realizes the ideal that pertains to it. Free trade, for example, was an attempt to make liberty the dominant ideal of economic life, and the history of recent times has shown that this cannot be. Free trade has given way increasingly to trade under compulsion. Political fraternities of the most varied shades led up to the World War, a sure sign that fraternity cannot prevail in politics but rather tends to the treating of one neighbour as a brother and another only as a step-brother.

Dr Steiner wanted to guide these things into their true and original channels. I was well aware that a frontier official might not trust himself on the spur of the moment to decide whether a document proposing to eliminate political frontiers or to make the economic life world-wide should be allowed to pass in war-time. Fate willed it, however, that the document got through. The man who kept it to himself and did not submit it to his monarch while there was time must answer for what he did at the bar of history. In a short conversation I had with him at a later time I realized, I must admit, that he was a man who could scarcely have acted otherwise.

My visit to Berlin in July 1917, with all the strange circumstances attending it, was therefore the occasion of my first acquaintance with the threefold idea of Rudolf Steiner. My own reason for the visit had, however, been to show Dr Steiner my dissertation, the manuscript of which was now complete and bore the triangular stamp of papers allowed to pass the frontier. I must now tell a little more about this dissertation. I had received the theme from Dr Steiner. The difficulty was to find the professor who would accept it and let it pass as given to me by himself. It was Professor Arthur Stöhr of Vienna who eventually declared himself prepared to do so. I met him on the staircase when I called. What did I want? A subject for a doctor's dissertation. He had no time at the moment. 'I must go and get a shave,' he said. 'The barber's shop is round the corner in the adjoining street. If you have time to suggest a subject on the way there, good and well.' 'That will be easy,' said I. 'The difficulty only is, when I have worked out the subject, will Herr Professor recognize it as the one that he agreed to?' 'Write what you like,' he replied, 'only please do not let it be such nonsense as I have had to read this morning. What is it you want to write about?' 'I want to compare the ideas of nature and the theories of knowledge of Goethe and of Rudolf Steiner,' said I. 'I want to show that human consciousness is only a special kind of consciousness, that there are other forms of consciousness to which we are able to evolve. I want to classify the possible forms of consciousness and examine their relation to what science teaches us about the real world. I want to show the middle way between Locke's one-sided sensualism and Berkeley's denial of all matter.'

By this time, however, we had reached the barber's shop. The Professor stopped, looked at me keenly, and said: 'I shall remember all right. But one thing more. You are taking the psychology examination too, I suppose?' 'Yes, Herr Professor.' 'Well now, there are two possibilities. Either I shall be examining you, or else my colleague Höfler.* But if you come to me and tell me Höfler's things, you will probably be ploughed. On the other hand, if you go to Höfler and tell him my things, you are ploughed before you get there. What will you do?' And at that he disappeared into the shop.

There is a good example of the way in which in Austria they enable many different individuals to make their way. He could not have been more helpful, and from thenceforth I had every reason to love Professor Stöhr — the more so later on when he came to examine me. Here was a soul who was fully at home in the philosophy of Ancient Greece. His eyes shone as he spoke to me about Ephesus. He knew Heraclitus off by heart, and recited in the Greek fluently for fifteen minutes while he examined me. And when I enumerated the different kinds of fire according to Heraclitus, and did not forget the ethereal fire, he was deeply gratified. Adolf Stöhr is the author of a book, *Heraclitus*, which begins with the words, 'The God of Heraclitus is named, according to the body, *Pyr Aeizoon*, the eternally living, primeval Substance. He changed a portion of His spirit and of His body into this universe, which will exist for a period of time determined by Him. After that He will receive the world again into His Divine repose. And a like change will be repeated in future epochs.' The path of *Pyr Aeizoon* through air, water and earth is called 'the downward way' and the returning path 'the upward way.' 'The way upward and the way downward are one and the same,' says one of the Fragments of Heraclitus. When I told Professor

---

* In Austria, as in other Continental countries, the great majority of examinations are viva voce.

Stöhr about the fire out of which all things that are have become and into which all things will return, to rest for a certain season in the quietude of God, he replied that I had evidently learned to live in thoughts akin to those of the Ephesian philosophy. And he was deeply touched when I told him in reply to his question where I had these ideas from, that I had them from the works of Rudolf Steiner.

Altogether this examination and the consequent attainment of my doctor's degree was an important event in my life. But it happened at a considerably later time. I took my degree because Dr Steiner hoped I would. For myself I should probably no longer have done so. Actually it was not until after the War, seven years after I left the *Schotten-Gymnasium*.

Professor Stöhr asked me during my examination: 'Can you give me a description of the course of Greek philosophy as a whole and of its inner meaning?' I spoke for an hour and showed the development of Greek philosophy as an evolution of consciousness, from the mythological consciousness which had still been founded on an old clairvoyance to the pure thinking which reveals itself fully for the first time in Aristotle. Stöhr was interested in the early Greek philosophers, and especially in the Ephesian doctrines. I told him of Dr Steiner's ideas on the subject, and he was greatly astonished at some of the points of view which emerged, which were quite new to him and yet intelligible and capable of confirmation.

My examination at the hands of the other professor of philosophy was not quite so easy. He gave me the interesting task of showing how the *I* comes to expression in the philosophies of Fichte and of Karl Marx. To one whom Dr Steiner had advised to study how the act of knowledge is the essential thing in Fichte, and the all-embracing facts of world-existence in Aristotle, the field was not unfamiliar. In Fichte, Schelling and Hegel, willing, feeling and thinking were revealed in action. Marx, as a disciple of Hegel, took his start from Hegel's principle of independent thought, but failed sufficiently to appreciate the activity of the individual *I*, and ascribed the effects of life too one-sidedly to the influence of the environment, failing to see that the individual transforms his environment no less than the environment the individual. I criticized the materialistic conception of history as representing only one aspect of the problem. Hegel only had the *concept* of the soul; he only *thought* the life of soul. He failed to reach the real soul, just as Marx failed to reach the real individuality, the spirit. Marx's own life, powerful in its individual influence upon the masses of the people, seemed to me to reveal the very thing to which he did not do justice in his teachings. The professor began to feel uncomfortable. At length he asked me, referring to my quotations from Dr Steiner: 'Herr Kandidat, will you please answer me the question: Why is it that I cannot understand Rudolf Steiner's books?' 'I am prepared to give you the answer,' I replied, 'if you are prepared to receive it.' 'If you please,' said he. 'You have trained your thinking in a too one-sided way in the school of Kant,' said I. 'Kant looked for the reality of things *behind* the phenomena instead of in their mutual relations.' The professor stopped in his examination, and gave me the highest mark.

In the mathematics examination things went well, as the professor of geometry asked me questions on a subject I had studied thoroughly, the geometry of multiple curved surfaces. The other examiner, who had to test my knowledge of higher mathematics, was Professor Escherich, an old friend who knew what I knew and what I did not know. So his examination turned into a friendly talk about the ideas of Rudolf Steiner, whom he had known in old times in the Café Grinsteidl, which both men had frequented. 'Look,' said the aged councillor, 'never would I have thought that the quiet Steiner with his dark eyes would have become such a famous man as to be the subject for this dissertation.' What questions Professor Escherich did ask me on mathematical subjects I was able to answer with a repetition of his own jests and examples, so that he soon perceived that he had before him one who had conscientiously attended his lectures.

I must not leave unmentioned the professor who examined me in geometry. He was an excellent teacher, and used to draw his figures in the air. He was so skilled in doing so that if you followed him well you could catch the figures in the air, where he had fixed them with deft movements of his hands, his elbows, and his nose. I was fond of this man in spite of his eccentricities; he was a geometrician of genius, and I owed him much.

I passed the examination, and sent a telegram to Dr Steiner at Dornach. Telegram in hand, Dr Steiner came up to my wife, who at that time was a eurythmist at the Goetheanum. 'How do you do, Frau Doctor,' he said, and went on repeating the same words until at length she grasped the point. Dr Steiner, by whose encouragement I had gone back to take my doctor's degree after the war, was very glad that I had passed. He liked to see anthroposophy represented in a scientific way, as something complementary to and not inconsistent with the established science of our time. He felt it to be one of my special tasks to show that this was possible.

Rudolf Steiner had set me the task of writing a theory of knowledge for spiritual cognition; this was to be my dissertation for my Ph. D. My dissertation actually had another title* and I adopted a rather different terminology from what would naturally have been my own, so as to conform more nearly to the accepted academic standards. Nevertheless, the theory of knowledge for supersensible cognition is contained in this work. I avoided the use of Dionysius the Areopagite's names for the three hierarchies and spoke instead of three hypothetically possible kinds of consciousness, each of which again contains three subspecies, so that the whole description answers, indeed, to the nine hierarchies. All this will be found in the concluding chapter of the published dissertation.

The work remained almost unnoticed, its essential content being well concealed by the terminology in which I also followed Dr Steiner's advice. I went through it all with him point by point, and the essay, such as it is, contains many things which would have awakened no little interest in the age of Scholasticism. For in all detail the theory of knowledge for the Angels, Archangels, and Archai; Exusiai,

---

* *Die Moderne Naturwissenschaftliche Vorstellungsart Goethes, wie sie Rudolf Steiner vertritt.* (The mode of thought of modern science and the world-conception of Goethe as represented by Rudolf Steiner).

Dynamis, Kyriotetes; Thrones, Cherubim, and Seraphim is here expounded.

It happened again on each occasion when I came to treat of the spiritual hierarchies, that something of outstanding importance took place in my own life. The contents of my dissertation were worked out on the battlefield, in daily meditation and constantly in face of death. Sentence by sentence, on the long marches and in the noise of battle, the dissertation was elaborated, without ever writing down a single word. When I came home from the front, the whole work was before me in my mind's eye, completed. It took me only ten days to write it down; that was in a little Hungarian village remote from any libraries or archives. The subject was so familiar to me by now that I was able to write it all down straightforwardly, even including the quotations. It was only necessary afterwards to read them through and confirm them.

The village in Hungary was Magyarkersztur; it was the home of Nora von Baditz who afterwards became my wife. When I came back from the front I had found her at home as the guest of my mother. Our conversations had led me at that time to concentrate my studies upon the being of the Christ. She, too, was deeply interested in the spiritual hierarchies, though she approached the problem along quite other paths than I had done. She had been a friend of my brother, who in a strange way had made an end to his life during the War, as I have already related. Several times wounded, he had again and again returned to active service. At the last he was in command of a battery in the fortress of Przemysl. To be made prisoner by the Russians seemed to him unworthy. He concluded his diary which he had always kept with care and diligence, addressed it to our family and having finished it and signed it entrusted it to the matron of the hospital. Then he went back to his battery. He had the bore of the cannon filled with ecrasite and laid a fuse, then having convinced himself that all his men, his own orderly included, had left the battery, he lit the fuse and exploded the battery along with himself while the fortress fell into the hands of the Russians. Rudolf Steiner sent us a telegram and wrote an epitaph for my brother whom he had dearly loved:

In life his meditation
was turned towards the Spirit;
So may he find in death
the Spirit's life.
With him are the thoughts
of all those who love him.

And so it proved to be. Those who had been his friends could not forget the brave young man. One may think a heroic death of this kind superfluous. My brother, Friedrich Stein, knew what its meaning was. His destiny, which was profoundly connected with the Russian soul, did not allow him to be taken prisoner by the Russians. It is only in the light of other lives — earlier and later incarnations, too — that such a deed will find justification; for the immediate present it is shrouded in mystery.

Rudolf Steiner, able as he was to follow the dead in their after-life as others did the living, was deeply interested in the destinies of this soul after death. I do not hesitate to relate these matters, as the time has come when humanity, for its true progress, must know more and more about such things.

On one occasion when I was walking beside him along the Michaelergasse in Vienna, Rudolf Steiner suddenly came to a stop and drew me aside into the silence of the Augustiner church; we went down the steps into the crypt where the Austrian rulers lie entombed. I did not immediately understand why he did so; later on I realized that he wanted to get away from the noise of the street for the sake of a moment's concentration.

Before entering the church he had pointed with his umbrella in the direction of a silversmith's shop in the Michaelerplatz. 'Here, in the face of this shop-window, here it was,' said Dr Steiner. 'Here I sat writing the book which your brother is now working through in thoughts as crystal-clear as mathematics — the book on *Goethe's Theory of Knowledge.*' 'How so?' I asked in some astonishment. 'Here was the Café Grinsteidl,' was his reply. Rudolf Steiner in his youth had been very poor. At home he had neither light nor warmth. Thus it was in the café that he wrote his deeply important works. Often he had not even proper paper to write on. And now he experienced the soul of my brother after death, working through — point by point, thought upon thought — the book which he himself had been writing at this place, so many years before. My brother's premature death had not rendered him inactive. I was deeply moved, for I had never yet encountered in so practical a form the fact that the dead live on and that a living man can be aware of what they are doing. Moreover, I was able to put to the test to some extent what Rudolf Steiner said on this occasion. The last book which I had put into my brother's hands before the outbreak of the War had been Dr Steiner's book, *Goethe's Theory of Knowledge*. The book had long been out of print, the new edition had not yet appeared, and it was difficult to obtain a copy. My brother read it most diligently and I could see from his letters how deeply he was interested in it. Now, following his death, he was living through the memories of his life in backward order, beginning at the time of death. Rudolf Steiner was accompanying him in his thoughts, confirming in practice what he had once said to me: the occultist must accompany every soul who has once become his pupil. 'Whoever,' he went on to say, 'has read but a single line of the book *Knowledge of Higher Worlds and its Attainment*, I must follow him through all his succeeding lives to continue helping him. Such is the rule I must obey.'

Here, then, I had a definite example before me. Rudolf Steiner taught his pupils to live with the dead, and if one lived in sympathy with him one learned to know the work which they accomplish; the separation between the two worlds was no more. While I was writing my dissertation and was in frequent conversation with persons who had been near to my brother in his life, a portion of this otherwise hidden world was revealed to me. The contents of my dissertation are in part due to this.

When the World War came to an end, like so many other young men I stood before an empty void so far as my outer prospects in life were concerned. My mother, having lived throughout the War in Switzerland and helped in the carving of the first Goetheanum, was again resident in Vienna, except for the summer months which she still spent in Switzerland. I for my part, in the closing stages of the War, had undergone a training in mensuration and was about to return to the front for special service. Immediately before this I was married. But at this point, events followed one another in unexpected and quick succession.

The Peace of Versailles, dismembering Austria in the most senseless way and with a stroke of the pen destroying what had been a natural economic unit, is among those things about which one cannot speak without bitterness. Wilson was not to blame; he was not in a condition to be fully responsible for what he did. Those who allowed the articles of peace to be drawn up by a man who died of a disease of the brain from which he was already suffering at the time when he re-formed the continent of Europe, failing to recognize what they were doing, cannot, however, be exonerated by history; they are responsible for untold misfortune. Wilson knew nothing of the peoples to whom he imagined himself to be giving a new form of life. Europe no doubt will continue paying for these blunders all through the present century. The balance of economic life which was thus upset will not be restored so easily.

These matters played no little part in my own life at that time; having laid aside the uniform of a first lieutenant, I resolved to give lectures on the social question. Dr Steiner had for a moment considered making me his and Frau Marie Steiner's secretary in Berlin; he now gave up this plan and sent me as a lecturer to Vienna. I began with a small sum of money, given me by my friend Count Ludwig Polzer-Hoditz. It is not uninteresting to relate how this came about.

Count Polzer had been in Stuttgart seeing Dr Steiner. On his way back, owing to a disturbance on the railway-line, he had an unexpected stop at Crailsheim. He telephoned from there to Dr Steiner. I happened to be with Dr Steiner and heard the conversation. Dr Steiner had just been offering me the secretaryship when Count Polzer rang up. Dr Steiner asked him what he wanted. He did not know, he replied; he only wanted to let Dr Steiner know that he was still in the neighbourhood. Dr Steiner then asked him if he could help me make a start in Vienna; Count Polzer consented, and thus I came to be diverted from Berlin to Vienna.

I was extremely poor during this time in Vienna; my wife meanwhile was studying eurythmy in Switzerland. I had enough capital to hire a hall but not enough to put up posters. I could not therefore afford to make any break in my lectures, for I always had to announce the next lecture during the one I was giving. I earned just enough to keep me from starvation. I felt very lonely and rather hopeless. While I was in this situation I wrote a letter to Dr Steiner containing no less than sixty questions. Dr Steiner was accustomed to such letters and generally put off his reply until the next time I saw him. He had too little time to write. The letters from his hand which I possess were all of them due to some special circumstance; as a general rule he did not answer in writing. Others, too, have had the same experience in this respect as I. On this occasion, however, he answered at once; the answer came through Emil Molt, head of the Waldorf-Astoria cigarette factory in Stuttgart, who telephoned to me. 'Dr. Steiner,' he said, 'has had your letter, containing sixty questions. He cannot possibly answer in writing, but he invites you to attend the course of lectures he is just about to give to the teachers in the school which is being opened for the children of my employees. He asks me to tell you that all your sixty questions will find an answer in this lecture-course.' So then I went to Stuttgart; I caught the very next train and took no luggage with me. In any case I had few possessions; what little I had was afterwards brought on by my friend Dr Karl Schubert in an immense rucksack. For my part I never went home again, and for the next thirteen years remained in Stuttgart. I attended the course of lectures for the Waldorf teachers and at the end was just about to leave when Dr Steiner called me back and asked Herr Molt to appoint me as teacher. Thus I became a teacher in the Waldorf School at Stuttgart in Southern Germany.

Much could be said about the lecture-course, which was given especially for the Waldorf teachers and a few invited guests. In my life at any rate, it was an epoch-making event. There opened out before us a science of Man beyond our largest expectations. The human being in his development arose most wonderfully before our inner vision through Rudolf Steiner's lectures.

I was a mathematician and had also studied the history of philosophy, and psychology. At the University of Vienna I had, moreover, taken a course in experimental physics for several terms and in chemistry for one term. I therefore imagined I should have to teach scientific subjects. Rudolf Steiner, however, gave me history and literature. I still remember my despair when Rudolf Steiner told me, at two o'clock one night, that I should have to take a history lesson the next morning. 'But I do not even know in what century Charlemagne lived,' said I. Dr Steiner was not perturbed. 'Begin by teaching what you know,' he said. 'Give them the history of the World War, for there you surely were yourself, were you not?' I was speechless. Later on I understood that Dr Steiner, wanting to renew everything, put every teacher in a place where he would have to work up everything anew, out of his own initiative. Dr Steiner led the school sternly and on a grand scale. Emil Molt, who was responsible for the financial side, appointed me as a teacher subject to a fortnight's notice. Now, therefore, all of a sudden, I had a position in life. Subsequently Dr Steiner called my wife too to Stuttgart, and there we lived for thirteen happy years of active work and study. My wife became a eurythmy teacher at the school; so there arose a most harmonious co-operation. In 1920 my daughter Clarissa Johanna was born; Dr Steiner not only gave her her name but himself baptized her.

When the Waldorf School rose to its height we were more than sixty teachers — all of us more or less on terms of personal friendship with one another. So there arose a quick and active spiritual life of an unprecedented kind. Dr Steiner, though he still lived in Switzerland, shared all important events of the school life with us, and there was not one of us who did not often find his way to Switzerland. Dr Steiner himself also came frequently to Stuttgart, and there we had the unforgettable teachers' conferences with him — conferences in which all the knowledge of our time, and the wisdom of the Time-Spirit too, were fully present. Dr Steiner once, in jest, called the College of Teachers of the

Waldorf School the Intelligence of Middle-Europe, — not that there was no intelligence outside Stuttgart; his implication was that the sixty-four Waldorf teachers, gathered around him, might between them represent the best attainments of science and scholarship in all essential domains.

In the Waldorf School Dr Steiner sometimes provided children of elementary school age with class-teachers who had been university lecturers before. According to the usual ideas of our time, this would be a kind of degradation. Dr Steiner, however, said, 'To teach children really well, may often require more knowledge and a larger heart than to teach grown-up people.' As to social distinctions, there was no such thing in the Waldorf School. The count was equal to the son of the working-man; each human being was fully received for what he really was.

But it would be a false picture to imagine that we were like doves, full of sweet harmony with one another. Often enough we had very painful rows, and in the last resort there was no other way than for each one to say what he really thought. Dr Steiner showed endless patience, and could sit with us in conference until two or even four o'clock in the morning; the main thing was that everything twisted should be put straight, that the truth should come out, and we forgive one another. Sixty-four individualities around a common table are not so easy to manage!

The children had a good time in the true sense of the word; they were excellently taught and cared for, medically too, and throve under such treatment. Stuttgart's Medical Officer of Health, an impartial judge, found that the Waldorf children had the largest average chest-measurement and the best teeth and eyes, and wondered how this result had been attained.

Rudolf Steiner's educational method has much in common with that of Aristotle, or even Thomas Aquinas. Read, for example, the *Tractate on the Education of Princes*, by Aegidius Romanus de Colonna, favourite pupil of Thomas Aquinas, and you will find whole passages apparently the same as what Dr Steiner gives. Yet there is a very great difference. In the Aristotelian pedagogy and in its medieval, scholastic adaptations, the essential point is that the *inherited* predispositions come to the surface in the successive seven-year periods of life, and that the method of education should reckon with these gradually liberated inherited faculties. Dr Steiner, on the other hand, regards the inherited faculties as something essentially incomplete — even to some extent as a burden to be overcome. His essential aim is to develop the child's *individual* faculties and predispositions.

Faculties are forgotten thoughts and ideas. Inherited faculties are the forgotten experiences of earlier generations. Rudolf Steiner introduced the method of teaching by periods. History, for example, is given morning by morning for a period of six or eight weeks, followed by mathematics for a like period, and so on. This gives the children the opportunity to *forget* what they themselves have learned, and thus to supplement or even to replace their inherited faculties by their own individual ones. What you are allowed to forget for a certain time, afterwards bringing it to consciousness again in a new form, becomes your very own — filled with the will and strength of your own individuality.

It is, of course, not possible at this place to give an adequate introduction to Rudolf Steiner's educational system; we can only touch in passing on its most essential aspects. A whole world dawned on me as I began to understand the real difference between Scholasticism and Anthroposophy.

An important event in my own life took place in the year 1924, the last year during the whole of which Rudolf Steiner was still with us. Those children of the Waldorf School whose parents did not wish them to have the conventional (Protestant or Roman Catholic) religion lessons, attended the independent religion lessons which were arranged for by Dr Steiner and given by teachers of the School itself. In connection with this was a weekly service for these children on Sunday mornings — a simple Christian ceremony.

There was something deeply impressive in this Sunday morning service, and on one occasion I was moved by it more deeply than ever before. The experience became so concrete as to merge at last into spiritual vision. I could experience quite clearly how I was entering into a more or less unaccustomed condition, become free of the bodily

nature. From this time onward I knew by my own experience what it was to enter the spiritual world free of the
body and to perceive without the bodily sense-organs.

Rudolf Steiner, who explained the experience to me, told
me it corresponded to a certain degree of a pathway of
spiritual experience which was well known to him. He wrote
me a long letter of explanation, to which he afterwards added
verbal instruction. For the first time I was now entering into
a form of conscious experience which carried my thoughts
out into the cosmos, my feelings into the planetary spheres,
and my will into the elements: fire, air, water, earth. Rudolf
Steiner gathered it up into a meditation which he gave me:

My Head bears the being of the resting Stars,
My Breast is harbouring the life of the wandering Stars,
My body lives and moves amid the Elements.
All this am I.

Other experiences followed, and I soon recognized that I
was able to enter now by my own experience into the regions
I had so often heard him describe. I afterwards ascertained
that many of the things which I was thus experiencing had
been known for centuries in the traditions of spiritual movements, and I thus felt myself to be living within a certain
degree of a particular path of knowledge. Rudolf Steiner
confirmed me in this and wanted me to raise into fuller
consciousness things I had only faintly experienced to begin
with. It may be justified to give some further indication of
the nature of such experiences, since Rudolf Steiner gave me
the explanation of them, which may also be of use to others.

I saw my own being in a kind of cave or grotto. The
grotto, however, was not made of rock, but was alive and
moving. Dr Steiner explained that I was seeing my own
blood-circulation, the pulsations of which, instead of flowing
from within outward to the skin, appeared in a reflected
picture, working from without inward. Such experiences
being repeated, I learned in this way to see the whole of
physiology in a quite new aspect. I made acquaintance with
a world in which the biological-organic life and at the same
time the moral life of the soul finds its reflection, and I could
recognize the mathematical laws according to which this
reflection takes place.

66

Another cognate experience arises when one grows able to project outside oneself the sensitiveness which pervades all the flesh of the body. Where sensitiveness ceases, that is to say where the space inside our body is normally filled by the skeleton, the skeleton itself becomes visible. Where empty *Nothing* is, so far as the aforesaid sensitiveness is concerned, there — as in the negative of a film — there appears *Something;* one sees the entire picture of the skeleton.

Thus I encountered death, saw my own skeleton from outside, and felt the taste of ashes in my mouth. I knew myself to be in a world free of the body. Dr Steiner described this as an experience of a certain degree, which he also named and wrote down for me. Today, many years later, I understand these experiences and know that they are by no means unusual. They occur when the consciousness of a human being finds its way to independent spiritual experience. But Dr Steiner died soon after this time, and this resulted in great difficulties for my inner path, for it was now that I most needed him.

In Dr Steiner's lifetime, these spiritual experiences had, however, already taken on a form which enabled me to look back into previous lives on earth. I had experienced my own death in a former century. Thenceforth I knew who I am. Dr Steiner, who knew of this experience, too, gave me to understand that I had seen truly.

The reader may object, 'How is it possible to have such experiences, and even if one has them, how can one be sure of not confusing reality with mere fancy?' Such questions and objections are justified. To test the reality of such experiences, one would have to indicate the methods which make the distinction possible. But to do so at all fully would go far beyond the compass of this biography. Since, however, these experiences go back into history, there are also ways of testing them by historical tradition. Tradition is inexact, while spiritual experience is exact. You can learn more through experience than is extant in historical tradition. But you are thereby better equipped to seek things out in history, till you discover one day that what you saw in the spirit was the true history, which others have only concealed in order to attain specific ends. In the last resort, external history, too, will confirm what is seen in the spirit. Yet without vision you would not have known where or how to seek. There are such ways of confirmation, and he who goes along them knows them to be reliable. There are other ways of confirmation too.

For my own life the consequence of these experiences was that when Rudolf Steiner died the connection of my life with the spiritual world did not cease, and it became possible to continue many things which seemed lost to others. This very fact, however — not only in my own case, but through others too, undergoing like experiences — brought about dire conflicts which in the end divided the circle of human beings who had gathered around Rudolf Steiner. It is not my task at this moment to write a history of the spiritual movement which Rudolf Steiner inaugurated, or of its fate after his passing. It would, indeed, be an interesting contribution to the history of mankind, but it could only be made intelligible by including not only the present but also the past history of spiritual movements which are connected with this one.

2. Historical Periods and the Fate of Nations

Trithemius of Sponheim (1462–1516) has left a rare historical work in which he depicts world history as an ordered sequence of events into which the deeds of humanity are fitted. He maintains and proceeds to prove that similar configurations make their appearance in history every 2,480 years. He arrives at the number 2,480 as a total of seven long epochs, each of which lasts for 354$^1/_3$ years. A different impulse holds sway in each of these shorter epochs, and in accordance with the conceptions of the Middle Ages he personifies these impulses. He speaks of seven different leaders of history, endows them with the names of the seven planets and places them in the opposite order to our days of the week: Saturn (Saturday), Venus (French *vendredi*, Freya, Friday), Jupiter (*jeudi* from the Latin *Jovis dies*), Mercury (*Wotans*-day, *mercredi*, *Mercuris dies*), Mars (*Mardi*, Tuesday), Moon (Monday), Sun (Sunday). Apart from this half-mythological phraseology, Trithemius teaches a totally unmythological historical theory, namely, he claims that world history runs in epochs of about three and a half centuries each, and that these impulses can be clearly described.

Putting this theory of the medieval thinker into modern terminology, we may say the following. Seven epochs are clearly discernible in the course taken by history since the time of Christ, and we have been in the seventh epoch since the year 1879. That 1879 is a year which modern writers also place at the beginning of an epoch is shown, for instance, by Marshall, the English economist, in his work, *Economics for Industry*, which was published in 1879, and in which he says: 'The time has now arrived at which the phrase "political economy" should be shelved, and the word "economy" substituted on the ground that the adjective was misleading since political interests generally mean the interests of some part or parts of the nation.' Since the year 1879 we have had such an ever-increasing mutual interweaving of interests of all states in the economic field that the phrase 'political economy' is indeed beginning to be inappropriate. From that time onwards we should speak of 'world economy'. Trithemius of Sponheim is not altogether wrong when he describes this epoch beginning with 1879 as one radiating forth like a sun and representing something *universal*.

From Michaelmas 1879, the concluding point of his prophetic history, he works backwards in epochs of $354^1/_3$ years and arrives at another sunlike, cosmopolitan period, 2,480 years earlier, at the time of Alexander the Great. Going back still another 2,480 years, he comes to a period which he is unable to describe in detail owing to the many gaps existing in historical knowledge of that time. We, however, may be certain that it was indeed a cosmopolitan epoch, for it was the time when the Babylonian King Gilgamesh travelled to the West, This event is depicted in detail by the reliefs in the British Museum. Three times we see the question of the relationship of East and West rising before humanity. The third time is clearly in our own epoch, and we may be sure that up to the end of the twentieth century no question of greater importance is likely to arise than that of how East and West can live in peace together. As the prophetic Trithemius of Sponheim has given us a conception of history which in his day was still indeterminate both as regards the far past and the distant future, but has become for us an open book proving that he was right, should we not venture, in line with him, to envisage what the end of this century may be?

In this sense, the twentieth century should present a repetition of events strongly reminiscent of those of the epoch 2,480 years previously. This coincides with the year 480 BC, the date of the battle of Salamis.

For this reason we shall speak in some detail of this battle, after a brief outline of the historical periods mentioned by Trithemius.

The period of the coming of Christianity represents for Trithemius the time at which Light penetrated Darkness. Christ, the Light of the World, shone into the dark age of Saturn. Study of Gnosis clearly indicates that philosophy at

70

this time consisted in portraying the fullness of Light newly shed over the ancient mysteries that were now darkened. The next period is that of 'Hate and Love' (Venus), the era of the martyrs and the persecutions of the Christians. The next is that of 'Order and Chaos' (Jupiter), the epoch of the migrations of peoples and of the ordered monastic life. The next period is that of 'Illness and Healing' (Mercury, or in the language of the Church, Raphael), the time of a St Francis of Assisi, or of a 'poor Henry' (a novel of the Middle Ages depicting the miraculous healing of a knight), or of the Holy Grail and the wounded Amfortas. The next epoch belongs to Mars. It is the period of the Crusades and Orders of Knights with their warlike stand for Christianity, and lastly, the courageous discovery of new regions of the earth. The next epoch belongs to the Moon. Its character comes to expression in the prominence assumed by the theory of heredity, and the idea of race. The leading figure is Gabriel, the Christian representative of the Moon, who proclaims birth. Then comes the last epoch in which we are now living. It is the Sun-Age of Michael.

Mythological as the phraseology of Trithemius is, the divisions stand the test of scientific knowledge. It is the true classification of world history.

The author is fully aware that every doctrine concerning epochs is theoretical, appearing to be arbitrarily constructed and incapable of proof. He allows himself, however, to apply Trithemius' methods to an example. He would like to contemplate the end of the present century in the light of the fact that this view of history embraces and then describes what happened 480 years before Christ, and that in our present time events will again take place, in a different form, of course, but yet having a certain similarity. From this point of view let us picture the time of the battle of Salamis, 480 BC, 2,480 years before the end of this century. It was not Greece alone that was in the scales at this time. The continuance of the whole of European culture was in the balance. If the Persians had remained victors, the East would have overrun the West. Greece would have become a European-Greek satrapy of the Persian Empire, and all that is still today the basis of our culture, of classic learning, would not have come into being. If Athens had not been burnt, the Athens we know today as the great centre of art would never have existed; the philosophy of Plato and of Aristotle which dominated the Middle Ages, the whole of our classical culture — none of this would have come into the world.

The whole of Asia was stirred when the armies of Darius and, later, after his death, those of Xerxes began to march. The royal messengers went forth from Susa in the direction of all the points of the compass to assemble these armies: to the Danube as well as to India, to Jaxartes as well as to the upper valley of the Nile, to the shores of the Archipelago, to Pontos, to the Arabian and Persian Gulfs, to the coasts of the Syrian and Lybian Seas. This preparation lasted for two years, and in the third year a migration of the peoples began, emanating from the eastern boundaries of the world and gathering together peoples of many different languages and accoutrements — a gaily coloured throng. This onslaught was opposed by only ten Greek tribes.

The Greeks were by no means united to the point of being a national power. To bring the fleet to its prime was left to the far-seeing mind of Themistocles, and inner conflicts were far from being overcome. The nobility and the people were not of one mind, and the foremost poets, for example, Pindar, as well as the Oracles and the centres of religious rites which were connected with the leading ranks of the community, were of opinion that they must deny their support to this movement for national defence.

It was left to a few men by their courage in leadership and by their executive abilities, to accomplish that which preserved Greece, and with Greece the whole of European culture.

All previous undertakings on the part of the Persians had been of a local character, concerned with punishing towns in revolt or other smaller groups. Now, under Xerxes, the movement involved the whole of Greece and thereby influenced all European culture, for the first time beginning to bud.

Starting at this point and extending to the time of Alexander the Great, who by his Asiatic conquests hellenized practically the whole of Asia of that time, a complete inversion took place. It was not power from the East that swept Greece, but the Greeks wandered East of their own accord, delving gladly into all the cults and philosophies of the East, learning from and entering into each one with love, and precisely in this way forging the link with the Grecian world and conception of life. Alexander the Great was a pupil of the world-embracing Aristotle, and he believed in the reality of the single, all-comprising truth in which all religions and philosophies share. For this reason Alexander could feel himself to be a son of Jupiter Ammon or a worshipper of Jehovah or a disciple of Serapis, without being untrue to his own convictions. For him, there was only one all-embracing truth, recognized in all the mysteries, pointed to by Aristotle as the highest goal, the manifold manifestations of which should not confound devout disciples. It was necessary for him to withdraw under military protection. But he was much less warrior and conqueror than a philosopher hungry for knowledge and a bringer of culture, a true pupil of Aristotle.

At Salamis the highest goal of Europe was at stake. Free-willed union with the whole earth must take the place of subjugation by Eastern despotism. Human dignity must triumph over brute force; freedom and love must replace lust for domination. On this depended not only Greek but European culture.

The individual soul had not reached its full development in this epoch of Greek culture. Aristides was still in banishment 'because he was too just,' and 'so just a man might easily become the object of too much worship and in this way too dangerous to the common weal.' 'For the individual is of lesser account than the common weal.' Such were the arguments of the peasant who, being completely illiterate, was at a loss to know how to write the name Aristides on the slab in order that he might be banished. The peasant sought the help of his neighbour who, unknown to him, was Aristides himself, requesting him to inscribe the name Aristides on the slab. 'Why do you wish that he shall be banished?' asked Aristides. And then came the peasant's reply: 'He is too just and would attract too much admiration.'

This argument, which would puzzle our present-day

consciousness, came naturally to that period. The common weal was of more value than the individual. The idea of individual leadership had not yet arisen. Half a century later, in the person of Alcibiades, we find consciousness of individuals being awakened for the first time. His peculiarities must be understood in the sense that they are experiments on the part of the individual becoming conscious of the 'I am'. Whether he actually cut off the noses of the Hermes statues or not, this and other similar stories narrated of him in his day prove that the 'I' of the self-conscious personality was just awakening. In Herostratus this impulse was turned to some account. The same impulse was in Alexander, but ennobled in his case by the education he had received. The 'I' broke through and the Platonic Dialogues, the methods of Socrates, the philosophy of Aristotle are all expressions of this personal intelligence which was born for the first time in this epoch.

Themistocles was already a great leader. But he failed to convince the Athenians that now was the moment to finance the building of a huge fleet, as this was essential for the very existence of Greece. It was necessary for him to take small frictions with the inhabitants of the Aegean Islands into his pretext, in order to cloak his actions. He planned the far-reaching idea, but he carried it out by means of trifling tactical means.

The fact that he was able to persuade the people, who up to now had shared the income derived from the mines, to allot this money to the building of the fleet, shows his influence and his wide perspicacity. Aristides, who opposed him, feared to see the populace ruined by undertakings on too great a scale. Fate led to his banishment, whereby it was his lot to become the first eye-witness of the approaching Persians, and it was he who brought Themistocles the news that meant so much to him, namely, that the Greeks had already been surrounded in the Bay of Salamis by the enemy so that there was now no way of escape, the decisive battle being the only possibility left. Fate could not possibly have allotted the roles more wisely in allowing the great men to act together, their ways having first separated — for the good of the whole — and then again uniting. Themistocles, knowing his people, had desired this very surrounding by the enemy and Aristides was his prime witness, used by him to convince the irresolute members of the war council that the decision must now be taken.

It is of inestimable value to study how the destiny of peoples, indeed of whole spheres of culture, is formed through individuals and the links between their destinies. That which made Aristides and Themistocles first into opponents, rivals, and finally into friends, affected the whole world, saving culture and civilization.

The Battle of Salamis would never have been won without the intervention of wind and waves, without the adroitness of the skilful Greeks which had been practised for decades. Nature and human nature combined to mould destiny's work of art.

In this connection the conduct of the Lacedamonians is also very significant. They had always held back, had safeguarded themselves by the excuse that they were waiting for the full moon before attacking, and so forth. Owing to this attitude their co-operation had always been feeble. But now that the crucial point had arrived they were on the spot, actually under the royal command of Leonidas, and they died the death of heroes, gaining for the Greeks the necessary time to transfer their defence from the mainland to the ships. That in spite of treachery they died heroically, in loyalty to others, consciously sacrificing the lives of the few for the salvation of the life of the whole — this is highly significant.

The day of the Battle of Salamis, September 20, was a holy day for Athens. For on this day, the 19th Boedromion, the image of Iacchos, the God of the Eleusinians, was carried in procession to Eleusis. While Themistocles was prevailing upon his people to embark upon the decisive battle, the torches of the procession lit up the Bay, indicating as it were in a picture, that the God of the unfoldment of the 'I' should remain protected and the ship with the holy pictures of the Aekides approached from the Aegean. The sacrificial flames blazed as it passed by.

At that time the Greeks could not appreciate the full significance of what was taking place, but they had some inkling of it in the panorama presented by the events.

The battle, which had to be fought out against an over-whelmingly majority, was won by the co-operation of all parties, the laying aside of all ancient feuds, the uniting of rivals, the message of the exile, the religious fervour of the Eleusinians, by storm and weather, and lastly by the moon goddess, who at the decisive finale shed that half-light which was needed by the Greeks who knew the locality. In grati-tude, the Greeks united the festival in memory of the victory to the festival of Artemis the moon goddess.

In the meantime the storm had wrecked the bridges of Xerxes over the Hellespont and this accelerated the with-drawal of the mighty king, who now began to fear for his own safety.

The incredible had happened, the future of Europe was saved. What lessons for our time can we learn from these things?

The situation as it was at Salamis is practically at hand again. We are confronted, not by the ships of Persia, but by the ever-increasing power of the East. The 'Greek lack of unity' has not become less. While we are trying to deal with our rivalries and quarrels, the 'mighty king' is arming once again. By the end of the century, will there again have sprung up that Aristotelian-Alexandrian culture which can make it possible for Europe to permeate the East with loving comprehension? The question must be asked. It is only when this takes place that the 'hellenizing' of the East, that is to say, the assimilation of the two poles of culture, the Eastern and the Western, can occur.

When the end of this century dawns the day of Salamis will be renewed. Men and gods will bear other names than of yore but the problems will have remained the same. May it be that a Themistocles and an Aristides, may it be that all opposing rivals will then stretch hands to each other in the torchlight of the renewed Eleusinian mysteries. May the God be borne in truth into the mystery. Then, and only then, will there arise once again the Aristotelian-Alexandrian cul-ture which in Europe was the wisdom-culture, but which must meet the East with love; then, and only then, can there happen that to which Trithemius of Sponheim refers, when he says that humanity must know that after the lapse of the appointed time, epochs of cosmopolitanism come again to the world, prepared for by other periods which serve different ideals. We are living in this period of preparation. May our epoch understand the preparation and the goal and, learning from history, find the direction in which the present age should proceed.

3. England and the Foundation of Commercial Towns

The Origin of the Lohengrin Saga Traced According to English History

The period in the Middle Ages when, at first in England and then extending over the whole of Europe, towns sprang up as centres of a new economic order, corresponds actually to the time at which humanity passed from the dream world into the modern economic order.

Towns serve not only as protective means against attacks by wild neighbours who, devastating the land, terrify the population so that the latter are driven to seek refuge behind strong ramparts, but are also centres of commerce and industry. In the Middle Ages the towns served both ends: as strong fortresses and centres of economic life. English towns which were attacked by the Danes had almost all succumbed to their conquerors who, from thence, held the surrounding country in a state of constant excitement, fear, and armament. For this reason Edward the Elder rebuilt Chester as well as Witham (Essex), Towcester, and Hertford. His sister Ethelfleda erected castles for defence against the Welsh and Danes at Bransbury (Hereford), Stafford, Tamworth, Scergeate (Sarratt, Hertford), Wardborough, Warwick, and others. A newly discovered method of constructing fortresses by means of walls of rock and bricks made the erection of these fortresses an easier task (*Anglo-Saxon Chronicle*, AD 921).

In Germany the Hungarians stormed victoriously forward, and Henry the Fowler had to protect his people just as the English had to protect themselves against the Danes.

The fact that the towns served not merely as fortresses but also as acknowledged centres of economic activity is due primarily to the laws enacted by Edward the Elder. He commanded that all trade transactions were to be carried on only inside the city gates. The German king laid down the law that all business transactions were to be carried on only within the towns and that all festivities and meetings were to take place therein.

William of Malmesbury, in the fifth chapter of Book II, tells of the deeds of Edward and his sister Ethelfleda. 'He invented a plan, by means of which he circumvented the onslaughts of the Danes, namely, at appointed places he re-erected old towns and built new ones, supplying them with armed men who protected the inhabitants and warded off the enemy.'

Edward had a brother called Ethelward. The son of the latter was named Turketul. Towards the end of Edward's reign Turketul took over his father's inheritance. The latter died in 918 or 920. The King offered Turketul various ecclesiastical honours, for example a bishopric and the episcopate of Winton. Turketul, however, declined all these honours, so the King, recognizing his worth, raised him to the position of High Chancellor and entrusted to him all temporal and spiritual affairs. This Turketul has been honoured in saga as knight of the Holy Grail. Wolfram von Eschenbach mentions him in his poem *Parzival* (III, 364) as a knight of the Holy Grail, and writes his name thus: 'Turkentals.' More recent saga converted him into the knight Lohengrin.

After the death of King Edward in the year 924, Turketul continued as Chancellor in the reign of Edward's son Athelstan, who, according to the chronicle of William of Malmesbury (Book II, ch. 6), had been reared at the court of Ethelfleda and her husband Ethelred. During the reign of Athelstan an insurrection occurred of Northumbrians, Scots, and Cumbrians. It led to a battle at Brunford in which Danes and Norwegians also fought against Turketul and Athelstan. In this affray Turketul led the Londoners and Mercians. In the battle Turketul fought Constantine, King of the Scots, but was almost slain while attempting to take the King prisoner, and was only saved by the bravery of one of his men, the centurion Singinus, who killed the King of the Scots. Turketul gave thanks to God for his salvation, and was thankful that he had not been called upon to kill or wound anyone. Ingulph, in depicting the battle, mentions Turketul. Henry of Huntingdon and Roger of Hoveden also refer to this battle.

As conqueror in this important battle of Brunford, Turketul was now given the honour of escorting two English princesses, Eadgitha and Elfgifa, to Germany to present them to the King's son in order that he might choose one in marriage. Roswitha von Gandersheim explicitly refers to this incident. Otto, the son of Henry the Fowler, fell in love at first sight with Eadgitha, the elder daughter, and decided to marry her (*Hrotsuith*, 117, 324).

Eadgitha was about seventeen years of age at this time. Elfgifa was affianced to the Burgundian Duke Alberich (Waitz, *Jahrbücher* p. 10).

Turketul conducted the two English princesses to Cologne on the Rhine. This event is mentioned in the poem *Lohengrin*. Lohengrin comes as ambassador from England, as the messenger of the Holy Grail, sent by Arthur to Cologne. He then accompanied Henry I on all royal missions and processions, and took part in the battle against the Hungarians. Thus runs the saga.

It has been historically established that the towns were founded and defended on the same economic plan as Turketul introduced into England. In this sense it is also associated with the repulse of the Hungarians.

Eadgitha received the town of Magdeburg as the bridegroom's gift. She lived happily by the side of the German king for over sixteen years, and presented to him a son Liudolf. Eadgitha and Elfgifa had three more sisters; one of these, called Eadgyifu, married Charles III. Ludwig Ultramarinus is the offspring of this marriage. The latter was espoused to Gerberga, daughter of Henry I. The Dukes of Lower Lothringia are descended from him.

From this we can see how tradition, making use of historical events, according to the account of Wolfram von Eschenbach, calls Turketul by his real name, converting Lothringian, Loherain, into Lohengrin. The legend of Godfrey of Bouillon, who is supposed to be descended from the Swan Knight, that is Lohengrin, is also well known. Below is a genealogical tree from which a comparison between saga and history can be made.

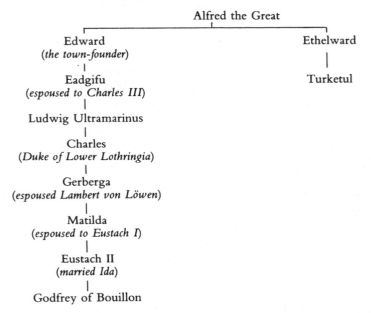

Alfred the Great

Edward
(*the town-founder*)

Eadgifu
(*espoused to Charles III*)

Ludwig Ultramarinus

Charles
(*Duke of Lower Lothringia*)

Gerberga
(*espoused Lambert von Löwen*)

Matilda
(*espoused to Eustach I*)

Eustach II
(*married Ida*)

Godfrey of Bouillon

Ethelward

Turketul

Elgive, another sister of Eadgitha, married Ludwig of Aquitania, as recorded by William of Malmesbury and Ingulph. Lastly, Eadhilda was espoused to Hugo of France, the forebear of the Capets (forebear, at all events, by his first wife, Hadwiga, daughter of Henry I).

From this we can see that the English princesses were espoused to all the principal European dynasties, and this fact opens up a most important, far-reaching Continental political issue underlying these matrimonial alliances, of equal weight as regards legend and history.

Ingulph relates the following:

> When the news of the victory of Brunford spread throughout the whole Christian world, all the Kings of the earth desired to contract friendly relations with Athelstan and in some way or other to conclude a holy peace pact.

He then goes on to relate how they

> all sent ambassadors to solicit the hands of the royal

princesses of England. In this process of courting the English princesses the ambassadors brought many rare gifts such as the English had never seen nor heard of in centuries: portions of the Crown of Thorns of Jesus Christ set in crystal, the sword of Constantine the Great, the banner of Mauritius the Martyr, as also the lance of Charles the Great to which the French attach no small importance.

These presents are likewise mentioned by William of Malmesbury (Book II, chap. 6).

As we already know, Eadhilda married Hugo the Great, the son of Robert, Duke of Neustria, Burgundy, and France. The bridegroom was a cousin of Athelstan, Adalof, Count of Boulogne, son of Baldwin of Flanders and of Aelfthryde, sister of King Edward, who in Hugo's name conveyed the numerous valuable and rare bridal offerings to the collection of the nation's display of treasures at Abingdon. And then the gifts are described as we already know. By the marriage of Eadgitha's sister Eadhilda they were transferred from Carolingian possession to England. Amongst them was to be found the Holy Spear which is mentioned in the Grail story by Wolfram von Eschenbach as the 'bleeding spear' which is carried in front of the Grail, and which was then at Malmesbury at the Court of Athelstan. In the Lohengrin poem this spear is referred to and is identified with the lance of Longinus, and it is therein related that Henry I captured the spear from Rudolf II of Burgundy, who in turn had it from Count Samson, the Councillor of King Hugo of Italy.

The actual history of the spear is a novel in itself. It once rested in the secular treasury in the Royal Palace at Vienna, whither it was brought from Nürnberg for safety during Napoleon's campaign. It belonged to the insignia of the German Empire.

The Lohengrin poem runs as follows:

As blood and water emanated therefrom
The blind man (Longinus) touched his eyes therewith
They were instantaneously restored
They spear belongs to the Kingdom.

For the history of the spear, see Waitz, *Jahrbücher* p. 67.

The marriage of Eadgitha and Otto took place in the year 929. In 930 Eadgitha gave birth to a son Liudolf, and in 931 to a daughter Liudgard. But Turketul returned to England. Turketul's most trusted friend was Dunstan, who was banished for a time, recalled however at Turketul's request and made Abbot of Glastonbury. Turketul presented to him, for his monastery at Glastonbury, a most valuable chalice, which was preserved there up to the Norman epoch and was famed as Turketul's chalice. Edmund the Magnificent succeeded Athelstan, and, after his assassination in 946, Edward's youngest son, Edred, came to the throne. In the second year of his reign the Northumbrians made an insurrection, and Turketul was called upon to undertake an embassy. He was here honoured and appointed lord of sixty benefices. On his journey he came upon the Monastery of Croyland, which is situated near Peterborough in the English province of Holland. We have here the origin of the Dutch Lohengrin Saga. To this very day, whoever goes there is astonished at the Dutch character of the landscape. One can see windmills, canals raised high above the ground, ponds, and swans. As Turketul arrived, three monks came forth to greet him, and led him into the ruined monastery in order to show him the relics of Saint Guthlac. At that time Croyland was an island. The monastery had been founded in 716 by King Ethelbald. Saint Guthlac and his sister Saint Pega were living here. Coelwulf demolished the monastery. Turketul listened to the account of the Danish invasion of 870. He was seized with compassion, and promised aid to the monks. Then he appealed to the King that he should do something for Croyland. Turketul himself wished to become a monk there, but the King would not allow it; he needed his Chancellor. The King actually went on his knees to Turketul, beseeching him not to forsake him. But Turketul invoked the Holy Apostle, Paul, and the King gave way.

Then Turketul wended his way to Croyland. He found but three aged monks alive. With a large retinue he travelled round the island. The chronicler here relates: 'It is here worthy of note that at this time such a drought reigned that over the whole of England there was no rain for a period of three years, and this drought was for the most part referred to as the "Drought of Elias".' In the Dutch saga the knight known as Lohengrin is not called Lohengrin, but Knight *Helias*. Turketul returned all his sixty principalities to the King and became Abbot of Croyland. Here he established a very special cult.

Meanwhile the death of King Edred took place in 955. Edwy succeeded and reigned till 959, when the sixteen-year-old Edgar became king, at whose birth the saintly Dunstan had heard the singing of angels. The chronicler, when speaking of this king, writes as follows: 'He was what Romulus was to the Romans, Cyrus to the Persians, Alexander to the Greeks, Arsases the Parthians, Charles the Great to the French, and Arthur to Britain.' Turketul visited him in 966. He was known as Edgar the Peaceful. This was the sixth king during whose reign Turketul lived. Turketul received a privilege for Croyland, and met Dunstan once more.

What joy! Turketul was now approaching his closing years. He had Croyland's history chronicled. He lived in retrospection. This history embraces the period from the foundation up to 973. He lived in his memories of the past, relating them to others. He presented to the monastery a golden chalice and two silver cups lined with gold, which had been given to him by the German Emperor, Henry I.

Now his hour drew nigh. He was surrounded by his highly prized friends. He outlived them all, and tended them during illness with devoted fidelity. First his beloved Clarenbald died, next Swarling followed by Brun, then Aio his notary, and lastly Turgar, who as an eye-witness had related to him the history of the monastery. By 973 they had all departed, the old and trusted companions. And now approached the year 975, in which King Edgar also died. Turketul became ill. For three days he lay in a fever. On the fourth day he called for the relics given him by the German Emperor, Henry the Town-planner, Hugo of France, and Ludwig the Aquitanian.

For him they were not merely relics; they were the landmarks of his life which he now reviewed. They were the emblems of the history inaugurated by him. In his mind's eye he saw the five princesses whose migration he witnessed from England to the Continent, thus inaugurating history by forming alliances with the highest continental rulers. He viewed this history, studied England's connection therewith. His gaze rested on the relic of the Apostle Bartholomeus, who corresponds to the same person called Nathanael in the Bible, the fifth apostle chosen by Jesus (John 1:45–51). Jesus had designated him as a representative of his people. This relic served as a reminder to Turketul that he also had fought for his people, fighting for all he held sacred. He had received it as a young man when, for the first time, he put on the warrior's girdle at a festive ceremony. The monarch who had initiated him had made him a present of this relic as a reminder that he also should fight for his people. The monarch had received it from the Duke of Benevent. Every article surrounding him represented holy or secular history, emperors and kings had handled or worn the objects. His mind now dwelt on this fact in retrospect. In storm and stress this relic had protected him by virtue of its admonishing power throughout all the battles. They then appeared in his mind's eye — the battle of Brunford as well as others. In spirit he reviewed the attacking Danes, the Hungarians on their steeds. He experienced what it signified to consolidate and protect Western civilization, behind walls and fortresses, in peaceful cities. He had lived through the reigns of six kings, the last of these having earned the title of the Peace-maker. Then his gaze fell upon the relic of Saint Leodegar. The Duke of Aquitania had presented it to him. He saw Leodegar, the Bishop of Autun, whose mother Sigrade was the sister of the Duke Eticho, father of Saint Odile. Leodegar belonged to that princely family from which it is claimed by the old chroniclers that all European rulers were descended. Maximilian I was proud to trace his origin to this family. Rudolf of Habsburg, Robert the Brave, and Hugo Capet did likewise. The latter bishop lived at the period at which the battles took place, which lent the background to certain parts of the Nibelung Saga. He died a martyr's death, enveloped in the tragedy of such occurrences. To Turketul he stood as the representative of those races who, on continental soil, depicted the protectors of the precious blood, of the Holy Grail.*

All these facts were passing before the soul of the dying Turketul. He viewed his own life bound up with the history of Europe, and he mused how, introduced into the intermingling of nations by royal matrimonial alliances, the secrets of Christianity had achieved a perpetual mission, not yet complete. He realized that it was a matter of import to promulgate this Christian mission in the future, and turning to the monks and lay brothers around his couch, whose immediate concern this future was, he addressed his farewell words to them, 'Preserve the fire of your zeal,' and expired. He now addressed the peoples of Europe. 'Preserve the fire of your zeal.' He said these words at the end of his life, which had been dedicated to the task of connecting the history of the Continent to that of England, knowing full well that the establishment of towns would continue for a thousand years. We are now at the end of this thousand years.

At Cowbit, close to the Monastery of Croyland, there stands a chapel. There is a document preserved in a niche in the wall of this chapel. It contains particulars concerning the swan mark, which was branded on the foot of the swans as an indication that the latter were the property of the King. This swan mark is a remarkable sign.

What is the significance attached to it? It is Turketul's lamp, which it was customary to hoist in Cowbit, the most elevated point in the surroundings of Croyland, as a signal that the Danes were about to launch an attack. The hoisting of the lamp served as a signal for the populace that they should seek refuge behind their ramparts. The old Chancellor of the

* Proof of this fact is in my book *Weltgeschichte* (*Ninth Century*) where I have shown that Hugo of Tours, a descendant of Eticho, conveyed the relics of the Holy Grail to Charles the Great.

King, the founder of towns and builder of fortresses, warned his people. This symbol was branded on the swans, as Turketul was known as the Swan Knight. The saga of the Swan Knight, however, does not, as some would have us believe, derive its origin from Brabant, Holland, or Cleve, but in the English province of Holland in the vicinity of Peterborough. But in this case it is no longer saga — it is history. The time has now arrived, after the passage of a thousand years, when history should be retrieved from the mists of legend.

Sent forth by Arthur as Knight of the Grail, fighting for sanctity, finally serving the peace-loving king, the messenger of the Holy Grail founded the cities. Now, at the expiration of a thousand years, these cities have become what they are — gigantic forces. Thus we see their development throughout history, but the mission still remains, even if changed in outward formation. Just as of old, the peace-loving economic character was bestowed on the development of towns by means of valiant encounters; in like manner we of today are called upon to fight for a similar peace-loving, economic significance in the evolution of the countries throughout the world. This can no longer be achieved by matrimonial alliances. It is possible today only by appropriate co-operation in concrete fields of endeavour; yet the mission still remains — to impregnate the world with the economic impulse in the light of the precious and most unselfish Blood that was shed for all humanity. The task has still to be undertaken — the method alone has altered.

Thus we can see that the warning has now once more to be extricated from the mists of saga and presented in the light of history. And now one is constrained to ask: Where is the kindling fire to preserve it? Should it not be possible, delving back into the veritable all-embracing depths of the history of England, to renew the fire that slumbers in the souls of men, and thus consciously to tread the path leading from town culture to world economic culture from the year 1000 to the year 2000, from slumbering saga to present-day transactions?

4. Portugal as the Preparer for the British Mission

Portugal and Spain, which together constitute the Iberian Peninsula, are not really differentiated from one another geographically, geologically, or even in point of language, for the Portuguese tongue is no more different from the Spanish than the Castilian, Catalonian, or Basque. Nor are the political frontiers between Portugal and Spain in any real sense natural frontiers. The independent existence of Portugal side by side with Spain is indeed one of the riddles of history, but in truth this independence, seemingly so unfounded, is deeply rooted in the history of mankind — more so than a history of Portugal from the merely national aspect can reveal.

It was in fact the transition from the medieval to the modern consciousness of mankind which gave birth to Portugal as an independent entity. One might even say that the new age created for itself, in Portugal, a destined instrument for the progress of all mankind. The immense change from medieval bonds of consciousness to the free and world-wide outlook of the modern age is profoundly rooted in the history of the Portuguese, more especially in their voyages of discovery, whereby the Far East — India, above all — was brought into more intimate contact with Europe. What in antiquity, in Alexander's time, had been but an isolated adventure, now became a firmly established relationship of commerce between East and West.

Vasco da Gama's discovery was followed by Francisco Almeida's conquest of India on behalf of the Portuguese crown, and what was thus achieved was made into a lasting possession by Albuquerque. Thus there arose the world-embracing trade of modern time, which became a thing of far wider than merely national significance. Men of all nations indeed took part in these voyages, whether as merchants, scientists and scholars, or simply adventurers. Martin

things to do

- ○ Rose quartz
- ○ Blue Howlite
- ○ Jade
- ○ Carnelian
- ○ cherry quartz
- ○ Mookite
- ○ Clear quartz
- ○ Smoky quartz
- ○ Sodalite
- ○ Moonstone
- ○ Crackled quartz
- ○ Unakite
- ○ Red tiger's eye
- ○ Rhodonite
- ○ Dalmation jasper green
- ○ Green aventurine
- ○ Hematite
- ○ Amethyst
- ○
- ○

Behaim constructed his famous globe, which can be seen to this day in the Nuremberg museum and bears witness to the extent of his knowledge — a knowledge founded still in ancient spiritual traditions. He too, in the spirit, accompanied the bold seafarers. In the State Library at Munich there is a manuscript account of the journey by a German who accompanied the Portuguese on their voyage to India. Members of nearly all the European nations were present there. Indeed, there can be no doubt that the voyage was inspired by the great orders of chivalry, all of which were cosmopolitan in character. These knightly orders — I mention for example those that were founded in England with the renewal of the Arthurian legends by Henry VII — were intimately connected, above all, with the Order of Knights of St James of Compostela (Santiago). Maximilian too, the Roman king, had his share in these international communities of the spirit.

The Portuguese voyagers owed their knowledge and their skill to the School of Navigation at Sagrés in the south of Portugal, the founder of which was Henry the Navigator. The latter was Grand Master of the 'Order of Christ,' which had been founded by the Portuguese king Dinis after the dissolution of the Knights Templars, with the intention to protect and carry forward their valuable impulses. These orders, too, stood for an international community of spirit.

Henry the Navigator himself was half Portuguese and half English. His mother was Philippa, daughter of John of Gaunt, who was the third son of King Edward III of England. Philippa's mother was Blanche of Lancaster. Thus the Red Rose of Lancaster is also interwoven with the history of the Portuguese discoveries. Azurara has bequeathed to us Henry the Navigator's horoscope. In the interpretation we read that Henry was well fitted to seek out things that were hidden from other men, as is shown by the position of Saturn, the guardian of secrets. If ever a horoscope was of significance it was this one, which, though recorded and worked out at the time of his birth, was literally fulfilled by his life; for Henry was chosen by destiny to discover the hitherto unknown African continent, and it was his ocean map which at a later time guided Columbus to the West.

Henry the Navigator was a man of extraordinary features. The mighty and prominent chin was some indication of his unusual character. He was a mathematical genius, knowing in advance, with intuitive feeling, what others had to calculate. Small wonder if the things which he initiated worked on into the future. Englishman and Portuguese at one and the same time, he united realistic common sense with fine sensibility. Thus he became not only a national hero of Portugal, but a representative of the spirit of the coming time.

What the Portuguese had discovered and had made into the lasting foundation of a new world-commerce, was inherited by the Dutch. At the end of the sixteenth century, when Spain put an end to Portugal's independence and the reactionary spirit was threatening to gain the upper hand once more, the united Netherlands were separated off from the same Spanish empire. The two events were simultaneous. It was as though the spirit of modern time, at the moment of losing hold on Portugal, created a new instrument for itself in the Netherlands, the heroic characters of which, by their strong sense of liberty, appeared as the true children of modern time. The Dutch trading companies inherited what the Portuguese seamen had achieved in the Far East, and the Dutch inheritance was taken over by the English in their turn. England can therefore look back on all this as on a page of her own history.

It is a wonderful thing to observe how the earth-embracing impulses of the new time, sustained by a spiritual community of individuals belonging to nearly all the countries, eventually gained the day in conflict with those older forms of society which were still based entirely on community of interest brought about by way of marriage. This conflict is most distinctly shown in Spanish and Portuguese history of the epoch we are now considering. At the death of Henry IV of Castile, when the question arose who was to succeed him, Alphonso V of Portugal believed that the right of inheritance was his as brother of Joanna, Henry's wife. But Henry IV of Castile also had a sister Isabella, famous in history as the consort of Ferdinand the Catholic.

The issue lay between Isabella, Henry's wife Joanna, and Juana, the daughter of the latter.

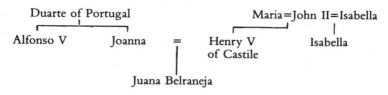

Duarte of Portugal ⌐——————⌐ Alfonso V | Joanna = Henry V of Castile | Maria=John II=Isabella | Isabella | Juana Belraneja

Isabella and Henry IV were children of the same father, John II, but of different mothers, John having been twice wedded. Juana (the child of Joanna, Alphonso's sister) was held to be illegitimate, her father Henry IV being deemed incapable of begetting children. The fatherhood of Juana was attributed to Beltram de la Cueva, who was on terms of friendship with Juana's mother, Henry himself, however, with good reason, declared her to be his own offspring. He too was twice married; the first union had been dissolved as being childless. It was his second wife, Joanna, who in the year 1462 bore him the daughter Juana, known to history as Juana Beltraneja. The terrible fate of this child, which cannot but awaken the sympathy of every feeling heart, reveals the ultimate *reductio ad absurdum* of politics based on heredity and conflicts of succession. The unhappy maiden was betrothed, one after another, to the various aspirants for the throne of Castile. At last she pined away her young life in prison and monastery. No one inquired what was her own will or inclination. She became the mere tool of high politics. When she was only two years old, Henry IV had offered her to Alphonso V of Portugal for his son Joao, hoping thereby to enlist the help of Portugal against his own noblemen with whom he was in conflict. At the age of four Juana was betrothed to the twelve-year-old son of Juan II, half-brother of Henry IV, but her bridegroom died in his fifteenth year on July 15, 1468. When Juana was eight years old the plan arose to betroth her to the brother of the French king; this, however, was prevented by the Castilians. The union was put off, and in the end it did not come about.

After the death of Henry IV, the Portuguese king, Alphonso V, himself resolved to marry Juana, but the necessary dispensation was refused by the Pope, and the union was not consummated. Juana was only twelve years old when she became Alphonso's wife, while the king was already in the twenty-sixth year of his reign. In her seventeenth year she was divested of all honours and dignities, had to resign the title, Queen of Castile, and was no longer allowed to call herself Infanta or Princess. The intention was to unite her with the son of Ferdinand and Isabella when he should reach the age of seven. Till then she should remain a prisoner, and she was only to be released if the boy should reach the age of fourteen without claiming her hand in marriage. Juana now had to decide what she would prefer, the prison of Moura or the monastery of the Order of Poor Clares. She chose the latter. Her eyes filled with tears, and accompanied by the lamentations of her friends, she laid aside the title of Queen, her royal garments and decorations, and from now onward wore the dark garment of a nun of the Order of Poor Clares. She became known as Dona Juana, and the monastery of Santarem closed its doors behind her. The probationary year passed by, and Juana still elected to remain in the monastery. Fear for her life gave her no other choice. On November 15, 1480, she was solemnly consecrated. Alphonso left the conduct of these matters to Prince Joao. The latter was married to the daughter of Ferdinand and Isabella, and of their union was born a son, Alphonso. It was Joao's plan that this child should in due course unite the thrones of Portugal and Castile. But the world-guidance of destiny, having to serve the spirit of the new time, could not allow Portugal's independence to be jeopardized until the northern peoples were ready to take over the Portuguese mission. For these peoples — the Netherlands and England, above all — the time had not yet come. Thus it befell that Juana, after so many trials and sufferings, was once again bereft of the husband who had been intended for her. From her window in the Monastery of Santarem she witnessed how the one on whose behalf she had been imprisoned fell from his horse and came to grief. They bedded him in straw, and he who was to have brought about the union of Spain and Portugal died in a fisherman's hut.

Juana could not know why fate had brought her so much

pain and suffering, but the fact was that through her sufferings two cosmic powers were battling for victory: the spirit of an age that was past and that had now become reactionary, seeking to form the destinies of nations by way of marriages and inheritances, and the spirit of the more modern age, desiring to give to the individual the free choice of his own destiny and to the nations world-embracing ways of communication. The latter spirit gained the day, and Portugal remained an independent country until the peoples of the North were ready to take over their mission.

It was the great knightly orders which were the instrument of this spirit of modern time. Fundamentally peaceful in tendency, for its aim was the development of world-wide intercourse and economy, the spirit of the new age had in that time no other means of preparing the way for world-economy than by the sword of chivalry. Oriental trade had to be wrested from the Arabs, in whose hands it lay.

In the name of Christ, that is to say with a religious motive, and by the power of the sword, the foundations were thus laid for the modern time — the time in which we live, wherein we must learn to lay aside the sword and to make all the Earth the bearer of a peaceful world-economy, embracing all the nations. We must transmute the courage of the warriors of the fifteenth century, and the great sufferings of that time, into thoughts no less world-embracing and courageous, but with full consciousness envisaging the aim of peace.

The struggle with the Arabian power reached its height in the siege and eventual conquest of Granada, which was the last stronghold of the Arabians in Europe. Across the snow-covered peaks of the Sierra Nevada the army of Christian knights draws near to the fortress of Granada. The plan of campaign had been worked out by the knights of St James of Compostela, Portuguese and Spaniards side by side. From the very outset, the leaders of the Order were fully conscious as to the far-reaching purpose of the campaign. And when, after a lengthy siege, the longed-for surrender was attained and the flags of Ferdinand and of the Order of St James of Compostela surmounted the ramparts of Granada, the knights of St James felt that this achievement — of deep significance for all Christendom — would not have been possible without the inner organization of the Order. Granada had been encompassed with such good fortune that one of the gates was seized from two sides at once; the defenders were assailed by the attacking knights in front and by artillery established on a high hill at the rear. The position can be seen to this day, including heavy cannon-balls that still remain there. It was a bold and brilliant piece of artillery work to bring about the fall of the strong castle by this means. With the short-range cannon of that time it was only possible by bringing the cannon comparatively near the gateway.

Among the Portuguese knights who took part with initiative in these events, was Francisco Almeida. With the leave of the Portuguese king and as a knight of St James he was among the foremost in the siege and fall of Granada. It was he who afterwards became, on behalf of Emmanuel I of Portugal, the first Viceroy of India. Documentary history tells us comparatively little of Almeida, who was closely connected not only with Emmanuel of Portugal but with Ferdinand and Isabella also. Almeida had been an eye-witness of the unhappy bargaining with the hand of Juana, for as ambassador of Alphonso V he had prepared the latter's journey to Louis XI of France. The awful nature of Juana's treatment had entered deeply into Almeida's soul, and had awakened in him the sure knowledge that a new age was coming, wherein the destinies of nations would be guided in quite other ways than by marrying and giving in marriage. He wanted to see Portugal and Spain united not by marriages but by brave and conscious deed, of significance for all mankind. It was indeed an event of the greatest importance when the Christian army assailed the rose-covered walls of Granada, and planted thereon the ensign of the Order, whose coat of arms contained the sword, it is true, but with a heart in place of the handle, for in the traditions of the Order it was known that in future ages love must take the place of the sword — only the time for this was not yet fully come.

In the hands of the Moors who held Granada there was at that time a sacred treasure, with the possession of which a kind of hidden knowledge was associated. It was a sacred relic connected with a form of alchemy. Destiny brought it about that this object and the knowledge associated with it fell into the hands of Francisco Almeida. Almeida felt that he had the right to dispose of it after his own insight, but the Order of St James did not agree with him, and desired to keep for itself the right of disposal, both of the relic itself, and of the hidden knowledge which went with it. Almeida however insisted on his right and eventually passed on the relic and the knowledge to a certain man from Alsace, whose name was Stefan Rautter. This individuality is known to history under the pseudonym *Basil Valentine*. His writings, preserved by his pupils and circulated in manuscript form, were at a later time collected and published by Thölde, secretary of the Rosicrucian Order. Thölde's edition contains a few biographical remarks by Basil Valentine himself, but the real name is not given; it is only inserted in handwriting in one of the extant copies of the edition. Basil Valentine here mentions, among other things, that he undertook in peril of his life a journey to Santiago de Compostela, and he remarks that those who may now benefit from the knowledge which he brought from thence should thank God that he was enabled to complete the arduous journey.

Basil Valentine's work contains the great secret of alchemy, which consists in the study of certain transmutations of carbon, referred to mysteriously as the *prima materia*. The secret is not revealed; it is only hinted at in a half-jocular form, where it is said that the disciple of alchemy must not take it amiss if he be called upon to dirty his hands with coal.

Basil Valentine also mentions that he came to England. Thomas Malory, who here became his pupil, repeats the same jest in the story of the knight, Beaumains. Indeed, the entire seventh book of Malory's *Morte d'Arthur* proves him a pupil of Basil Valentine; only what Basil refers to as the stone which goes through many colours is for Malory the knight of many-coloured armour.

It was Almeida, therefore, who withheld the knowledge from the Order of St James and was responsible for giving it to Basil Valentine. The hidden knowledge, and the preparation in question, were preserved thenceforth in the

Rosicrucian schools of alchemy. This knowledge is indeed very ancient, and in the last resort goes back to the time of Alexander the Great, who learned the secret of substance and of its medical use from his tutor, Aristotle. The 'coal,' the transmutation of which is the subject of alchemy, is indeed none other than the carbon which is contained in every living substance. In the living body of man this carbon does indeed take on all colours, inasmuch as all the organs are made up of its compounds. Carbon builds up the human body, which is not only alive, but permeated in its living substance by soul and spirit. What Basil Valentine calls the Philosopher's Stone is none other than the human being looked at from the threefold aspect of body, soul, and spirit. Therefore the Philosopher's Stone is represented as consisting of *three substances, though one in essence*. In the mystery schools of antiquity it was always known that the human being must experience a transmutation in body, soul, and spirit if the ordinary consciousness is to be changed into a higher, clairvoyant consciousness. To describe this transmutation in the language of carbon chemistry was the essential content of Basil Valentine's alchemy. Thus Almeida brought the royal art from Granada to Compostela and from thence, by the hand of Basil Valentine, to Alsace and to Thomas Malory in England.

Those who believed that the secret should have been retained within their Order brought about Almeida's recall from India, and on his journey home, in March 1510, he was killed by an unknown hand at Saldana Bay, in the extreme south of Africa. A lance of peculiar construction was driven into his face above the teeth and in this way he met his death. The lance was of steel, wrought in a peculiar wavy form. The chronicler Osorius says that he was killed by natives, but the strange form of the lance is inconsistent with this version, and the chronicle must in this point be corrected, without thereby imputing murder to any person. It was in fact an execution, and those responsible were avenging the betrayal of a secret; they only did not know that a new world-order was approaching, making necessary the transmission of certain sources of knowledge to the North. Almeida died for this. On his tombstone the words were written: 'Here rests Francisco Almeida, who never lied nor feared.' The tombstone and the tomb were afterwards removed by an unknown hand.

The destiny of this enigmatic person reveals the conflict of two different epochs, the earlier of which had always the tendency to possess, to conserve, and to inherit, forming the destinies of nations by alliances of marriage. The tragic fate of Juana — at the time when he was in the service of one of those who wooed her — had revealed to Almeida that this epoch was now past. So he became the one who desired not merely to conserve the alchemical secrets bequeathed to the world by Aristotle. He took the secret from the Order of St James, breaking thereby the power of the Order, and was quite ready to atone for this with his death. He passed the secret on into those regions where the knowledge of the mingling of substances within the human being might come to life again in a new way, as a knowledge of the working together of many nations for the development of a universal economic civilization. For the nations are in truth related to one another in the one world-economy as are the several forces in the human being. But to elaborate these things was the destined gift, not of the Latin but of the Germanic and Anglo-Saxon peoples; therefore he who understood this had to pass on the knowledge to northern countries.

Thus in the fifteenth century the foundations were laid on which our work is based to this day. Through the courage of the great discoverers a new beginning was made, in continuity with the world-embracing ideas of Alexander the Great and of his teacher Aristotle. Francisco Almeida was well aware that he was undertaking the same sea voyage, only in the opposite direction, on which Nearchus, admiral of Alexander the Great, had once upon a time set out. The voyage to India and the new age which it was helping to inaugurate signified a renewal of the world-embracing ideas of Alexander. Alexander died in the moment when Nearchus brought him the report that his fleet was lying ready in the harbour of Babylon to sail around Arabia. Alexander did not live to fulfil this, and so Arabia was not hellenized. Now, in the fifteenth century, the work that had then been interrupted had to be continued, and in this way the conflict with the Arabians came about.

The spiritual community, whose esoteric life was founded still on the alchemy of Aristotle, tried, as Alexander himself had done, to embrace the earth, but on this occasion in a more earthly, more realistic way.

In the letters of Almeida to King Emmanuel of Portugal, written on fine paper with a peculiar watermark, in the handwriting of his secretary Pereira, we can see Almeida's own signature in a rough sailor's hand. He justifies the measures he had taken, comparing them with Nearchus'. He writes: 'In Alexander's time the interior of the country had to be occupied; we, however, must rest content with fortifying certain points along the coast and thus securing the ocean path to India, for we must now wrest the trade from the hands of the Arabs and must take their place.' This letter indicates for the first time the great significance of the ocean-path to India on which the British Empire is founded to this day [1936]. In the time of Alexander the Great, the earth had had to be encompassed in a more spiritual sense. Alexander died a premature death in Babylon. The Arabs remained unhellenized. The Crusades and the wars against the Arabs in the time of the great discoveries, were the ultimate consequences of this failure. Thomas Aquinas had to put right what had been falsified in the Arabian version of Aristotle. Therefore the medieval pictures represent him with his foot planted on the neck of Averrhoes.

In the period of the great discoveries the world had to be conquered in a political and military sense, so as to prepare the way for the new age that was to come. In this new age, the third, we are now living, and we shall have to learn how to embrace the earth by peaceful, economic means.

Such is the Philosopher's Stone for our age. It is made up of culture, politics, and economic life. These are the three which are so hard to unite in one; they represent for our time the three that must be harmonized.

This is the task before us. It will be truly solved if the attempt is made in the consciousness of the world-wide responsibility which the present time lays on the shoulders of those peoples who possess the substance of the earth.

5. The Immortality of Nations Revealed in Myth and Legend

Whoever can exchange a view of existence in which life is limited by birth and death for one which traces the development of the individual through successive lives on earth, will find himself infinitely enriched thereby. Imperfection, incompleteness will begin to appear as a preparatory stage in development. Injustice is seen to be something which leads later to just compensation. The secrets of fate are revealed to him.

Whoever can rise beyond this outlook, which gives a meaning to the life of the individual, to the yet higher point of view from which entire nations and groups of nations are seen to repeat their life on earth, and to reappear after extinction in new places and new epochs, will gain insight into the destinies of mankind.

The creators of the great national mythologies and the outstanding legends of certain cultural groups gain the insight, from which they draw the wisdom of their mighty picture language, from the heights of such a world outlook. The past lies so clearly unfolded before their all-penetrating gaze that the present seems merely a transition to things towards which past development has long been moving. Thus the future is revealed to them, not prophetically, but because they know the laws which determine history. They therefore do not indicate all the details of the actual course of events, but only the main outline which can be foreseen. Thus the guidance contained in their message remains equally true after centuries. World history, as it advances, fills in with concrete facts the undetermined parts of their narrative, and what with them was intended as a mere general indication, a dimly sketched outline of the future, becomes concrete history to us, their descendants, for already it is seen that free human action has led along the paths they traced for it and confirmed, precisely by its individual additions, the basic law of destiny they knew.

It was in the light of such a high perception and outlook that the poems of men like Homer and Virgil were conceived. Schliemann, for example, as a schoolboy, felt the essential truth of these poems, and, grown to be a man, was able to realize the long-cherished wish of his heart and establish by excavations that the main outlines of the Homeric narrative were in accordance with historic fact. What a joy it must have been for the earnest scholar to find the dreams of his boyhood, still interwoven as they were with the dreams of the great mythologist, thus revealed and rediscovered as history.

The works of Virgil are similarly imbued with truth. In his *Aeneid* he recounts how, after the fall of Troy, Aeneas left Troy with his father Anchises to re-establish the destroyed Trojan culture in a new place and in a new form. They carry with them the statue of the goddess, whose possession, according to legend, ensures the continual rebirth of the passing culture.

It is the wooden statue of the Palladium through the preservation of which Aeneas is able to transplant the Trojan culture to Rome. The priestly culture of Troy was to be continued in that of the mighty Roman Empire.

The Palladium came from heaven, as did the entire Trojan culture, which was religious and divinely related, whereas the Roman culture was human and earth-bound.

The souls of those who had experienced the downfall of the ancient priestly culture during the Trojan period of development were to obtain a more earthly range of experience during the period of Roman culture. Virgil held the view that the souls of human beings pass through many lives on earth and that groups of people whose fate was linked together in one epoch reappeared, not merely as individuals but in groups, in other times and cultural surroundings — born in new bodies, but bound to continue, to complete and to equalize the fate commenced in former lives. He was not content to keep this idea to himself as a theory to explain the riddles of life, but had the courage and insight to apply it to concrete history. Thus he causes it to be explained to

Aeneas through the mouth of his dead father, Anchises, that the souls of those who formerly lived in Troy as members of her culture are the same as those now to be reborn to experience the Roman culture. Anchises dies on the journey, but remains in spiritual contact with his son, Aeneas, who is thus still inwardly connected with the soul of his dead father after death.

Arrived on Roman soil, Aeneas became a pupil of a prophetess, a sibyl, of whom there were several, and whose wisdom is collected in the Sibylline books. Reading the signs of wind and weather, they explored the secrets of the earth and reported on the life of the dead. They have been sublimely depicted by Michelangelo in the Sistine Chapel of Rome, where they seem to contrast with the quiet, earnest, earth-bound appearance of the prophets, Aeneas was thus admitted to the circle of one of these sibyls, became a pupil in the oracle cavern, and broke the golden twig at the entrance of the cavern, to which Goethe refers when he writes: 'Green is the golden tree of life.' Whoever could break this twig and keep it to light his way through the dark underworld obtained a knowledge of the secrets of life after death while yet alive on earth. Aeneas obtains his initiation and learns the secrets of the world of the dead. He is allowed to see the two great streams of motion in that world. He sees the souls of the just departed streaming towards the cosmos, there to be imbued with heavenly powers in preparation for new development, but he also sees the other stream: of those advancing to be reborn and to enter a new earthly life. There also appears to him, transfigured, the soul of his wise, dead father, who tells him that the creators of the great events in the Roman epoch will be the reincarnated personalities of the Trojan epoch. He sees the souls of Troy, well known to him, descending like an army, some quicker, some slower, to people the new Roman life about to arise.

A philosophy of history is here revealed in mythological form, which seeks to explain the manner in which mankind develops in stages. Successive national cultures are represented thereby as transformations of one another, and the development of mankind as a whole is seen as a wisely ordered series of phases. Fundamentally, this is the same idea as that developed later by Gotthold Ephraim Lessing in his *Erziehung des Menschengeschlechtes (Education of the Human Race)*.

This stage-wise evolution of mankind appears in the conception of Virgil as a development which, originating, like the Palladium, in heaven, takes a downward path, becomes humanized, and finally turns earthwards, to the earth itself. Virgil, however, who saw so clearly the history of mankind and its successive phases, also knew that the fall into matter must be followed by a re-ascent to the spirit and expressed this idea in his fourth Eclogue. This earned for him the place of honour in Dante's *Divine Comedy* and caused him to be regarded as the prophet of Christ by the Church. And so indeed he was, for like everyone who has learnt to think in terms of true mythology, he saw the great phases of world development.

However daring it may appear, it is equally inviting to continue Virgil's thoughts beyond the time of Christ, beyond the time of Christ's life on earth. Virgil himself had such an extension in view, for the Child he describes, whose birth is awaited with so much hope by the world and the earth itself, develops so slowly that his life up to manhood comprises more than mankind has yet attained.

A specimen of Virgil's words is here given:

A higher flight be attempted. The idyll become prophecy. Sense and meaning of mighty import. Verily new and great things are at hand. [Written forty years before Christ!] The world seeks completion, perfection. Wondrous times are about to begin. Times to which the sibyl refers when she speaks of the latter days. *Dike* (justice) returns. A better humanity. . . . And all that comes to pass through a child, whose joyfully awaited birth is immediately at hand.

O thou mysterious Power, protecting all that strives towards the light of life, watch graciously over this birth. Hold thy hand graciously over the boy who is destined to bring about the glorious Apollonian age.

. . . What a sublime vision for the eye of the

seer! A superman walks on earth again! A hero . . .
a new Dionysos!

. . . A ruler over the hearts of man . . . full of
peace. . . . Not immediately, however, will the
conditions we long for be attained. . . . But already
the first years of the child will bring incomparable
blessings. . . .

Then the child will grow bigger. It will be a
wonderful boy, with a noble desire to learn all the
best that the wisdom of all ages and nations can
teach. How could the hard nature attain its full
gentleness so soon? But the conflicts of the future
will serve pure high aims. They will serve great
ideas of moral progress. And then the lovely child
will be grown to manhood. . . . Then thoughts
and actions will be in harmony. Then the discords
in the social life of mankind will vanish.
(One sees that the child will live for centuries and represents
a long period of development.) The last traces of injustice
will disappear. Need and poverty will no longer exist.
Gone the haste and the noise of false work and
pleasure.

Gone the artificiality of crazy fashions. Gone all
brutality.

Even to lifeless nature and in particular to plant
life man will find a soulful relationship and
communion. Rejoice, O earth!

Tremble in ecstasy of expectation, ye nations. The
Fates are at work. The wheel is rolling.

And I shall live to see all that?

Ardently I desire it. [But that, of course, is
impossible, for he is describing enormous periods
of development.]

Still more ardently do I wish that the muse would
give me the power to sing gloriously of this
glorious age.

May the spirit *then* be equal to the task. [He means
in a future life on earth.]

Come, then, gracious child. Smile upon your
own. See the rapture of your welcome.

If we continue Virgil's thoughts in a concrete manner, the following stages of development appear. First phase: God-related humanity, priest culture. Second phase: man becomes earthly and strives after earthly power — the Roman state phase which succeeds the religious phase. Third phase: man unites himself with the earth as such, exploiting its material resources to the full to build up his economic and social life. We today are clearly in this phase which Virgil hoped would turn again to the spirit.

The priestly culture of antiquity has long since vanished and only survives in the great cultural institutions of mankind. The political state culture of Rome, however, has been multiplied in the national states of modern times and appears to be just developing its final and most perfect bloom. For these national states are still based in most cases on the institutions of Roman law. Nevertheless we already stand in the third phase in which, opposed by conflicting interests of the strong individual states, partly still striving to attain their full power, the third structure is beginning to take shape: the world organization of economic life. This third phase could not be shown by Anchises to his son. Rome fought against it in her early days in the form of Carthage. Had Carthage, the Phoenician daughter settlement, been victorious instead of Rome, the third phase would have come much too soon, and the commercial spirit would have overrun the spirit of courage and manly ideals. Hannibal's armies were driven back from the gates of Rome by the thunder and lightning of the gods, and the sibyls, with their knowledge of wind and weather, well knew where world history is in reality made. When, however, the time had really come for this third phase, the elements came to its assistance, as we know from the history of the Spanish Armada, whereby the nation of the third epoch was preserved against powers which still served the passing epoch. Had Anchises been required to instruct his son regarding these latter days, he would have shown him that the same souls, who became at the right time Greeks and Trojans, who became at the right time Romans, became in our time the sons of the material age. He would have been able to show him that nation which expresses in each epoch the present age.

This has always been known in European mythology. In the sphere of national consciousness whereby the history of England became separated from that of France after 1429, through the intervention of Joan of Arc, this knowledge has always lived. Joan of Arc was also a sibyl, though a Christian one, and knew when the full moon caused the spring floods to rise and reverse the course of the river. And, carried upstream against the river course, her troops took Orléans. The fall of Orléans separated English history from French for ever. England, for her good, lost her continental possessions and became *herself*. She never had a better friend than this enemy, who took from her the earthly possession of the lily and gave her the spiritual gift of the rose and self-experience. In the Wars of the Roses and at Orléans, England became herself, and was then preserved against the Spanish Armada.

The peoples, however, from whom the Anglo-Franco-Germanic cultural group developed, have the knowledge in their legends that they are repeating the culture of Troy, on a higher level and in a different form.

Other nations, also, have had similar mythological dreams, though it cannot be said that the nations possessing such legends believe in reincarnation. They usually allow the manner of connection to remain obscure, or subsequently invent artificial genealogies in support of existing traditions, an interval of a few centuries between father and son being often quite disregarded. The true connection was known, however, to the original creators of mythology. Only later has tradition been misunderstood.

The Portuguese ascribe the origin of Lisbon to Ulysses and consider themselves to be Greeks. Trithemius von Sponheim, the interesting historical philosopher, found such pleasure in collecting these traditions that he caused an edition of a chronicle to be published which has certainly never existed and was purely his own invention. Its contents, however, are no less valuable for that reason, for the majority of his indications, if not all, were originally living tribal traditions, and only their co-ordination under the name of an author appears to be his work.

In his chronicles he indicates the descent of European races and peoples from antiquity. Goethe took up the thread of Trithemius's work, and in the second part of his *Faust*, Act III, we find the following lines, showing the manner in which the tribes of ancient Greece live again in the races of Central Europe:

Thine, German, be the hand that forges
Defence for Corinth and her bays.
Achaia, with its hundred gorges
I give thee, Goth, to hold and raise.

Towards Elis, Franks, direct your motion.
Messene be the Saxon's state
The Norman claim and sweep the ocean,
And Argolis again make great!

It was Goethe's definite opinion that German culture was a repetition of the Greek. He himself, who was typical of German nature, felt himself as a Greek. Schiller strengthened him in this view. On August 17, 1794, Schiller wrote to Goethe:

For a long time I have watched, although from some
distance, the progress of your mind, and have
observed with ever-increasing admiration the path
you have chosen to follow. You seek the essential
in nature, but you seek it along the most difficult
path that would deter any weaker spirit.

In order to understand the particular in nature,
you consider nature as a whole; in the generality
of its forms and phenomena you seek the key to the
individual. Starting from the simpler organism,
you mount step by step to the more complex, till
finally you evolve man, the most complex of all,
from the materials of the entire universe.

By thus recreating man after the manner of nature,
you seek to penetrate and learn his concealed
technique. A great and truly heroic idea, which
shows sufficiently clearly to what extent your spirit
assembles and holds together in beautiful unity the
great wealth of your ideas.

You can never have hoped that your life would
suffice to attain this ultimate goal, but it is a greater

thing even to have started on such a path than to have reached the end of any other — and like Achilles in the *Iliad*, you have made your choice between the Pythia and immortality.

Had you been born a *Greek*, or even an Italian, surrounded from your cradle by exquisite natural beauty and an idealistic art, your path would have been infinitely shorter and might even have been rendered unnecessary. For then your first views of life would have shown you the essential forms of things and the grand style would have developed in you with your first experiences. But since you were born a *German* and your *Greek spirit* was cast in this northern creation, there remained no other alternatives for you than either to become a nordic artist or to replace to your imagination, by the aid of the intellect, that of which reality had deprived you and so, as it were, by feeling and reason, to create a Greece from within.

To this letter Goethe replied:

I could have received no more agreeable present to my birthday which falls in this week than your letter in which, with a friendly hand, you draw the sum-total of my existence and encourage me by your interest to a more industrious and lively use of my powers.

It is seen from these letters that Goethe, in portraying himself and his life in the character of Faust and the union of Faust with the Greek Helena, did not intend this to apply to himself alone, but to the entire cultural group. Karl Julius Schröer, the great Goethe scholar and commentator of *Faust*, fully agrees with Goethe's views on this subject. For him the Germans are Greeks and the Austrians Macedonians. The German-speaking 'islands' in Hungarian-speaking territory correspond to the islands of the Aegean. A study of books on the German literary history will establish this very clearly, and it will also be recognized that myth-creating powers were still fully alive in the nineteenth century. Schröer writes:

If we follow up the comparison between Germany and ancient Greece, and between the various

107

German and Greek states, we find a great similarity
between Austria and Macedonia. Austria's
important task is seen in an example before us: to
sow the seeds of Western culture in the East . . .

In his *Faust*, Goethe wished to depict a typical figure of
Germanic culture. He wished to show that such a figure, in
seeking the spiritual, must unite with the spirit of Greece —
with Helena. He feels, however, clearly that Helena represents only one side of this spirit, that behind her another,
more valuable and higher being must be sought. In his work
this higher being assumes a Christian form — the Madonna.
In the Graeco-Trojan saga, the second figure is the nymph
at the source of the golden river whom Paris leaves to follow
Helena.

Goethe feels clearly that these problems of the Trojan-
Hellenic culture are still fully alive and continue in other
forms in modern life.

The Anglo-Saxon character and spirit cannot be held to
be identical in this respect with the general Germanic spirit.
In the Anglo-Saxons we see a continuation of the Roman
state impulses, but carried a stage farther and appearing today in the form of an economic impulse striving to embrace
the world. In the place of the ideal of ruling nations by
might, there is seen ever more clearly the development of
this idea to the new ideal of leading the nations towards
economic co-operation.

No longer the idea of a world-embracing empire based on
political power, but instead the idea of a commonwealth or
community of more or less independent nations who work
together in the interests of a common life devoted to culture,
government, and trade. And yet this is more a continuation
of the Roman than the Grecian impulse, which latter experienced a revival mainly in classic German literature.

One feels that this is correct when, visiting the British
Museum, with its treasures comprising all times and nations,
one first walks along the line of Roman Caesars.

In order to determine the place in which British consciousness feels itself at home, let us return to the saga of Troy.

Before Aeneas reached Italy on his way from Troy, he
made a landing on the island of Crete. Here we find the

remains of a culture which is clearly something intermediate between the ancient priest culture of the Orient and the more earthly culture of the Roman epoch. It was here that Theseus slew the Minotaur with the help of the wise Ariadne. The Minotaur was a monster who lived in the labyrinth, a maze of tangled passages, and required human sacrifices from time to time. King Minos bears the same name as the first human king of Egypt: Menes. The kings *before* him are considered in the saga as having been gods or demi-gods and it ascribes to King Minos the construction of the labyrinth, of which there was one in Egypt. The name Menes or Minos is related to the Latin word *mens*, reason, intelligence, and recurs in the German word for the human being, *Mensch*, also in Sanskrit as *manas*, reason. Thus reason built the labyrinth, the brain with its many windings; and without the thread of logic man could not have escaped confusion when the picture consciousness of the old time passed away and gave place to the age of cool reason. To this new age belonged Theseus, who knew how to use the thread of Ariadne to escape from the labyrinth, so also the wise Odysseus, the wise Menelaus, Agamemnon. They stand in sharp contrast to the representative of the older form of consciousness that still dreams in pictures and confronts them in the person of Achilles. The Trojan War stands at the point of development where the old myths and the old priestly culture are overwhelmed by reason. The serpent attacks the priest Laocoön and his sons.

The labyrinth was thus a temple representing the convolutions and windings of the human brain, to remind the beholder that without the thread of intelligence, without logic, escape from the labyrinth was impossible. Only Theseus, the man of intelligence, could, with the aid of the Ariadne thread of logic, overcome the animal man, the Minotaur.

This legend, which has a general and thoroughly human character, is now revived in the Tristan story.

Tristan is the Western Theseus, overcoming Morhold instead of the Minotaur. The scene of his fight is not Crete but the island Samson in the Scilly Isles. The same typical situations arise in his life as faced the heroes in Trojan War times. Tristan also stands between two women: Isolde with the golden hair and Isolde with the white hands, as Paris of Troy stood between the nymph of the golden river and Helena. Paris, by marrying Helena, loses the nymph. He meets the three spiritual powers of thinking, feeling, and willing, represented by the three goddesses Athene (wisdom), Aphrodite (beauty), and Hera (power). Instead of deciding for all three, as full development would demand, he chooses Aphrodite, who promises him the most beautiful woman, Helena, for whose sake the Trojan War is fought. As representative of the Grecian epoch, Paris decided for beauty and gained the woman who bore the name of the Hellenes.

Wherever the seeker after higher knowledge decides in a one-sided manner and fails to find the balance which should prevail between wisdom, beauty, and power, the fourth entity, love, which is the power of the individual consciousness in its unselfish form, must lead to a tragic end.

So it was in Troy, which as representative of the ancient priestly wisdom was overwhelmed by the clever Greeks, and thus, after this culture of wisdom had become united through Paris with the search for beauty in Greece, no other sequence was possible but the one-sided power cult of Rome.

Western culture now links up with Crete, intermediate between the ancient culture of wisdom and that of Rome. In Theseus-Tristan love should prove triumphant by showing that it is not born to rule but to raise.

Goethe coined this expression in his fable of wisdom in which he depicts the three world-ruling forces of wisdom, beauty, and power in their efforts to divide the dominion of the world among themselves. Finally, he shows that all three powers must work together in harmony, under the leadership of the fourth power — love; for love, he says, does not 'rule but raises.'

So Tristan, who strives after this ideal, after harmonizing inner discords, must overcome the chaotic in the human soul opposing him in the figure of Morhold, the modern Minotaur. The Minotaur requires the sacrifice of youths and maidens at the age of puberty, because human nature is then disturbed by chaotic sense impulses, and the fighting power of the reason (Theseus) is often not sufficient to win. For

110

this reason Tristan, besides the equipment of knowledge, is armed with the harmonizing power of music.

He wins the fight, but receives a wound, which no one can heal but the woman who is able to develop the highest degree of love in the most individual manner: Isolde.

All these characters are not merely symbols. Tristan and Isolde are as real as men and women are real who give representative expression to the culture of an age. The Western world should recognize itself in them.

They are individual because they are real, and yet they show in the mirror of their individual fate the fate of all Western people. Thereby they serve as symbols. United by personal, individual love, they suffer a fate which proves that love is stronger than all other powers, stronger than death, and a possession which cannot be transferred to others, because it belongs alone to whom it is given.

Tristan could not give Isolde to the sinister King Mark for whom he had fetched her from sunny Ireland, for the light of the maid with the golden hair could not unite with the darkness of the gloomy Mark. Only there where there is light already can the magic lamp of higher wisdom shine. Only when 'light kindles light' can love result from the highest mutual revelation and knowledge, so mysteriously, that the miracle may well appear to be the result of a magic potion.

But in reality the two drank the cup of knowledge, revealing in such radiance the true nature of each other that they fell into each other's arms in mutual recognition.

In the Bible it is written: 'And Adam knew his wife.' The writer thus knew that love is the highest act of mutual revelation. It is not right to say that love is blind. Rather the reverse may be said: that he who loves sees more in the loved one than all others who remain blind and do not love because they do *not* see. Love opens the eyes to sight and true knowledge as we are told by Rudolf Steiner in his *Philosophy of Spiritual Activity*.

And so it was with Tristan and Isolde. They loved one another, bound together by the magic potion of superhuman love, because they knew each other, not only in their present form, but as they had met repeatedly in previous lives on earth. And such a bond is stronger than all convention.

Nevertheless Tristan brought Isolde from Ireland to King Mark and delivered her to him. But how could he do otherwise than keep her whom he loved so much? He could only leave her outwardly. He did so and went to Brittany, there becoming united with another, Isolde with the white hands, whom he married.

This happened so because human nature is such that we can realize and cling to the eternal for long, but cannot keep it for ever, and because, being human, we must return to the affairs of earth and time.

It was not otherwise with Paris in Troy, who had to lose the nymph of the golden river. He exchanged the sun-gold of the eternal for the woman whose name in Greek signifies the silver-gleaming moon (Selene) — Helena.

And Tristan exchanged Isolde with the golden hair for Isolde with the white hands. But on the bridal night after his marriage with Isolde with the white hands there appeared before his soul the pure gold of his eternal love for Isolde with the golden hair, and he drew his sword and laid the bare blade between himself and his bride.

Next morning Isolde with the white hands complained to her brother Kaherdin.

He wanted to kill Tristan. Tristan did not defend himself, but asked him to hear his story. And when Kaherdin had heard from Tristan's lips the 'Story of Tristan and Isolde,' he was deeply moved and forgave Tristan. He fitted out a ship and bore Tristan back to Isolde with the golden hair, who still lived on the coast of Cornwall.

Is that not the story of the West and its development? It has wedded itself to earthly things, to the world in which things are bought and sold, but has not forgotten its connection with the eternal. Even in the bridal chamber the sacred mission is remembered and the naked sword laid between itself and materialism. This the West should not forget: that the sword still lies where Tristan laid it, and that Kaherdin in Brittany has heard and remembered the story. It is not a French legend, but a Cornish reality, for he heard it from Tristan's own lips. Having heard the story, he cried: 'Come, let us seek Isolde!' And they sought and found her, and will always find her, for the story is eternal and can never die.

The legend relates that Tristan and Isolde met again, and once again lost each other. Finally, Tristan fell ill. The old wound opened and death was near. Then he remembered the healing powers of the golden-haired Isolde. He sent Kaherdin to fetch her, who delivered the message, and sailed with Isolde across the sea.

Tristan was already weak and the shadows of death were around him. His head lay in the lap of Isolde with the white hands. He was unable to lift it. He had arranged with Kaherdin that white sails should be hoisted if Isolde returned with him, and black sails otherwise. The ship approached with white sails. Tristan, who could no longer lift his head, asked Isolde with the white hands to tell him the colour of the sails. In a fit of jealousy she replied, 'The sails are black.' Then Tristan died. But at the same moment Isolde with the golden hair lay over him, kissed and died with him.

The story of the black and white sails is taken from the Theseus legend. King Mark buried Tristan and Isolde. Each one was laid in a separate grave: Tristan in a coffin of beryl, the stone that induces clear thinking, and Isolde in a coffin of chalcedony, the stone that can assume any colour.

From Tristan's grave there grew a rose-tree. The roots branched down into Isolde's grave. King Mark had them cut away. Then a twig from the rose-tree sprouted and grew into Isolde's grave. King Mark let it remain.

Thus it is with development in the West. The divine powers that guide our development have given us the most beautiful legend in the world, the story of the power of love, a story which, though highly individual, has a meaning and value for us all. The gods that guide our path have no illusions. They know that Tristan united with Isolde with the white hands. But beyond birth and death the power of the rose rises up to the eternal spheres; in the end victorious over death itself and uniting the material efforts of mankind with the spirit — not to the end of wisdom, or beauty, or power, but of love which does not rule but raises.

6. Is King Arthur a Historical Character?

In the time of the first English printer, William Caxton, who brought over the art of printing from the Continent to England, the legend of King Arthur, which up to this date was found mainly in French romances, began to take form in England. Its roots lay much deeper, beginning in the tales and stories of the Cymri, those Celts of Cornwall and Wales who took heart and flourished again after William the Conqueror had subdued the Anglo-Saxons (Wueleker, *Die Arthursage*). In Geoffrey of Monmouth's story (1132–35) Arthur was shown as ruling over all peoples who successively conquered the British Isles. In this story he does not appear actually as a historical personage but as the ideal, the personification of the eternal evolution of the island and its development. While the legend is unquestionably Celtic in origin, we find it wandering from one people to another, growing and developing and assuming a universal rather than national character.

In the original form of the story, Arthur is pictured as a mighty warrior and general, dominating all the kings of Britain (see Henry of Huntingdon), but in later records he is portrayed as a wise and mild ruler. When the Normans settled on English soil the whole Norman Anglo-Saxon culture and community was created round the figure of Arthur. This community made him their central figure. (Severin Ruettgers). The Norman form of Geoffrey of Monmouth's story is given to us by Wace. Layamon used this source, adding to it many other Celtic legends giving Arthur new characteristics, whereby he became the mild and generous hero of all the later stories. Scotland also had its Arthur, described in *Huchown of the Awle Ryale* (see G. Neilson).

Behind the historical figure of Arthur works a superhuman spiritual being leading invisibly, but most powerfully, the whole history of the island kingdom. The question as to whether he was a historical or mythical figure should never arise, for the legend certainly originated with a real person — with Ambrosius Aurelianus. At the same time appeared, behind this historical person, the whole English history in a superhuman personification. Putting aside all differences of race he seems to embrace Celts, Scots, Normans, French and even Germans in different epochs of history. He places the island kingdom as the centre, not only of a European, but of an all-embracing human culture.

The age in which Thomas Malory wrote his *Morte d'Arthur* saw him in this sense. This work could not appear before 1485 though it had been written fifteen years previously.

Caxton speaks of Arthur as one of nine heroes, of whom three were pagan, three from the Old Testament and three Christian. He enumerates them as Hector, Alexander and Caesar, Joshua, David and Judas Maccabaeus, Arthur, Charlemagne and Geoffrey of Bouillon. What he describes is really a ninefold hierarchy consisting of three times three heroes. For him Arthur is a spiritual power, and to doubt his existence would be senseless. We must understand that spiritual powers as eternal as the nine members of the hierarchy, 'the company of heaven,' are represented in this case by the nine human personages. In connection with these facts the name of Arthur was used as a title or designation of this special kind of leadership.

In his preface to Malory's work Caxton says: 'In the Abbey of Westminster, at St Edward's Shrine, remaineth the print of his seal in red wax closed in beryl, in which is written Patricius Arthurus, Britannie, Gallie, Germanie, Dacie, Imperator.' The name of Arthur is given to St Edward in the same way as William of Malmesbury, speaking of Ambrosius Aurelianus, the hero of the battle of Mons Badonicus, calls this man, having quite another name, 'Arthurus.' He says '*Hic est Arthur de quo Britonum nugae hodieque delirant,*' (from *Gesta Regum Anglorum atque Historia.*) This is the real Arthur of the British tales. The name is used as a synonymous term for a certain type of hero. There have been many King Arthurs and the title was given to all those who honoured and worked for the continuity of the evolution of the island kingdom in such a way that the progress and evolution of other nations were included. About Edward all these things can be said, so we can therefore understand that he was given this title. John Lingard speaks of him in his history of England: 'Edward enforced the laws of his Saxon predecessors' and 'whenever the people under the despotism of the Norman Kings had an opportunity of expressing their real wishes, they constantly called for the laws and customs of the good King Edward.' Many years after his death, therefore, St Edward received the title 'Patricius Arthurus' and it was sealed on his tomb. Such a seal as Caxton described was never in King Edward's possession. The complete preserved collection of his seals shows nothing at all like it and it is obvious that it was added to his shrine at a much later date. Those who did this must have had powerful authority behind them to have obtained the necessary permission and the existence of the seal must have been a fact which could be proved by any person who visited Westminster Abbey, Caxton speaking of it as common knowledge. This shows that a Society of Knights must have existed closely connected with the royal house. The name of Arthur was used by this Society because they worked for the historical continuity of the best traditions of the island.

'Imperator' was the title used for the master of certain medieval societies as is proved by a Rosicrucian manuscript.★ Here the constitution of a Rosicrucian Society is described, and the word 'Imperator' is used in the above sense.

The description of the founding of such a secret knightly society in England, using the name of Arthur, may belong to a time a hundred years earlier than its publication in book form. In the British Museum there is a book entitled *The Ancient Order Societie and Unitie Laudable of Prince Arthur and Knightly Armory of the Round Table*, by Richard Robertson, printed by John Wolf and published in London 1583. Here we have not 'King' Arthur, but 'Prince' Arthur. This change of title was brought about by the fact that a hundred years previously Henry VII of the House of Tudor (which came originally from Cornwall) was anxious to connect his own House with Arthur. He called his eldest son Prince Arthur,

★ Theol. et Phil. 4 No. 514 Thesaurus in the Landesbibliothek in Stuttgart.

and saw to it that his son was born at Winchester. The event took place on September 20, 1486. T. W. Shore in his book, *King Arthur and the Round Table at Winchester*, bases his story on this connection. The king created round the person of the prince an order in which the Arthurian tradition was regarded highly, and we can assume that Thomas Malory was enabled to publish his work *Le Morte d'Arthur*, and Caxton was encouraged to print it by the King and the royal circle who had this subject very much at heart. Probably, the following words of Caxton's in the preface to Thomas Malory's work, refer to this fact — 'Many noble and divers gentlemen of this realm of England, came and demanded me many and oft-times, wherefore that I have not made and imprinted the noble history of the Sangreal, and of the most renowned Christian king, first and chief of the three best Christian and worthy, King Arthur.'

There is no doubt that this Knightly order was international. We can see this from its whole character, and its world-wide significance is shown by its particular use of cosmological symbols. Richard Robertson tells us that the fixed stars, the planets and the four elements play an important part in the symbols, and they were very similar to those used in the Solomonic Temple. There the twelve groups of the zodiacal stars were indicated by the table with the twelve shewbreads. The seven planets were shown in the seven-branched candelabra, and the four elements through the four times three bulls looking to north, south, east and west, and bearing the molten sea of brass. All these symbols had already been used by Charlemagne, the measurements and proportions of the dome in the Cathedral of Aachen (Aix-la-Chapelle) being the same as those in the Temple of Solomon. Caxton enumerates Charlemagne as one of the nine heroes, therefore it is natural to suppose that the symbols used in the ceremony and culture of this knightly society, having the nine symbolic heroes, were similar to those used by Charlemagne, and the inclusion of David as one of them indicates the same. Alexander, David and Charlemagne were kingly knights; Caesar, Judas Maccabeus and Godfrey of Bouillon, Knights of the Sword, and Hector, Joshua and Arthur, Knights of the Word. This Society, centred in

England, included in its membership men of other countries, some of them even having been rulers of importance in Europe as, for example, Maximilian I, who, one year after the publication of *Le Morte d'Arthur*, was elected Roman Emperor. On his monument in the Royal Chapel in Innsbruck (the design of which had been made under his instructions during his lifetime) we find twenty-eight figures as torch bearers, one of whom is King Arthur of England. This great monument was begun in 1509 and finished in 1583, the same year in which was published Robertson's book, *The Ancient Order of Prince Arthur*. Maximilian was counted as the last knight, and there is no doubt that he was fully acquainted with all the knowledge of the Arthurian traditions.

Prince Arthur married Katherine, the daughter of the Catholic King Ferdinand and Isabella his wife (1501). There were many signatories to the marriage contract, amongst whom was the Archbishop of Santiago (St James) di Compostela. Maximilian himself was the son of Leonora of Portugal and, without doubt, all the important personages of Spain, Portugal, Austria and England belonged to the knightly order and were carrying on the Arthurian traditions. The only difference was that in the southern countries, strongly under ecclesiastical influence, the name used for the great leader was the 'Priest—King John' not 'Arthur'.

It was through the extensive research of H. Oscar Sommer, who republished Malory's *Morte d'Arthur* in 1889–91 (London, 3 Vols.) that the sources used by Malory for all except Book VII of his work were made known. Book VII, however, can be traced with certainty to alchemy. Thomas Malory used the writings of Basilius Valentinus. These writings tell us that their author learned alchemical wisdom at Santiago di Compostela and that he had been to England. What he tells us of the primary matter which is coal, Malory represents as a knight whose name is Gareth. This knight appears first as 'Kitchen Knave,' but the lovely lady to whom he is allotted as protector, is warned not to despise him for his name and lowly calling. He also has the ironic name of 'Beaumains' or 'Beautiful Hands,' showing that he, as Kitchen Knave and as a beginner in alchemy must not be afraid of handling the *prima materia* — otherwise coal — for by the alchemistic process, black and dirty coal becomes the shining diamond which only consists of carbon, but radiates in many colours. The body of the human being is also created from carbonic matter and so we see him described by Malory as the 'Knight of Many Colours' (Ch. 29, Book VII).

Here too, the knights who have the secret of knowledge of the Philosopher's Stone are arraigned and counted; Lancelot of the Lake, Tristan of Lyonesse, Lamorak of Salis and Beaumains (or Gareth) of Orkney, Son of Lot. The alchemists expressed the process of cleansing the soul in chemical symbols. The dark, unenlightened soul was likened to coal as it was unlit, dark like a raven, and the name 'raven' was used for the alchemist handling the *prima materia* and being in the first stage of education. In like manner, the Bible mentions the ravens of Elias. When the cleansing began the black raven became changed into a black and white magpie as described in Wolfram of Eschenbach's *Paszival* and when the cleansing process was complete, the white dove indicated the holiness of the spirit.

The Philosopher's Stone has to go through many colours, as told in the history of the Holy Grail, until at last the red substance of the Holy Blood indicates the completion of the inner way, appearing in such beauty that over it the white dove of the Holy Spirit can hover. Christ's blood in the crystalline vessel shows the final aim for which the Philosopher's Stone was created. The aim of the alchemistic process was to provide a vessel fit for the blood of Christ and his selfless sacrifice. The way from the black coal to the white diamond, radiating in all colours, is the way of purification. Before the purification there is darkness and after, many coloured visions.

What alchemists taught through the symbology of the chemical substance, Malory expressed by replacing knights for the chemical substance, and whoever grasps both meanings will easily understand the connection. In the Tristan legend the pure stone of the alchemist, shining with many colours is pictured as a dog called 'Petit Cru' or 'Little Creature'. The alchemist thought out these pictures and symbols in the following way. He said: 'All organic substance is only coal (carbon), but man is not coal, but a soft diamond — in the colour of the skin, the Soul Painter has employed all colours to arrive at his lovely rosy brown.' The true *inkarnat* was the Philosopher's living Stone appearing in many colours. The chemical kitchen was the actual body of man. The *materia prima*, the original matter from which all organic substance was created, was carbon, but the whole alchemical work was the work of 'women and children' as Basilius Valentinus says, and can be finished in ten months, because the whole creation of the stone was the creation of the human being. The purification was the wisdom and knowledge of how to become again 'as a little child.' The parallel, which indicated how the body is created and how the soul is purified, was studied with interest and the interplay of soul and body was likened to the painting of the soul on the canvas of the skin. The study of the Incarnadine was that of the interplay between soul and body. The human being, as this work of art, was studied with the greatest admiration.

It is interesting to follow the 'soul painting' of the skin. Anger brings red-blue. Envy brings green. All colours must play to give the stone its perfect clearness. Where love works in the right way, red and white appear in their proper proportion. When the emotion of love works properly, it paints all red and white. The idea was that the cleanness of the soul appears as the beauty of the body. In the Parzival saga all these alchemistic symbols are used. Konduiramur, the bringer of love, is red and white. Feirefis is black and white like a magpie. Parzival is the red knight. Malory himself was a scholar of the alchemy of Basilius Valentinus and the whole company of knights who grouped themselves round Arthur and the royal house were secret masters in alchemy. Their goal was international, cultural life.

No one who has followed English history through its legends and stories can believe that these things are dead. It is only necessary to translate them today in other language than that of alchemy and medieval symbols.

Something eternal — universal — the very breath of freedom lives in this land. It stretches out, embracing the whole of humanity. It still speaks to us through the hills and the valleys, the rocks and caves mentioned in the Arthurian legends. The winds and the waves sing of it, the atmosphere is full of it. It is necessary to find contact with this invisible Power which, in only one of its forms, appears as the Arthur of the legend. This Power in reality is the Eternal Spirit of this country which we shall meet again. Could we but realize this, a cultural element would be born again, English in its innermost depths. It speaks to all human beings wherever they live and to whatever nation they belong. The Round Table is the whole world, says the saga (Malory xiv, 2). Its knights still live, their search for the Grail still goes on and the Grail, as we now know, is the secret spirit which must unite all mankind in love and brotherhood.

7. King Arthur and the Problem of East and West

The figure of King Arthur stands as a token of England's innermost being, for in him is incorporated a part of that power which overshadows the history of England, illuminating it with a radiance in which its spiritual mission becomes perceptible. As the star-cluster of the Great Bear illumines the Pole and rules the hosts of the other stars, in like manner there gleams, amid the circle of the Round Table, the figure of King Arthur. In this Arthur circle we behold a brotherhood that is ordered according to the laws of the starry heavens.

King Arthur stands out in history as a personality who was engaged in mighty conflicts against a power that arose from the south and was directed northward. Herewith are connected certain historical facts concerning the Anglo-European north and the power of Rome in the south. But it is not merely a historical reminiscence that is interwoven into the legends of King Arthur. We have to do also with a deep secret of human nature. That which appears as the pole of the heavens is also to be found in man and is represented by the human head. That which streams upwards from the south is what is carried in the human blood. We find these same images in the mythology of many peoples.

If we look towards ancient Persia, we find similar ideas. The original divine humanity first descended upon the earth at the Pole, and the polar and neighbouring regions formed the first habitation of mankind. The Greeks, too, describe this land as that of the Hyperboreans, a land whither Apollo, god of the spiritual power of the sun, returned again and again. Gradually, and through long ages, the human race spread from thence over the face of the earth. The other and opposite pole only later entered into the story of evolution. This occurred when the development of humanity of the earth reached the equatorial region. All this is found in the conceptions of the primeval East. When humanity had developed so far that it had attained an existence which, according to our scientific investigations, we designate that of the warm-blooded organisms, then the other side of the world began to play its part. The Germanic peoples called this other side of the world the southern 'Muspelheim.' It is the polar antithesis of the northern 'Nifelheim.' The Persians said that the Ahuras — who were gods of light like Apollo — inhabited the north, and the Devas — gods of darkness — streamed against them from the south. The beings whom the Persians called *Ahuras* and the Indians *Asuras*, were addressed by the Germanic people as *Asen*, and the Indian word 'Deva' (in the Persian *Daeva*) we find in the Germanic as *Wanen* (pronounced V). In the name 'Wanen' we have again the German word *Wähnen* because the Wanen appeared to the human soul in dream and in presentiment or dim feeling; while the Asen of light were met with in waking life. Such an Asen-figure — but in terrestrial and human form — is King Arthur. He rules the world; he represents the link between humanity and its original divine home. That is his mythological background; and from this background he comes forward into history.

We must picture Arthur to ourselves as a being of light. He and his knights are guardians of what is noble and just. No wonder that these primal guardians of 'Rights' still live on, as they do, in the present-day organization of the 'life of rights,' of the social life, of Britain.

There was a time when the guardianship of human rights was held only in the pure hands of the priest-kings. Wherever Arthur and his knights appeared, wherever the Round Table was set up, there the sinister forms who hate the light were compelled to withdraw from their presence. Arthur and his sun-radiant knights brought law and order to every place as a reflection of the heavenly ordering of the stars. These traditions remained alive in England up to the time of Queen Elizabeth. From those Knights of the Sword whose strokes had smitten the countries of Europe with the glancing light of sunlike law and order, there came all that still lives on as the life of social rights in Britain. Then the sword was put aside and only the red sash from which the sword had once hung remained as representative of the rights of man. Even today the young aspirant to jurisprudence, following a definitely established ritual, is obliged to eat a certain number of dinners before he can enter his profession at the Bar. These dinners are taken in the Temple quarters, where an ancient custom prevails that from year to year a little piece of pie paste is set aside and baked into the pie of the following year. This custom can be traced back into Elizabethan times, when it vanishes into legendary obscurity. During the reign of Queen Elizabeth the traditions of Arthur's Round Table became transformed into the traditions connected with the organization of rights which still exists.

One must not imagine King Arthur as merely a single and definite historical personality. In a certain sense 'Arthur' signifies the name of an order or rank; there have been many 'Arthurs' in the progress of time, just as there have also been many 'Parzifals.' For the name Perceval (or Parzifal) was borne by the seekers on a particular quest. Thus there were also Arthurs in other countries, and we have one of the greatest and most powerful in the personality of Charlemagne, who, together with his Paladins, represents the order of a true Round Table. Here we can still discover quite clearly the origin of the Round Table. It is connected with the traditions of Solomon's Temple, the same Temple which gave rise to the various Templar Orders, on whose territory in London the Round Table tradition still lives on.

It is related of Charlemagne that he built the Cathedral of Aachen according to the same measurements as Solomon's Temple, and the Emperor's throne is also said to be copied (as regards the steps) from the throne of Solomon. The names, too, of those who closely surrounded Charlemagne, which were conferred upon them by him, emanated from the Temple traditions. His biographer, Einhard, bore the same name as the builder of the huts, and this again shows a connection with an old Temple story.

In the knights of King Arthur we have a revival of a very ancient tradition appearing among more northern peoples, one which goes back to King Solomon and to those currents of evolution which are the basis of his real significance. A primeval wisdom, which we find repeated in the mythology of many peoples, interprets the Temple as representing the body of the Godhead. It echoes, too, in the words of Christ when he speaks of the 'Temple' that shall be rebuilt after three days.

It was Rudolf Steiner who recognized that the mission of the Hebrew race was, in a marvellous way, a different one from that of any of the other peoples of the world. Other peoples created wonderful sculptures and built beautiful temples for their gods, but the Jewish people had to deny themselves these things. They might build no outwardly visible temple for their God, the mighty 'I AM,' who proclaimed himself as 'I AM THAT I AM,' nor might they make any graven image of him. That was indeed profoundly significant; for how could the 'I AM' be known save in the inner holiness of the soul? At the same time the Temple did play a tremendous part in the life of the Jewish people. But its mission consisted in the fact that the stream of inheritance throughout the generations had to be kept pure in order to build up that body which should arise as the temple of the Godhead — the body of Christ.

It was Solomon who inaugurated a second stream by the side of this stream of preparation within the generations. He built the Temple in the *outer* world. Naturally he required for this the help of the Phoenicians which was brought him by King Hiram. The stream which flowed through Charlemagne is to be regarded as similar to that which owed its origin to Solomon, though with a certain difference.

While in Hebraism, on the one hand, we have a religious stream in which everything depends upon inheritance, and because of this tendency must pay special attention to all that is connected with the development of the embryo, which in its turn is linked with and follows the laws of the mysterious rhythms of the moon, so we have, on the other hand, a second stream, apparently similar to the first, but differing from it in certain essentials. This second stream comes before us in the book of the laws of Manu. Here we find declarations which are verbally almost identical with those of Moses. But, in effect, what is revealed therein is not a moon religion, but a sun religion. In what was given by Moses there is also a solar cult, but it is concealed; and long ago it was correctly surmized by Lenormand that hidden behind the lunar cult of the Jews, yet connected with it, there is to be found that other monotheistic stream which is a solar cult and is now known as that of *Akhenaton*.

Who — spiritually discerned — was this King Akhenaton? He lived in the Egypt from which Moses later led the children of Israel. He lived in that same Heliopolis of which Manetho tells us that Moses himself had been a priest. Manetho calls him *Osarsiph*, and only later do we find him with the name Moses, after he had undertaken to be the leader of the Jewish people in their flight from Egypt. It was then that he transformed his sun monotheism into a moon monotheism, and we must try to form some conception of this change and its meaning. All agricultural peoples, all settlers, naturally adopt a solar cult, for they regard the harvest of the earth as a gift from the sun. All nomadic peoples adopt a lunar cult, for they look upon their herds and their multiplication by reproduction as subject to and a gift of the rhythms of the moon. Thus a people who, having been settled, becomes nomadic, must of necessity change its solar cult into a lunar cult. The sun monotheism nevertheless still remains hidden, as it were, behind the lunar cult, and this fact is everywhere to be discerned.

Now King Akhenaton was placed in a remarkable position. He knew that after a few centuries, with the returning Saros-period (and this connection is also a discovery of Rudolf Steiner), the power of the ancient clairvoyance must vanish. He knew that in no very distant future the worshippers of Ammon would no longer be able to perceive the living divine revelations directly but would know of them by tradition. Rather than submit to the onward advance of this shadow, he took the splendid and courageous decision not to leave things to take their course with the inevitable silencing of the Word of Inspiration, but to change over, with complete consciousness of what he was doing, and with a clear spirit, to the worship of the world as it is revealed to the senses, and to the worship of its ruler, the disk of the sun, Aton.

When one reads the hymns of Akhenaton, when one allows his magnificent rhapsodies to the sun to work upon one's feeling, one cannot but be stirred to the depths by this tremendous revolution taking place within a human soul, and one is profoundly moved by his really 'modern' words. Here there speaks to us a human being of our own times, one who belongs to our world, who has inclined himself towards the earth and towards a materialistic culture.

That which we can study in this Egyptian example, appears before us also among the northern peoples in the figure of King Arthur. In Arthur and his knights there lives the knowledge that they are the last who will be able to look with clear vision into the revelations of a spiritual world that is growing dim and dark.

In these few words we have sketched what lies behind English jurisprudence. It has been born out of a great and noble spirituality; but the important question we must ask is whether there is still something remaining over which has not crystallized into the frozen forms of tradition. The problem of King Arthur is more alive today than ever before. For such problems arise again and again; they are always there, and it is only their outer forms that supersede one another on the horizon of world-history.

The relation between England and India is not merely a question of political issues of the first magnitude, but it is concerned with a tremendous spiritual problem. For it is not only material interests which are in opposition to one another, but primarily two distinct spiritualities, polarically different. We shall endeavour to consider the question from this standpoint.

In looking at the historical evolution of mankind, and especially at the majestic ascent of the English-speaking people, one asks oneself: *Who are they*, in reality? Mythological history gives us the answer.

The English-speaking people have developed a new consciousness for themselves and this consciousness is to be found exemplified in the figure of Parzifal. This too is a discovery of Rudolf Steiner. He calls the peculiar nature of the consciousness of the English-speaking peoples, and in particular of the British themselves, the 'consciousness soul.' And he describes Parzifal as being the typical representative of this consciousness soul. This may seem rather surprising, for it is not easy at first sight to find a resemblance between Parzifal — filled to overflowing with holiest spiritual aspirations — and the materialistic trend of the British consciousness. And yet it is so. The resemblance is there. Yes, even a completely identical attitude of soul. We will first of all try to show how Parzifal also had material interests, and then we will turn our attention to what are the spiritual interests of Britain.

We possess a most precious account given by Chrétien de Troyes in which he describes how the youthful Perceval meets with three knights who are pursuing another knight who has seduced a woman, and they ask Perceval if he has seen him. But Perceval is not interested and will not give any information. Instead of answering these questions he puts questions himself. He asks: What are you wearing on your head? And the knight has to answer that it is a helmet and to describe the purpose of the helmet. Then he again asks Perceval for information, and again obtains only another question, this time about his shield and then about his spear; and so it goes on for some time. The narrative is given in such a way that one can distinctly feel that Perceval is one for whom the material, sense-perceptible things constitute the most important problems, and who is unable to make the other person's interests his own. In this way Perceval reveals himself as a modern human being, and not as one really belonging to the Middle Ages. This too is a great discovery of Rudolf Steiner: that Perceval is the first 'modern' man, the first westerner of the modern age, for he has entered this Age before its time, while other men have still to develop by slow and gradual degrees to the point where he already stands.

But now the Grail story goes on and describes just how such a man actually finds his way to the Holy Grail. Precisely this kind of soul is able to find its way to the highest spiritual possession. And it is this which is so wonderfully described by Wolfram von Eschenbach: how this same Parzifal, after many wanderings, achieves the quest and is permitted to take *one other* with him to the Grail. He chooses to take Fierefis, who is 'black and white' and is his step-brother on

128

the father's side. The father is the husband of Queen Secun-dilla of India. With this, something of the deepest signifi-cance enters the Grail story. It shows us that the western man is brother of the eastern man, and that the eastern man can achieve his goal in no other way than with the help of the western.

If this is a legend, it is at the same time a prophecy. For Britain stands today before the task of fulfilling the pro-phecy. The Anglo-Indian problem cannot be solved in India, but only in Britain. The Orient looks expectantly towards the West. The Orient is waiting for the West to discover a form of social organization which shall be a moral one, yet able at the same time to incorporate within itself the mechanical civilization of the western world. If the West succeeds in creating such an organization, then the East will recognize that the West also possesses a light; that a new Light is able to approach the *ex Oriente Lux*. If this does not take place, then the Eastern problem will remain unsolved.

The organization of the British Empire had its foundations upon the last fleeting remnants of the Arthurian organization. But the present age demands not Arthurian knights, but knights of the Grail. And that means that a new social organ-ization is needed, not built upon inheritance and tradition, but upon spiritual knowledge. This social order will have to reckon with certain demands which are a necessity of the age. And these demands will be recognized by the East the moment it is convinced that they are *morally* effectual within the social organization. The first of these demands is: *Indus-try, by virtue of its own natural legitimacy, must become a unity over the face of the whole earth*. The second demand is: *On the basis of the life of rights, all men are equal*. And the third is: *Every individual must choose his nationality with the same freedom with which he chooses his religion*.

A brotherhood of states of more or less equal standing is taking the place of the British Empire. The spiritual history of mankind demands that this transformation be undertaken and carried further in full consciousness of the goal to be attained. For evolution leaves only two ways open. Either the voice of the Spirit of the Age will remain unheard or unheeded — and in that case the East will determine to destroy Western civilization because it is unmoral, but it will be unable to put up a better social organization in place of the old and will lead the way back to primitive industrial conditions. Or — the call of the Spirit of the Age will be heard, and heard in that place where there is not only the possibility of knowledge but where action is also undertaken. And then, through a reorganization of the West which it will itself carry out, in the spirit of Rudolf Steiner's book, *The Threefold Social Order*, the problem of the East will be solved. This is the tremendous question which today emerges from the theme of King Arthur. To take up in earnest the suggestions of Rudolf Steiner would be to carry the Arthurian tradition livingly into the future. Any other way of dealing with this tradition is valueless, except as a matter of literary interest.

8. The Revival of the Arthurian Legend in the Fifteenth Century

The most comprehensive treatment of the Arthurian legend in England has been provided by Sir Thomas Malory in his book *Le Morte d'Arthur*, printed in 1485. It is easily accessible today in an excellent Penguin edition.

The book is notable as one of the earliest books to be printed in England. This was done by William Caxton, the first English printer, who had learned the recently invented art of printing on the Continent. The first work he produced was *Le Receuil des Histoires de Troie* (ca. 1474) in Brussels. In 1476 he returned to London and printed approximately a hundred books in his print shop in Westminster. One of these was the Arthurian legend by Thomas Malory in which English readers have always been very interested. A second copy of Malory's work, which had only been known in Caxton's edition, was later discovered, enabling an examination of possible alterations made by Caxton.

Malory's work was completed by 1469 but lay unpublished for sixteen years until Caxton printed it. Caxton claimed to have done so because 'many noble and divers gentlemen of this realm of England camen and demanded me, many and ofttimes'. Thus the book appeared at the behest of a group of English nobles who had close links with the house of Tudor which was about to begin its rule. The Tudors had good reason to revive the Arthurian legend. Shore points out in his booklet *King Arthur and the Round Table at Winchester* that the Tudors counted Arthur among their forebears and therefore it was in their interest to re-establish the Arthurian legend. We know that Henry VII of England, whose rule began in 1485, used Caxton as his printer and we may consider Caxton to have been Henry's court printer. Indeed, how could it have been otherwise? He had his print shop in Westminster directly under the eyes of the King, as it were. Henry VII called his first son Arthur and arranged for him to be born in Winchester, the traditional site of the Round Table. The book, then, existed as a manuscript but could not be printed so long as Edward V, the child king, and his brother Richard, Duke of York, were perishing in the Tower of London. This is not the place to discuss this highly significant situation in detail, only to mention a controversy as to whether Richard III, brother of Edward IV, was responsible for the death of the two children in 1483, or whether he is innocent, as Sir Clements R. Markham attempts to prove in his book *Richard III — his Life and his Character Reviewed in the Light of Recent Research.* Be that as it may, the period was not well disposed towards such things as a revival of the Arthurian legend. 1485 is the year in which England entered the modern age, with an associated victory for spiritual powers. For although it was dynastic interests which provided an opening for this spiritual impulse they allowed access to something which was of significance for the whole of mankind.

Thomas Malory's work ends with the marriage of Ferdinand and Isabella, the Catholic sovereigns, in 1469. It was printed at a time when a ruler ascended the English throne who sought links not only with the Iberian peninsula but also with the Holy Roman Emperor, for reasons which went beyond mere political considerations. An element of a renewed search for chivalry of a more profound kind, than that which was on the point of extinction, gained strength at that time. A booklet can be found in the British Museum which, although printed a hundred years after the events it describes, shows clearly by its title that it deals with those earlier events, for it refers not to 'King' Arthur but to 'Prince' Arthur. And Prince Arthur was the son of Henry VII. The booklet is entitled *The Ancient Order Societie and Unitie Laudable of Prince Arthur and Knightly Armory of the Round Table* and is dedicated to the chief customs official of the Port of London and to the Society of Archers. It demonstrates that the Tudors established some kind of society, but we do not know whether it took from the beginning the form described in John Wolf's booklet printed in 1583. However, history shows that it was effective. It is no accident that Maximilian I erected a statue of King Arthur in the Innsbruck court chapel. On the contrary, it is evidence that the attempt to revive the Arthurian legend was not only in line with the dynastic interests of the English royal family but, beyond that, was of concern to the members of the nobility in general.

Both Maximilian and Henry VII maintained lively relations with the Iberian peninsula. Maximilian was the son of Eleanor of Portugal and it was the wish of Henry VII that his son Prince Arthur should marry the daughter of Ferdinand and Isabella, Catherine of Aragon. This duly came about and the signature of the Bishop of Santiago de Compostela is among those on the marriage contract. But Prince Arthur died at an early age and Catherine of Aragon became the first wife of Henry VIII. Nevertheless, the short marriage with Arthur is of interest, for the liaison with the man whose birth was arranged to take place in Winchester, who was given the name Arthur and who had the Order of the Arthurian Knights created for him, was not without importance.

At the relevant point in Sir Thomas Malory's book we see that he used sources which lead back to Spain, to Santiago de Compostela. Let us therefore examine *Le Morte d'Arthur* to note the unusual links which governed the order of knighthood throughout several countries at this time.

Thomas Malory's sources have been comprehensively described by H. Oskar Sommer, a German who was responsible for the critical edition of *Le Morte d'Arthur*. However, no sources could be traced for the Seventh Book. Yet it is the sources for this book which I want to discuss, since it leads us to Santiago de Compostela. The book's content is pure alchemy. It could only have been written by someone versed in the alchemy of Basilius Valentinus. This alchemical author received his holy treasure from St James, as he himself writes. The order of knights surrounding Prince Arthur was learned in alchemy. The centre of this knowledge was Santiago. The knights of the Order of St James had Ferdinand the Catholic as their head. The marriage between Prince Arthur and Katherine meant that a seal was placed on the inner, metaphysical union not only of the two royal houses but of knighthood throughout the world.

The knighthood had its own specific impulses. A kind of

school, the school of the fifteenth century, is revealed at work here. The impulses which introduced the new age were disseminated through the symbols of alchemy and the romances of chivalry. What was clothed in the story of John, the priest-king, in the south, was at work in the north in the symbol of King Arthur. But they were linked by a common concern: the preparation of mankind for the modern age. The honourable attitudes of the chivalry of old were reaffirmed once more in order then to take leave of that chivalry for ever in exchange for journeys over the oceans, the discovery of new lands, the encirclement of the world with the instruments of technology. That is why Maximilian is the last knight. That is why the knights of St James, of Calatrava, of the Wing of Michael, of the Order of Christ are the great explorers. A new conception of the world was emerging. And its first lesson was: 'Do not despise carbon.' Alchemy had already taught that. But in the new age this teaching was to be given another, newer meaning. How was the modern world to emerge if carbon was despised? The alchemists had said: coal is black and dirty, but the diamond, sparkling in every colour, is transformed coal. Those who despise the black, dirty coal because it lies around in kitchens, because it can be found on every refuse tip, are not worthy of the diamond. It is worth while reading Basilius Valentinus' words on carbon. It is worth while reading the preface by Thölde;* they show that carbon formed the basis for alchemy. Malory deals with carbon under the name of Sir Gareth. The depiction is one of scorn since he is only the kitchen boy. But the story tells how, after many battles and transformations, with knights of many different colours, the knight who radiates every colour is finally victorious.

> 'What manner a knight is yonder knight that
> seemeth in so many divers colours? Truly,
> meseemeth,' said Tristram, 'that he putteth himself
> in great pain, for he never ceaseth.' 'Wot ye not
> what he is?' said Sir Ironside. 'No,' said Sir
> Tristram. 'Then shall ye know that this is he

* In *Basilii Valentini Chymische Schriften.*

134

that . . . was called in the court of King Arthur, Beaumains (the man with the sooty hands, the "beautiful" hands), but his right name is Sir Gareth of Orkney, brother to Sir Gawain.'*

It is astonishing to see how Malory has elaborated Basilius if one takes a copy of the *Twelve Keys* and compares them both. Basilius is not as easy to read, for the ordinary reader will not even find the *beginning* of Basilius Valentinus' alchemy. Basilius says that you should start no work without calling on God. If you forget that you will fail to understand anything in this book. For it is the case that all passages in which Basilius calls on God in the book, which comprises many hundreds of pages, must be collated in order to find the beginning. And that beginning is carbon. If carbon is treated with contempt the rest, which comprises a guide through all the colours until they radiate and shine as *one* at the end, will not make sense.

At this point I must bring in some alchemical concepts. All organic substance consists of carbon. But neither plants nor animals nor human beings are black. Therefore it must be possible for carbon to undergo a process in which it acquires all colours. The carbohydrates, for example, are also carbon in the language of alchemy. But what is the supreme achievement of Creation? It is the colour of the human skin. It can be black, it can be red and yellow. But it can also turn a hue of green in envy, red in anger, yellow in jealousy, white and red in a noble frame of mind. So what is the human skin in alchemical terms? It is the canvas on which the soul paints. Decadent ages believe that the skin has to be painted from the outside and they use make-up. But the use of make-up merely shows that knowledge of the paint-strokes of the soul and a healthy life has been lost. These do indeed conjure up marvellous colours from the blackness, carbon, the 'kitchen boy'!

Why is it specifically Sir Tristram who receives enlightenment about the secret of the colour of carbon? Because Tristram, Launcelot du Lake, Lamorak de Gales and Beaumains knew the secret of the Philosopher's Stone, that is, of the

* Malory, *Morte d'Arthur*, Book VII, Chapter 29.

constitution of the healthy body, the faithful soul and the victorious spirit, as Malory expressly confirms. For those are the substances which constitute the Philosopher's Stone. The Philosopher's Stone is the human being and Tristram knew this secret. Let us look to Gottfried von Strassburg's *Tristan* for confirmation. Tristan sends Isolde a small dog which shimmers with every colour. What is this other than the love which the artistic soul makes shine so marvellously on Isolde's countenance. This little dog has been given by every lover to his beloved. Of course, if the beloved applies 'rouge' the artistry of the soul is lost.

Petitcreiu (small creature = microcosm = human being), the small dog:

> It had been so ingeniously conceived in respect of two of its qualities, namely its colour and magic powers, that there was never a tongue so eloquent or heart so discerning that they could describe its beauty and nature. Its colour had been compounded with such rare skill that none could really tell what it was. When you looked at its breast it was so many-coloured that you would not have said otherwise than that it was whiter than snow; but at the loins it was greener than clover; one flank was redder than scarlet, the other yellower than saffron; underneath it resembled azure, but above there was a mixture so finely blended that no one hue stood out from all the others — for here was neither green, nor red, nor white, nor black, nor yellow, nor blue, and yet a touch of all, I mean a regular purple. If you looked at this rare work from Avalon [Avalon = the spiritual world] against the grain of its coat [in other words, from a spiritual perspective, from the soul], no one, however discerning, could have told you its colour. It was as bewilderingly varied as if there were no colour at all.★

That is the same Sir Gareth. Love is the greatest artist. It uses every colour to paint the soul on to the body so that it shimmers through. We should not forget the soul! But not

★ Gottfried, *Tristan*, Penguin Classics, pp. 249f.

despise the body either. Chemically it is nothing but black carbon. But the alchemist, the soul, makes this black carbon shimmer with every colour. Let the genuine spirit, the noble soul, shimmer in the healthy body: that was high ideal which the modern age inscribed on its standard. Such an attitude pervades all the legends of King Arthur and the priest-king John. It is the ideal of the age of discovery. People wanted to cultivate spirituality, but they also wanted worldliness to assume its rightful place. Travellers of the world, conquerors and brave hearts were produced by this age, not stay-at-homes. It was the time when mankind was taught in the heavens above to think in global terms, while Mars★ ruled on earth below through the ideals of chivalry. The spiritual sun above the earthly service below: that was the motto of the age. The heroes of the age of discovery wanted to show how earthly service could serve the spiritual sun.

★ The view of Trithemius of Sponheim, substantially confirmed by Rudolf Steiner, is that the consecutive historical epochs are each governed for approximately 350 years by one of the seven spirits of the planets. The influence of Samael, the spirit of Mars, extends to the early sixteenth century. See Chapter 2.

9. Basilius Valentinus in the Context of the Arthurian Legend

Alchemy, which played such an important role in antiquity and the Middle Ages, is a science almost completely forgotten today. It is thought of as the precursor of chemistry. We smile about the strange ways of times past and reassure ourselves that in chemistry we possess the real and true knowledge which the Middle Ages were seeking. That is certainly correct to a large degree; a whole series of discoveries were made in chemistry by the development of alchemical ideas. But that shows no appreciation of *real* alchemy, originally a teaching of the mysteries. The fundamental truths of alchemy are not primarily related to substances, although it does make all kinds of preparations particularly for medicinal remedies, but to the nature of the human being itself.

According to the alchemists and to the teachings of the mysteries, human beings are not constituted in the way they should be and must therefore be guided back to their original state. The alchemist sees the occurrence of the Fall as the cause of human deviation from the divine plan of creation, introducing not just a moral but also a physiological transformation which has to be reversed.

Alchemy has definite and immutable views on the nature of this transformation, its meaning on a cosmic scale and how it can be reversed.

Let us look at the rhythmical function in the human being. Human beings breathe. In breathing they depend on the plant world which transforms the carbon dioxide we exhale by separating carbon, which plants need to build up their own structure, from the oxygen, releasing it to be re-inhaled by human beings. Mankind would soon perish if the undoubtedly simpler organization of plants did not exist in parallel with the higher organization of human beings. It would suffocate in the carbon dioxide it exhales. The alchemist therefore requires the student of higher knowledge to begin not by despising what is beneath him but by recognizing the service it performs for more highly organized beings. Thus the carbon cycle is not a closed cycle but one in which more highly organized beings require lower organisms to complete it. This can also be expressed as follows:

You, O human being, have succeeded in developing to the level at which you now stand and lead a conscious life, responsible for your actions. But you developed drives alongside your original pure and divine nature. You liberated yourself from your animal drives to a certain extent by ejecting the animals from your being as separate entities. But you and the animal world could not exist if the plant world had not remained at an even lower stage of unconscious, vegetative life. Therefore, O human being, regard with profound gratitude the lower element which has enabled you to ascend.

After devoting himself to such thoughts and feelings, the next step for the student was to say to himself, in accordance with the teaching, that God originally endowed human beings with the ability to produce closed cycles. That is to say, human beings should be able to fix the carbon themselves and allow the oxygen thus released to return to the atmosphere. Our inability to do this, our exhalation of death and thus our breach of the commandment 'thou shalt not kill' is the Fall of Man. The alchemist wants to reverse this — at least to the extent that this is possible at our stage of development. He himself wants to perform what the plant world performs. He wants to replace the two open cycles with a single closed one.

'If you want to do that,' he says, 'you must possess the consciousness of human beings and the innocence of plants. The highest of secrets would be revealed to you if you were able to perform consciously what the plant performs unconsciously.' Those were common turns of phrase. Plato's explanations of the universe in the *Timaeus* were read with profound interest. What he says of the circle as representing nature in its perfection and being the highest motion revolving upon itself was considered to refer to breathing. It was said that the closed cycle is a property of the perfect being, of the being which represents the ultimate goal. In the incomplete cycle higher and lower elements are breaking apart. The one rises and the other falls. Development can only take place at the expense of others. That, the alchemist said, is the Fall.

It is obvious that the constitution of our bodies would be carbon if we did not exhale carbon but fixed it as the plant does. We would become walking coal, walking soft diamonds. We ourselves would physically be the Philosopher's Stone. We would be living, conscious, responsible stone.

Alchemists therefore spoke of producing a stone which was mineral, plant and animal; but they were really referring to the future evolution of mankind and all the realms of nature. The path of future evolution was described as we today describe geology or palaeo-botany or palaeo-zoology. The future was seen symbolized by the closed cycle. People who were aiming for such goals took plant names such as 'Flos' or 'Blancheflur'. Or a plant was chosen as a symbol, a rose or a lily for example, when the secrets of higher development were revealed in the form of fairy tales.

All these things had a meaning to those people who were aware of the context and were able to solve the riddles in their correct places. The fantastical element was introduced only by those ignorant of such things.

Alchemy might therefore be described as the teaching of closed cycles, and in particular the carbon cycle. *Prima materia* was referred to with carbon in mind, yet alchemy is not purely the chemistry of carbon but simultaneously a path of moral development.

We must not forget that the alchemists were all physicians. They were aware that carbon in the form of vegetable charcoal is a kidney remedy in certain preparations. It is called *carbo vegetabilis* today. This was a fact of inestimable consequence for the alchemist. It showed him that carbon was linked with breathing on the one hand and with the function of the kidneys on the other and he investigated this link. The reason why it is difficult today to show the extent of the alchemist's learning in this respect is that he had progressed beyond the common knowledge of these things. It was left to Rudolf Steiner to renew this knowledge in modern times from quite a different perspective, namely the medical one.

He noted that the kidneys have two functions. First of all, the well-known one of passing water. But furthermore, by acting as a kind of brain of the metabolic system they regulate the oxygen requirement. They regulate the amount of oxygen which we take in. And that can be modified with charcoal.*

Thus the more profound study of the chemistry of carbon provided a method for understanding the medical and cosmological aspects in equal measure and the corruption and restoration of human nature was the great alchemical riddle. There are, of course, open and closed cycles in nature outside the human being. The use of manure, for example, promotes plant growth and thus enters the vegetative process. The animals graze on the herbage which grows as a result and produce manure once again. The alchemist said in his earthy, medieval way: 'If you can understand how the stinking dung revolves in the same round as the fragrant flower so that the one may be transformed into the other, you have understood something of the secret arts of nature.'

In this context, Goethe's concept of metamorphosis is really only a popularization of those relationships which the alchemists understood a great more comprehensively. For not only does the part contain the whole, the leaf the whole plant, but 'the All is in the One' the alchemist said. 'Once you have understood the cyclical nature of the cosmos you will encounter it everywhere.' Goethe read these things in the 'Kirchweger', which was subsequently printed under the title *Anulus Platonicus*.† This essentially already contains all Goethe's ideas on metamorphosis. What Goethe did was to apply them to the plant and later to the animal world. The cycle of water, the secrets of which have by no means been fully explored, is dealt with in a particularly wonderful manner in the 'Kirchweger'.

It is not some fantasy of alchemy that rain water is something quite different from distilled water, that it contains cosmic forces in earthly form; the alchemists were able to make use of this knowledge. Today we are still at some

*See, for example, Rudolf Steiner, *An Occult Physiology*.

†Compare Rudolf Steiner's lecture 'Goethe's *Faust*' on this work.

ove from an understanding of rain: alchemy was able to the murky and sulphurous haze, later torn by lightning, a context and knew why lightning generates rain. This ole cycle of murky gases, lightning, rain and rainbow — the secret of the thunderstorm *without* and *within* human beings — was known. The lightning outside is the spirit lighting up within us; thunder is thoughts rolling within the human being; the rainbow is our imagination. It was known that the same relationship existed between blood and nerves as between thunder cloud and lightning. Classical antiquity knew it, of course, and ascribed both to Zeus. Everything that was recognized as part of the human being and which the alchemist endeavoured to transform could be compared with the cosmic archetypes. The essential differences between the inner and outer astrality could be compared and the damage caused by the Fall could be registered.

The alchemical path of training taught the *return* to *cosmic* origins. The content of its teaching was the method by which earthly human beings can become part of the *heavenly spheres*. The *spheres* did not suffer the Fall, it was said, but Lucifer, the spirit of Venus, fell. That is why a distinction was made between Uriel, the representative of the Venus which had not fallen, and Lucifer, the fallen Venus. Lucifer was the Sphinx whose riddles fill us with trepidation. Lucifer was the power which caused the body to suffer disorder. Indeed, this Fall could be studied from a developmental point of view in any investigation of the stages which are manifest in the positions of the organs. In the lower animals the heart is in the head, in fishes it is in the larynx, in mammals in the breast. The path of the sun was seen in these stages. But the kidneys show the three stages of the Fall of Venus. In three stages they move downwards in embryonic development until they reach their present position in the organism at the same time that the reproductive organs are completed. All this was noted, was read as the script of cosmic development and it was known that all of human nature had changed thereby. To change it back was the aim of the alchemists' art. All human beings are sick, they said. This sickness of sin was to be healed by the alchemists. In doing so they saw other human beings as their fellow monks.

Let the greatest alchemist speak in his own words. Basilius Valentinus[*] says in his preface to 'The Great Stone of the Ancient Philosophers':

> Being possessed with humane fear, I began to
> consider, out of the simplicity of Nature, the
> miseries of this World, and exceedingly lamented
> with my self the offences committed by our First
> Parents, and how little repentance there was
> throughout the world, and that men grew daily
> worse and worse, an eternal punishment without
> redemption hanging over the heads of such
> impenitents: Therefore made I haste to withdraw
> myself from sin, and bid farewell to the World,
> and addict my self to the Lord as his only servant.
>
> Having lived some time in my Order, then also,
> after I had done my appointed devotions, meddling
> not with frivolous things, least my vain thoughts
> through idleness should yield causes or great evils;
> I took upon me diligently to search into Nature, and
> thoroughly Anatomize the *Arcanaes* thereof, which
> I found to be the greater pleasure next to eternal
> things. Having found in our Monastery many
> books written by Philosophers of ancient times, who
> had truly followed Nature in their Study and
> Search (like Aristotle, for example), this gave a
> greater encouragement to my mind, to learn those
> things they knew; and though it proved difficult to
> me in the beginning, yet at last it proved more
> easie. The Lord so granted, to whom I dayly prayed,
> that I should see those things that others before me
> had seen.'[†]

He continues to relate that in his monastery — he meant in mankind — there had been another brother of the same order. After all, we are all brothers in the same order in so far as we are human beings. And he tells that this brother (that is, humanity as a whole) was struck by an illness which

[*]See Carl Kiesewetter, *Die Geheimwisseuschaften*, pp. 52ff on Basilius' life and works. On the authenticity of the works attributed to Basilius see Rudolf Steiner's lecture of April 26, 1924 in *Karmic Relationships*, Vol. II.

[†]This and following quotations are from 'A Practick Treatise'.

no person and no doctor could cure. It was so bad that all hope was vain. Basilius Valentinus himself could not help either. Neither earth nor water, air nor fire — not even the fifth element, the light which is contained in things, the *Quinta Essentia* — could help. Higher grades than represented by these five elements were required to heal this sickness. Thus Basilius studied for seven years, he tells, and left no herb untouched. And since none of them were helpful, he moved on in the sixth year from the plant to the mineral remedies. He included the metals as well. He studied their forces and effects by seeking them where they are created in the geological process. That is, he sought all these substances in their cosmological context. And that is when he saw that everything is part of the one process in the sense that one thing is derived from another. In other words, he finally grasped the *archetypal law of metamorphosis*. Indeed, he finally reached the stage of clairvoyance. He recognized that some things should be described as Saturn-like, others as sun-like, a third as moonlike. So the substances, the metals for example, resolved themselves into processes for him. For substance is nothing more than the process, development, viewed at a fixed instance. And thus, he writes, he discovered that everything passes through the same processes and that the difference is only one of evolutionary stage. By this means he finally succeeded in producing a mineral which had passed through characteristic stages of colour and finally shone with every colour. 'Amongst all those I happened on a certain mineral, composed of many colours, and of very great power in Art, I extracted its Spiritual Essence, and thereby in a few days I restored my sick Brother to his former health.'

This mineral is none other than human beings themselves. But *transformed* human beings. They shine in many colours in the eye of the spirit. If one considers their spiritual nature then Amfortas, whom all of us carry within ourselves, can be healed. Basilius did this in himself and he writes:

> For this Spirit was so strong, that it did much
> revive or fortifie the spirit of my Brother, who as
> long as he lived daily prayed for me for he lived
> long after, and then bid me farewell. His and my

prayers did so much prevail, that the Creator, discovered, and by reason of my diligence did demonstrate unto me, even that, which yet remaineth hid to the wise men, as they call themselves.

So therefore in this Treatise I will declare, and so far as is lawful for me to do, reveal The Stone of the Ancients . . . So that by my writings, the dictates of Philosophy which are very short and ænigmatical, thou maist attain that Rock.

That rock is the human being, but the transformed human being.

A stone is found which is esteemed vile,
From which is drawn a fire volatile.
Whereof our noble Stone its self is made,
Composed of white and red that ne're will fade.
Its called a Stone and yet is no Stone;
And in that Stone Dame Nature works alone.
The Fountain that from thence did sometime flow,
His fixed father drowned hath also.
His life and body are both devoured,
Until at last his Soul to him restored:
And his volatile Mother is made one,
And alike with him in his own Kingdom.
Himself also virtue and power hath gained.
And far greater strength than before attained.
In old age also does the Son excell
His own mother, who is made volatile,
By Vulcan's Art, but first its thus indeed,
The Father from the Spirit must proceed.
Body, Soul, Spirit, are in two contained,
The total Art may well from them be gained
It comes from one, and is one only thing,
The volatile and fixt, together bring.
Its two and three, and yet only one.
If this you do not conceive, you get none.
Adam in a *Balneo* [bath] resideth
Where *Venus* like himself abideth
Which was prepared at the old *Dragons* cost
Where he his greatest strength and power lost.

Its nothing else saith one *Philosophus*,
But a *Mercurius Duplicatus*.
I will say no more, its name I have shown,
Thrice happy is the man to whom it is known.
Seek for it there, and spare not cost and pains,
The end will crown the work with health and gains.
Exitus acta probat.

This is the whole secret. The stone can be found. It transpires that it is not expensive, if one knows where to look for it. It can be found in every kitchen, since it is coal. It is more valuable when it takes the form of the human body. The difficulty lies in separating the volatile spirit from the body in such a way that it can reveal its own nature. If the student can achieve this through the exercises he undertakes, he will soon recognize that *two* volatile spirits inhabit the human body. One is the bearer of feelings, the passions, the emotions. We usually describe it as the astral body. It is that element of the soul which is still tied to the body. The alchemist, who sees it as copper coloured, calls it the red spirit. The other volatile spirit is life. It bears the memories, our heredity and what we have acquired. It is described as the white spirit because in the Imagination it appears a silvery colour.

A stone is found which is esteemed vile [the human
        being],
From which is drawn a fire volatile.
Whereof our noble Stone its self is made [the spirit has
        made us, after all],
Composed of white [life] and red [the soul element
        tied to the body] that ne're will fade.
Its called a Stone [for it is carbon] and yet is no Stone
        [because it lives];
And in that Stone Dame Nature works alone.
The Fountain that from thence did sometime flow,
His fixed father drowned hath also.

This fountain is the life forces. When they leave the body, which occurs for example when our hand goes to sleep, we feel peculiar trickling like thousands of droplets. That is the fountain.

This fountain drowns its fashioned father, the body; it

trickles around him, indeed, it swallows him 'life and body' because if the spring streams out of him *completely* the whole body appears to be dead. The whole human being enters a deathlike sleep. But this sleep is 'not unto death'. Its sole purpose is to allow initiation to take place. The person to be initiated has to pass through a deathlike sleep in order to have the experiences which will enable him to appear transformed when his soul and consciousness return.

Thus while the body is caught up in its deathlike sleep, the soul and life are intimately wedded. The golden king finds his silver bride. That is to say, the things which the human being has acquired through his exercises, the control of violent temper for example, must become *permanently habitual*, not merely an *occasional* achievement. In other words, the new configuration of the astral body has to be imprinted on the etheric body, on our permanent stance in life. The astral body then appears like a sun, the etheric body as the volatile mother, a moon. The sun is much stronger, however and it imposes its character.

In order that the great god of transmutation, the blacksmith-god Vulcan, can make all this happen, the lifeless body left behind has to be protected from decay: the 'I', the centre of consciousness, has to descend into the body. Thus the whole process looks like this:

1. 'I' = eternal 'I', spirit
2. Astral body = illuminating thoughts or the murkiness of desire
3. Etheric body = formation of the body, memory, habits, permanent characteristics
4. Physical body = bodily form.

This is the human being in his normal form. But in sleep he is constituted thus:

1. 'I'
2. Astral body } are both *outside* the body
3. Etheric body
4. Physical body } remain *lying in bed.*

The sleep of initiation, which effects the transformation after long, preparatory purification of the astral body — called catharsis — is quite different: the transmutation of copper (the passions) into gold (purity, eternity).

The etheric body which is normally 'below' is now 'above'.

The astral body which is normally here, remains here.

The 'I' which is normally 'above' is now 'below'

The physical body remains where it is.

Etheric body
Astral body

The 'I' in
the physical body

The 'I' has *descended* into the physical body to preserve it from decay. Snake-like, it winds itself round the body of the youth, as Goethe depicts it in his fairy tale, grasping its tail, and preserves the corpse from decay. The etheric body, which otherwise remains below in the body, now floats above as a volatile being in order to join the other volatile being of the astral body.

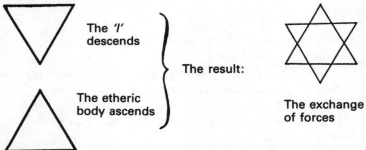

The 'I'
descends

} The result:

The etheric
body ascends

The exchange
of forces

'The earth has to ascend to heaven' says the *Aurea Catena Homeri, Homer's Golden Chain*. Goethe refers to it as the 'golden buckets' which the hierarchies pass from one to the other. And 'heaven must creep into the earth,' it says. In other words the 'I', the spirit, has to descend into the body to preserve it from death, and the etheric body, life, which is normally active only in the body, now has to ascend to vitalize the soul. That is the magnificence of the initiation process, that it *vitalizes the soul* and imbues the body with *spirit*.

Many exercises are used in preparation. They are all described in Rudolf Steiner's *Knowledge of the Higher Worlds:*

1) The purification of the astral body or probation.
2) Making habitual the self-control which is achieved (imprinting the astral body on to the etheric body).
3) Conserving strength (which otherwise has to be given to the body in sleep to repair it). For example, if I am angry I ruin my liver. It has to be repaired in sleep. But if I do not become angry, although the external cause is there, I save that strength. The strength which is saved by this method (called the six exercises by Rudolf Steiner) is carried by the 'I' to the body below and prevents the decomposition of the body during initiation. For initiation consists of removing life from the body.
4) Reconstituting all four parts to their normal state, but now containing the fruits of purification and initiation. The etheric body, for example, re-enters the physical body impregnated with astral currents. That, however, modifies the breathing process.

Indeed: during initiation 'body, soul, spirit are in two contained'.

I   Astral body (soul)
     Etheric body (life body)
II   'I' (spirit)
     Physical body (body)

And indeed: 'The total Art may well from them be gained'. For the astral body could never imprint itself on the etheric body as long as the latter is in the physical body. But now the volatile element, of astral and etheric bodies, has to be bound into the fixed element, the 'I' and the physical body, again.

Body, Soul, Spirit are in two contained,
The total Art may well from them be gained
It comes from one, and is one only thing [the human being]

The volatile and fixt, together bring.
It is two and three [body soul and spirit] And yet only
one [the human being]'.

'Adam in a *Balneo*' is the human being surrounded by the
currents of the etheric forces. Venus has forces in the astral
body which are related to the dragon. But now they have
been tamed. '*Mercurius Duplicatus*' is the two volatile substances of etheric body and astral body.

Adam in a *Balneo* resideth [etheric body]
Where *Venus* like himself abideth [astral body]
Which was prepared at the old *Dragons* cost [it was still
    prepared by the astral body but after the bath
    astral body and etheric body have become alike],
Where he his greatest strength and power lost [through
    the purification].
Its nothing else saith one *Philosophus*,
But a *Mercurius Duplicatus* [two volatile substances]'.

'*Exitus acta proba*' means: 'success will show if one has acted
correctly' or 'death (*exitus*) shows that one has acted
wrongly'. Death would be the consequence if one went
through the process *without* preparation. The body would
disintegrate.

Initiation, then, is the search for the philosopher's stone.
Those who want to find it must look death in the eye.

I once asked Rudolf Steiner whether Basilius Valentinus
was out of date. 'No,' he said, 'you approach him with new
sentiments and the path he describes is the same as that
represented in my book *Knowledge of the Higher Worlds*. His
path contains the esoteric substance of anthroposophy and
his conception of the world is ours too.' He recommended
the book to me as a book for meditation. He referred to it
as a compendium of higher knowledge. He said that its view
of nature was Aristotelian.

So when did Basilius Valentinus live and where can we
find the link which will bring us closer to this significant
historical individual?

As he relates himself, he travelled to northern Spain and
Santiago de Compostela* at the time of Ferdinand and Isa-

*See Chapter 8.

bella. 'Having made the difficult journey to Santiago de Compostela, which I had promised God to visit as a pilgrim, I did return to my monastery with God's help, wherefore I thank God to the present hour. But many other people were to be joyful together with me because of the holy object which I brought back with me and an eternal name for our monastery and all of mankind as comfort and aid.'

Basilius Valentinus, then, amid danger brought back to the north a holy object from Santiago de Compostela, as he relates. The significance of this deed consists of the fact that this holy object was a hidden one in Santiago, but when it came into Basilius' possession it became something which was made accessible to mankind. The history of this holy object has not been written yet. A Portuguese knight brought it from the court of Alexander VI to Santiago de Compostela. The knight, in Spanish services, had journeyed to Rome on behalf of Ferdinand, the husband of Isabella. A close relative of Ferdinand had been struck down by a serious illness. A miracle, which had to be ascribed to St Peter, cured the sick man. Thereupon Ferdinand vowed to build a chapel for St Peter at the spot where he had been crucified on the Janiculum in Rome. He sent his loyal knight to Alexander VI and the Pope gave permission for the chapel to be built. Bramante was given the commission for its construction. He built the rotunda of the Tempietto at a spot where a modest wooden building had stood before. The Tempietto still stands today. The guide usually picks up a handful of sand in the middle and allows it to trickle through the fingers of the visitor with the words: The blood of St Peter flowed into this sand. St Peter's church was later modelled on this rotunda. The knight returned to the Iberian peninsula. He took with him the holy object which the Pope had granted him. The Order of St James believed it had a claim to it, since the knight was a member of the Order. But the knight ensured that the holy object was passed to Basilius Valentinus who carried it to the north. The conflict which arose between the knight and the Order as a consequence led to the death of the knight in March 1510. But the holy object travelled to the north.

Basilius Valentinus journeyed to Santiago as a pilgrim of

St James. That is to say, he journeyed along the pilgrimage route which has been described by Emile Male. It linked Edinburgh with Santiago and passed through the whole of Germany along many side-roads. All the great Gothic cathedrals stand on this route. All important universities. It is the path along which the cultural life wanders through Europe. There is a St James street in almost all European cities. Together they make up the old pilgrimage route. The Goetheanum in Basle also stands on this route.

Basilius journeyed along this road. Near Edinburgh, Roslin Chapel stands at the Rose Burn. It was not built with mortar. Its stones are held together with the crushed scallop shells deposited there by the pilgrims of St James. The pilgrim fixed a scallop to his broad-brimmed hat. When he reached his goal he laid it down. The churches were built from these shells. Spiritual power similarly lay like a pearl in its shell. The alchemists wrote about this pearl and Basilius devoted several chapters to it. There is a pillar in Roslin chapel whose style appears rather strange. Legends have grown up around it. No one remembers any longer that the pillar in the market place in Sintra, Portugal, is of the same style. Cultural life at that time flowed from north to south, from south to north all the way through Europe.*

Basilius' manuscripts, which remained unpublished for a long time and were only printed much later by the secretary of the Rosicrucian Society, indicate that Basilius Valentinus stopped at the monasteries of St Peter. We know that he stayed in Erfurt. But Emperor Maximilian, who searched for him, could not find him: Basilius Valentinus was only a pseudonym. The man who bore it wished to remain anonymous. Rudolf Steiner said that Aristotle's view of nature continued to live in his writings, of which the only remaining complete originals are those about the Twelve Keys. His works contain Aristotle's lost writings. Nevertheless, when Basilius says that he read the wise masters who knew before him what visions he would have, we may assume that he is referring to the path of initiation, the school which leads to

*Details on Roslin Chapel are contained in W. J. Stein, *The British*.

higher knowledge and which he describes in the form it took in the fifteenth century. This wisdom heals the human being. It is eternal and only the form in which it is revealed changes. It flows through all development and is always renewed because serious seekers find in it what the wise masters knew before them, which is eternal. The gravestone of the knight who gave Basilius what belonged to him because he was initiated, has disappeared. It had written on it: 'Here rests the knight *sans peur et sans reproche.*' The inscription, the whole grave has gone. Jealousy pursued him even after death. But history is eternal. It progresses and reveals in later periods the knowledge of earlier times which has been extinguished.

10. The Hare in Myth and Alchemy

'The Easter Hare Book'

This winged comparison is too swift for unripe wits.
They lack the power to grasp it. For it will wrench
past them like a startled hare!

Wolfram von Eschenbach (Parzival *I*)

Introduction

It is of significance for mankind when ancient customs and
opinions are permeated with new life. The festivals of the
year are milestones in the course of human life when we
may think about the aim and direction of our endeavours.
While the meaning of the festivals can be grasped by the
adult, the festivals themselves with their colourful content
make a direct impact on the child. In this respect a true
relationship between adult and child can only be maintained
when the adult believes in what he brings to the child. A
purpose of this book is to show that the adult who stands
firmly in the present civilization can believe in the 'Easter
Hare' and so for the child the 'Easter Hare' can be saved
from the hypercritical scepticism of a materialistic age.

The Easter Hare is a profound symbol handed down from
the most ancient wisdom. It is the *animal of Venus*. The
Goddess of Love cherishes the hare in her sanctuary. Thus
it was in the ancient mysteries. Pausanias (III 22.9) mentions
the hare as the holy animal of Aphrodite. In the light of the
full moon the hares go gambolling, so the ancients tell us.
In the Middle Ages the hare was the symbol of alchemy.
Alchemy describes what goes on in the hidden inmost parts
of the human organism, deep below the threshold of
consciousness. What is produced in the retort of the human
organs escapes our consciousness. Only when we step forth
upon the path of inner soul development do we learn gradually to grasp those fleeting evanescent pictures which bespeak

the transformation going on within the physical organism. These fleeting Imagination-pictures in which, in the novitiate, the disciple of the alchemical master dreams the building-up process of his own physical organism, were called in the Middle Ages the 'fleeting hare'. The sevenfold human being at first shies at grasping this fleeting quality. He is sevenfold, for he bears within himself: corporeality, life, soul, self-awareness, eternal knowledge won from insights, the ability to practise what he knows to be good, and finally the ability to transform his own being. Existence, life, soul, and spirit which is aware of itself are what make up man in his present form of development. Anything beyond that is a goal and therefore only a potentiality in us. Alchemy strives towards this goal, not only seeking knowledge and its application to life but also to transform man himself. The human being who has dedicated himself to alchemy sacrifices the form in which he has been created in order to rise to his creator and to work at the transformation of his own being. The alchemist works at himself as a cognizant, moral and social being. The hare who freely gives his body to others is the alchemist's paragon; in fairy tales the hare appears as the 'white hare'.

The purely cognitive man in us uses his nerve and sense organization. With every act of cognition he destroys something of the organism given to him by Nature. Every perception is a destruction, for example, the destruction of the retina in seeing; every thought involves a partial destruction of minute portions of the brain. The perception of the complementary colours, however, is based on feeling. The feeling-man in us dreams the counter-pictures of what he consciously experiences. The will-man in us effects physically what the feeling-man has dreamt beforehand. The will-man regenerates. Alchemy endeavours to behold this regenerative process by means of a consciousness higher than our ordinary consciousness.

What goes on in synthesis and simultaneously in the human being is seen by the alchemist as occurring separately and consecutively on the earth in the seasons' change. He sees the objectivity of the sense and nerve process in the rigidity of winter. In spring he experiences the regeneration as brought about by the forces of the will–organization. The regenerating element in sleep, and in our sleep before birth, is seen by the alchemist as connected with the moon. The embryo in the womb develops according to moon rhythms. Vegetation is controlled by the vernal full moon. Whether the full moon falls early or late in one year determines whether Easter is early or late. As the moon moves round in the sky it consumes itself and then it regenerates itself. The waning moon works on the degenerative forces of the sense-nerve system, that is on the upper man. The waxing moon works on the regenerative process, on the lower man. The Middle Ages symbolized this polarity in hare and hound. The hound, the animal of the senses, barks at the full moon, while the hare as metabolic animal gambols in it. The hound is for ever hounding the hare, as degeneration follows regeneration. The hare's forte is in the metabolic-limb system.

Thus the hare is the symbol for *Nature's regenerative forces*; and the hare's egg is the moon. Prosaic modern man says that hares do not lay eggs. But the Easter Hare brings them and hides them under the bushes for the children to find. This again is ancient lore derived from the original wisdom: the world came from the egg. The world–egg and the hare belong together as the waxing moon belongs to the metabolic system. The eggs are brightly coloured because the brightly coloured picture-world of imagination escapes from them. It is the imagination stimulated by the moon. The ancient wisdom says: 'When Easter comes seek the brightly coloured picture-world, the heavenly food, as the children search for the brightly coloured eggs, — then thou shalt not stand by the empty grave, but the Risen One shall teach thee.

As Nature orders the process of generation in the rhythm of the year so the alchemist also deliberately integrates his soul-life in this rhythm. At Easter he receives what at Christmas he gives birth to. Christmas is the festival of Inspiration: then the angels' message sounds: 'Unto you is born this day a Saviour.' Easter is the festival of Imagination. The earth decks herself in bright colours, and inwardly the swiftly flitting picture-life awakens, a life open to the initiate's inves-

156

tigation but which for the uninitiated remains a 'startled hare' (see the quotation from *Parzival* at the head of the chapter) which eludes him. At St John's tide (June 24) we can immerse ourselves selflessly in Nature. There Nature encourages Intuition. Michaelmas (September 29) is the festival of action. What we have experienced in Imagination, Inspiration and Intuition should become action at Michaelmas. In olden times in Central Europe that was the time of social contracts. Servants — the assistants in activity — were engaged. Well then, Easter is the festival of Imagination. It is beautiful, this brightly coloured picture-world, the world of Venus. But one must not fall in love with it. Therefore the Rosicrucian, in the *Chymical Wedding*, written down by Valentin Andrae, says: 'He who would see Lady Venus uncovered must not wish to possess her and must not take Cupid with him.' Renunciation and sacrifice are demanded by this first view of the Imaginative world. One must be prepared to forego it. It was Jakob Böhme's greatness that he renounced it for ten years. At Easter we must bury our picture-world so that it may rise again. The Risen One gives us the picture-world, but first he must bring Good Friday. For centuries Easter remained merely the experience of Good Friday. It is when the Risen One, the Christ appears in the world-rhythm that Easter Sunday can be experienced.

What mankind's ancient Imagination has given us can be renewed at Easter. This is attempted in the following Buddhist tale and in the Rosicrucian images of the *Mons Philosophorum* where it is shown how the hare is the enlivener in sleep. Waking man is beheaded to bring about supersensible experience, for in waking the regenerative processes are thrust back into the rest of the organism by the senses and by the central nervous system. In waking man the etheric body which permeates the organism with life is beheaded. In sleep the organizing forces of the etheric body surge back into the head. The head is now replaced: renewal of the head takes place. This is the actual preparation of the Grail-supper for the senses and nerves by the root of life. The hare (alchemy) brings the root of life. This divided root is the breath-stream, entering the lungs from the mouth through the air-passages.

157

The metamorphosed process in sleep effects the regeneration. The Beheading of the Baptist and the Awakening of Lazarus are Imaginations of this process. Thus fairy tales are profound, and worthy not only of preservation from oblivion but of being kindled to new life. Rudolf Steiner whose knowledge we have followed closely, does this for them. Following in his footsteps as well as we can, we are enlivened by what superficial civilization consigns to cultural death.

The Hare in the Moon
A Buddhist Tale Renewed*

There was once a wise king. He died and entered heaven. The angels led his soul before the throne of God, and God said to him: 'My king, because thou hast led the people of earth in goodness and in loyalty thou shalt enter into eternal bliss. Speak what thou desirest and I shall grant thee thy wish.' The wise king, whose soul stood before God, answered: 'Lord and God, have mercy on me, frail mortal. No one is good save God alone. I feel sorely how little I have been able to do for the furtherance and freedom of mankind. If howsoever it pleaseth thee, my God, send me back to the earth that I may learn to do my task better. But grant me one thing out of the abundance of thy might: give me the gift to transform myself into any shape that I may desire.' Then God said: 'Go in peace.'

When the wise king came down to earth again he changed into the form of a hare, and as such he lived in the forest. On one side of this forest lay the mountains, on another

* Rudolf Steiner speaks about this tale in *The Gospel of St Luke* (lecture of Sep 17, 1909) and about its connection to Buddha.

In a funny but puzzling way Rudolf Steiner once made this hare motif known to Nora von Baditz (later W. J. Stein's wife). She tells how she was rather dejectedly sitting backstage when Dr Steiner suddenly stood before her and asked her cheerfully, 'Have you seen the hare in the moon?'

Her mood quickly changed to wondering. He laughed, and then so did she. 'Have you not seen the hare in the moon?' he repeated impudently.

She looked a little baffled, not knowing what to say. Then he laughed with such warmth and energy that all her sorrow disappeared.

'Yes, you have to keep a good look-out, then you will see the hare in the moon,' he said, gave a friendly nod, and disappeared.

The glowing seed of this meeting stayed in her memory for a long time. It was only much later that she came across the hare in the above lecture.

there was a river and on the third side lay a village. The wise king lived thus in the forest and had three friends there. They too were wise like him. They too had received the gift of God to cloak themselves in an inconspicuous form. One took on the form of a monkey, the second that of a jackal and the third that of an otter. They never revealed themselves in their human form to other people and so no one in the whole country knew what wonderful human beings those animal forms concealed. During the day each went out to seek food in his own particular terrain. The monkey went to the trees of the forest, the jackal to the fields and the otter to the water. After their day's work they would meet together in concealment, and only then would they take on their true form. In the evening the hare would teach them, telling them of his life, of his talks with God and with the angels, and of his former lives upon earth. He would say: 'To the poor man who begs of you, you should grant his request from the fullness of your knowledge. You should keep the commandments of God and bear patiently your renunciation and your fasting.' They took his exhortations to heart, and each then repaired to his retreat and remained there.

Thus time passed. One day when the wise king in the form of a hare was leaping across the fields he looked up and saw the moon. And because he saw that the moon in its course through the sky had almost consumed itself, and that all that was left of it was a very thin golden sickle in which the heavenly bread lay like a dark disc with a silvery edge, he knew that the time for fasting had come. Thus he saw the heavenly bread prepared, and knew that a man could only make himself worthy to receive it by foregoing all earthly food. Therefore he said to his friends, 'Tomorrow is the day when the heavenly bread is to be eaten. It is a day of fasting and no one must eat food. You three shall keep the fast by remembering our teaching, for you have vowed solemnly to keep the commandments of God. Whoever follows God's dictates of love shall receive heavenly reward. If a beggar approach you give him of your food, but you yourselves must wait till afterwards to eat food.' They declared that they were ready to follow this rule and each remained in his home.

Early next morning the wise man who had the form of an otter went out. He went as usual to the place where he was wont to seek his food, to the banks of the great river. There a fisherman had just caught seven scarlet fishes, tied them together on a string and covered them with sand by the bank. Then he went fishing further down the river and slipped and fell into the water. Meantime the otter smelled the fish, scraped away the sand and pulled them out. Then he called out three times in a loud voice: 'Does anyone own these fishes?' When no owner appeared the otter picked up the loop in his teeth and took the fishes home. 'Only when it is time to taste food shall I eat them,' he thought. Then he lay down to ponder the teaching of the wise hare.

The jackal too went out to look for food. In a game-keeper's hut he saw two spits with meat, a squirrel and a pot of milk. Three times he cried aloud: 'Does this belong to anyone?' and when he did not see any owner he put the cord of the pot round his neck, seized the spit and the squirrel in his mouth and carried them off into the bush where he had his home. There he set them down, lay down himself and thought: 'Only when it is time to taste food shall I eat them.' Then he pondered the teaching of the wise hare.

The monkey too went into the forest and took a bunch of mangoes from a tree and carried them back home into the bush. 'Only when it is time to taste food shall I eat of these,' he thought and lay down to think about the teaching of the wise hare.

The wise hare however did not go out. After he had spent the day deep in thought, he lay down saying to himself: 'Only when it is time again to taste of food, shall I go out and eat some grass.' To be sure if beggars should come to me I shall have nothing to offer them. But the food which I eat I cannot offer to beggars, for they cannot eat the grass upon which I feed, nor have I rice or anything else fit for them to eat. But when he grew sad because he could not offer a beggar any food he comforted himself with the thought: 'If a beggar comes to me I shall give him the flesh of my own body for food.'

Thus reassured the wise hare fell asleep. But he did not sleep like other creatures who shut their eyes when their eyelids began to droop. His resolve to sacrifice himself if it should be necessary had the effect of allowing him to sleep with open seeing eyes. And so in sleep he saw the dark disc of the moon. But now he could look right through the moon and he saw the far side which we humans never see, and the far side was brightly lit, and there was a shining white stone. This stone was the throne of God, and the hare saw God sitting on his bright throne. Now the wise hare saw that the throne of God and the seat of the angels had grown warm through the power of his sacrifice of love. The moon which otherwise is icy cold grew warm. When God noticed this he rejoiced over the hare and decided to put the hare-king to the test. He came down from heaven to earth and in the guise of a poor man came first to the place where the otter dwelled.

'Poor man,' said the otter, 'why are you standing there?' 'Wise man,' said the poor man, 'give me just a little to eat. If I could but eat a little of your provender I should have strength enough to last out the fast, and to live fasting as God has commanded.'

'Very well,' said the otter, 'I shall give you something to eat.'

And this is the speech between the otter and the poor man:
'I have seven scarlet fishes
Landed on the river bank
Take and taste them now, my friend
Eat and sojourn in the forest.'
'Keep them till next morning early,'
Spoke the poor man of mild nature
God's reward shall never fail thee.'

Having spoken these words the poor man vanished. God went on in this guise through the forest and came to the jackal.

The jackal also asked: 'Poor man, why are you standing there?'

And the poor man answered: 'Give me just a little to eat. If I could but eat a little of your provender I should have

161

strength enough to last out the fast, and to live fasting as God has commanded.'

'Very well,' said the jackal, 'I shall give you something to eat.'

And this is the speech between the jackal and the poor man:

'Squirrel, milk and meat on spit
Caught by cunning for the keeper
This I give thee for thy banquet
Thou mendicant sent out from God
Refresh thyself in heaven's halls
Eat and sojourn in the forest.'
'Keep them till next morning early,'
Spoke the poor man of mild nature,
'God's reward shall never fail thee.'

Having spoken these words the poor man vanished. God went on in this guise through the forest and came to the monkey.

The monkey also asked: 'Poor man, why are you standing there?'

And the poor man answered: 'Give me just a little to eat. If I could but eat a little of your provender I should have strength enough to last out the fast, and to live fasting as God has commanded.'

'Very well,' said the monkey, 'I shall give you something to eat.'

And this is the speech and answer between the monkey and the poor man:

'Ripened fruit and water here
Shady peace on lovely hill–side
This thou mendicant I give thee
Eat and sojourn in the forest.'
'Keep them till next morning early,'
Spoke the poor man of mild nature,
'God's reward shall never fail thee.'

Having spoken these words he vanished. God went on in the guise of a man asking for spiritual gifts until he came to the wise hare.

When the hare saw him he said, 'Poor dear man, why are you standing there?'

162

'Give me,' said the supplicant, 'only a little of the food that feeds you, so that I may be strengthened by your power to endure the fast that what is divine in the world may be strengthened.'

Then the wise hare spoke: 'Thou man of God, thou hast done well to be strengthened in body by me. Behold I shall give thee a gift, such as I have never given before. But thou must not destroy the life of that which nourishes you. Go and seek wood and kindle fire from coals and tell me when it is done. I shall sacrifice to thee my body, and I shall leap into the fire, and when the flames have roasted my flesh thou shalt eat of my meat, nourishing thyself from obedience to the divine will.' And the wise hare also spoke thus:

'Lo! I am the food for journey
Seek not earthly nourishment
Take me with thee for thy wayfare
As I am consumed in thee,
On the white stone the new name
I shall glorify. — Amen.'

When God heard these words he made a fire of coals with his supernatural power and called the wise king, who was sitting humbly and lowly before him in the guise of a hare. The hare then arose from his bed of grass and herbs and went to the coals. 'If in my fur there should perhaps be little animals,' he said compassionately, 'they should not be killed.' So he shook himself thrice. Then he offered his body as a sacrifice. He leaped and plunged happily into the burning coals. But the same miracle that had warmed the icy moon and the throne of God and of the angels now cooled the fire. The fire could not even warm the skin of the wise king in the lowly form of the hare. It was as if he had leaped into snow. Then he turned to the divine wayfarer and said, 'The fire which thou hast kindled is cold. It cannot even warm the skin of my body. What does this mean?'

'Wise King,' answered the divine pilgrim, 'Thou hast recognized me. I am he who has led thee into the ordeal by fire, and thou hast prevailed.' Then the wise king standing as a humble hare gave forth a lion's roar: 'O thou holy pilgrim on earth, though the whole universe should try me

my good will shall not be quenched as it flows out in love.'
After these words he gave forth again the lion's roar.

'Wise King,' said the divine pilgrim, 'Thy power in the doing of good shall be known through a whole aeon.' Thereupon he seized upon the rocky frame of the earth and with the hot stream of rock that had melted in his divine love he drew the picture of the hare in the disc of the moon. Then he bade farewell to the wise king who had thus shown the greatness of his sacrificing love, and bedded him softly upon his bed there in the deep forest and ascended to his resplendent throne. The four wise men still live together today, fulfilling the spiritual requirements of mankind, reading in the stars the signs of the times and they shall live eternally in divine bliss.

The Mountain of the Philosophers

When Parzival came to the hermitage the hermit taught him about the fall of Lucifer and Adam and about the stone which gives man the power to raise himself once more to the divine heights like the Phoenix. (Wolfram von Eschenbach, *Parzival*, Book IX)

The picture of the *Mons Philosophorum*★ shows a Rosicrucian mystery centre and at the same time is an illustration of a Rosicrucian path of development as expounded by Rudolf Steiner.

The individual who is still living in his lower consciousness cannot grasp the fleeting pictures of the Imagination. The pictures, like the startled hare, escape him. He cannot pass the guardian of the mystery. What he is to grasp appears like the fleeting hare. The ability to grasp what is fleeting comes by constant practice. The brooding hen indicates to him that nothing can be achieved without perseverance. Unless he can permeate his own being with soul-warmth he cannot attain illumination. The fetters of earthbound understanding must be cast off at the entrance gate. The hermit guards the gate of death. In icy loneliness the soul meets the ice-grey old man who brings to us that part of our being which we cannot comprehend in our physical bodies. The

★ See also W. J. Stein, *Weltgeschichte*.

spirit-seeker recognizes the thought-mode of this stage as a grey shadow.

As soon as the spirit-seeker's soul realizes that it has become free from the body it must cease to become a prey to fear. In the supersensory world we find the counter-pictures of organic activity. The temptation to experience in the body what has been seen in Imaginative pictures is exceedingly great. What proceeds from us is reflected as something coming towards us. If the individual succumbs to the temptation to imitate the mirror-image of his organic activity which the Imagination shows to him, he will destroy the healthy functioning of his body. This temptation alchemy calls the battle with the lion. The lion is the heart. The more the lion-fighter opposes, the more savage grows the lion. He must recognize that in the spiritual world one is active by being the reverse of what is active in the sense-world. If we let the lion do what it wants to do, and if we do not oppose it we shall get it into our power. We discover that its savagery is only the counter-picture of our own struggling. Once we have acquired acceptance and serenity we can apply conscious will in the spiritual world. The heart comes under our control. We ride the lion. The second gate is opened and the feeling man can pass through. The third gate is guarded by the dragon. In the symbol of the dragon the spirit-seeker experiences his metabolic man, the digestive organism. Coloured-pictures arise from there: dragon wisdom. We must renounce these. At the lion's gate we learned to blot out the pictures. So now we blot out our dragon-wisdom too. The dragon sinks down into the abyss. All grows dark. Now we recognize what the black raven is. But the development goes on. What had sunk down into the abyss of darkness in the shape of the dragon now reappears above our heads. The activity of thought is now seen as the metabolic activity transformed and raised on high. The brain with all its windings is a frozen intestine. The mobility of peristalsis reappears in extra-physical (body-free) thinking. What is in motion below is rigid above. What is rigid below is in motion above. In the language of alchemy the body-free thinking risen into mobility above is the white eagle. But the Imaginative experience still lacks the fullness of colour. This is given to the spirit-seeker when he learns to submit himself to his destiny, and then in the counter-picture to this submission he will receive the cosmic rays shining in upon him. The spirit-seeker implants in his earthly man what sun and moon have to give, and so the star-tree of higher knowledge can flourish. He comes to behold the high castle of the Grail, the place of the royal art, wherein man lives in harmony with the cosmos.

11. The Death of Merlin

Legend relates that Merlin had the gift of knowing everything that was going on in the world at any given moment.
His consciousness and perception were all-embracing; all that
was happening at any present moment, no matter where in
the world it might be, was accessible to him.

The legend goes on to tell that this consciousness was later
on transmuted and that Merlin was thereafter able to embrace
the future rather than the present. Indeed, there are many
prophecies attributed to him.

There can be no doubt that Merlin was a seer, to whose
vision the spiritual beings of nature were perceptible. In
woods and caves he would encounter the nature-spirits. In
the Bay of Tintagel to this day we are shown 'Merlin's
Cave'. Out of the trees, too, spiritual beings came to meet
him and he was able to converse with them. They took the
form of nymphs and he united with them in love. For
modern consciousness such things are difficult to understand;
yet they were a reality for that other kind of consciousness
which existed in all parts of the world in ancient times, and
to the dreamlike impressions of which we must ascribe the
origins of all mythology. It was due really to a mutual
penetration of the dreaming and waking life. What a man
saw as a tree by day appeared to him in dreams by night as
a spiritual being. The more active forces of nature appeared
in the figure of a masculine and the more passive forces in
the figure of a feminine being.

Trees have indeed a dual nature. Out of the cosmos, out
of the universe beyond the earth they are formed — endowed
with characteristic form after their kind. Take an apple-tree
for example. Not only the fruits, the apples, but the leaves,
too, are round, and the tree as a whole has the same rounded
form. The identical principle of form works throughout the
tree and appears again in every detail. A pear-tree has more
longish leaves and fruit, and the entire form of the tree is
like the pear itself once more.

Such is the formative principle in trees. But there is also another force at work there. Unlike the plastic forces which give the tree its form, this other force comes not from the surrounding universe, but from within the earth. It opens out and ramifies as it goes upwards. To begin with it shoots upward in the trunk, then it divides and divides again in branch and twig. This second force is more musical than plastic. Indeed, for spiritual hearing the basic note or 'tonic' resounds in the main trunk, the 'second' in the first main branches, the 'third' in the next stage of ramification, and so on, and we shall find that most trees come to an end of the branching process in the 'fifth.'

In the human being, too, these twofold forces are at work. The plastic forces, coming from the universe outside the earth, form and mould our head and nervous system. The brain, above all, is a most perfect work of plastic modelling. In the skeleton on the other hand, in the repetition, sequence, and enhancement of the several bones, the more musical forces are at work. Where the two polar forces — plastic and musical — encounter one another, rhythm arises in the human being. This finds expression in the repeated vertebrae and ribs. We see the same rhythm in the plant, in the sequence of the nodes along the stem.

Now the primeval clairvoyant consciousness saw on the one hand the physical appearance of the tree, while on the other hand with dreamlike imagination it apprehended the dynamic working of these inner forces, which was so like the play of the same forces in the human being that the seer of old time, in his dreaming consciousness, actually perceived a human figure that emerged out of the tree and came to meet him. And so it was in Merlin's case; nay, more, we are given to understand that his experiences of this kind were so real and so intense as to make possible for him a personal relationship of love to such a being or spirit of a tree. Such experiences would lead to the development of an ever widening cosmic consciousness, to which the secrets of nature would be unfolded.

Not only Merlin but a great number of spiritual seekers of olden time experienced the world of nature in this way. Beings spoke to them — beings were revealed to them out

168

of the stars, the planets, and the elements of earth. Indeed, this kind of consciousness was the prevalent one through many thousands of years. But in the course of time human consciousness underwent definite changes, which it is most important for us to observe and study. In Merlin's time the nature-beings spoke to man out of the woods and forests, out of the world of plants, and from the waves of the sea, surging and beating into the caverns of a rocky cliff. In still more ancient times it was the heavens themselves, the world of the fixed stars, which spoke to man. Orpheus brought forth Eurydice from the netherworld, from which man had to take his leave when he turned his soul's attention to the heavens, to the stars. The Orphic songs, preserved, for example, by Apollonius of Rhodes, are a description of geological events, which in their turn were a terrestrial echo of the changing constellations, the varying positions of the axis of the Earth in its relation to the fixed stars.

Stage by stage, the universe was bereft of living soul. The first to fade away were the great pictures of the heavens and of the constellations, which at long last became dead symbols — 'signs of the zodiac' as we now know them. But in an intermediate period the planetary gods still spoke to man, until they too at length grew dumb, one after another. The realm of Chronos or *Saturn* fell away when Zeus or *Jupiter* began his reign. Thereafter came the epoch of *Mars* or of the Titans. Comparative study of all religions will prove that the dream-picture-world of mankind drew nearer and nearer to the earth, while stage by stage the farther reaches of the cosmos faded away — their Word is reduced to silence.

It was as though the gods descended to the earth to unite with men. And at the last, the Logos himself became flesh. The cosmic distances were now unpeopled of the gods, and the time came when John the Baptist had to prophesy: 'Change the way of your thinking, for the distant realms of the heavens have now come near at hand.'

At the time of Merlin an important transition was just taking place. During the period immediately before him, the gods and demi-gods, whom the human being met in his dreams by night and in his day-dreams, too, had still been revealing themselves in the phenomena of air and water. The adventures of the Knights of King Arthur have to do with this stage in the evolution of human consciousness. The nineteenth century artist, Böcklin, reproduces very truly in his paintings the mood and feeling of this epoch.

Then came the time of Christianity. Long, long ago Persephone, the power of clairvoyance, had disappeared in the dark realm of Pluto. Isis, the human soul, wandered a widow through the world, filled with longing for the realm of Light and Imagination — for Osiris, her husband. The time had come when this universal realm of Light and spiritual Imagination was dismembered into so many isolated symbols. Sadness and grief spread out among the seekers of the spirit. The fair world of their dreams receded ever more, and the plain, matter-of-fact everyday world alone remained. This was the time when the Round Table of King Arthur gradually became a place of loneliness. When the Knights, for lack of spiritual experiences, had nothing more to relate, they stayed away.

The point of time was not always the same in different lands. The peoples, it is true, all of them, passed through the different phases of consciousness, but they did not all do so at the same time. Yet for every nation, sooner or later, the moment came for which the word of Christ was spoken: 'Blessed are now no longer they who behold, blessed are they who believe.'

In Christianity itself, the historical event of Palestine and the tradition which took its start from thence replaced the ancient spiritual visions. Christian tradition tells of the Crucified One, no bone of whom was to be broken. The prophets had foretold this, for it answered to a piece of ancient knowledge out of the mysteries. The meaning of it is that in Christ the spirit penetrated even to the skeleton, to the most mineral-like, most deathlike substance in the human body. Indeed, it was only thus that the spirit overcame death. Thereafter the power of the visionary light rayed forth renewed, out of the very symbol of death, — out of dead mineral substance.

The blood of Christ must be sought for in the crystal cup. Thus did the Knights of King Arthur seek. They took their departure from the Round Table and set out on their quest of the Holy Grail. The word 'Grail' is derived from the Latin word *gradalis*, signifying a gradual or step-by-step descent. The Grail in pre-Christian time had been a vessel the interior of which was graduated in a threefold form. Dedicated to the goddess Ceridwen, it had contained the mysterious 'red substance' of alchemy, — that which became in Christian times the sacred blood of Christ. It was the substance which induced the power of clairvoyant vision, which at one time had still borne witness to the realm of the fixed stars, which at a later stage spoke only of the planetary spheres, and in the latest pre-Christian times became restricted to the kingdom of the elements.

Clairvoyant vision was henceforth to be enclosed in the cup of crystal, that is to say the very substance of the Earth. This was the point in evolution when Christ celebrated the first Holy Mass, in the institution of the Last Supper as described in the Gospels. He took the heavenly bread of Imagination which had once upon a time rayed forth from the entire cosmos, and, as Osiris of old had been broken into many fragments, so now he broke the bread and distributed it among the twelve disciples. The 'white substance' of alchemy, erstwhile the silvery power of the moon, which leads us out into the world of dreams, was now transformed into the sacred Host. And in place of the 'red substance' of alchemy Christ distributed the wine. Wine is, in fact, the substance which brings about in man the eventual extinction of clairvoyance. This was the darkest moment in the world's evolution. The ancient world of the mythologies was blotted out; the new world of Light, or of the Gnosis in which the Risen Christ should shine forth, had not yet dawned — for the Resurrection was not yet accomplished. Judas had received the Sacrament. The Lord had steeped the bread in the wine and had given it to him. Judas went forth; it was night. He took the wages of betrayal, for he knew not that the absolute darkness would only last for three-and-a-half days, from Holy Thursday until Easter Sunday.

Christ died and was laid in a rocky tomb, and Joseph of Arimathea gathered up his blood in the crystal cup. Ancient clairvoyance and inspiration were extinguished. The spirit

171

penetrated through and through the skeleton. The world lay dumb and blind, bereft of vision. The sun was darkened and the earth trembled. The power of the light, the power of spiritual vision, penetrated into the very depths of the mineral kingdom.

This moment had been foreseen in the great mystery schools of antiquity. They knew that Dionysos would be seized by the Titans and dismembered in the realm of the elements. They knew too that Persephone would be robbed by Pluto and would dwell in Pluto's kingdom under the tree of dreams, in whose interweaving branches the dream-pictures weave to and fro. They knew, too, that in Pluto's kingdom the cup would be offered to her with the potion in whose surface nothing else could be reflected than her own human countenance.

This 'I' or ego-point of human evolution, the point where man utterly loses the divine world and is alone with himself, had been foreseen in the mysteries of Iacchos. It was this moment which Christ himself experienced in the Garden of Gethsemane on the Mount of Olives. In a little chapel somewhere in Hungary this scene is remarkably portrayed. Christ prays in Gethsemane to the Father from whom he receives the cup. On the one side we see the disciples sleep; mankind is asleep during the greatest event of all history. On the other side we see the angels turning their faces away. They, too, do not understand what is going on; they cannot comprehend how an immortal god should undergo death. Then Christ in utter loneliness takes the crystal cup. The eternal *I Am* of man is here revealed at the historic moment of decision.

English mythology has experienced this event of human evolution in the Merlin legend. Merlin was the seer whose power of vision had at one time embraced the universe. But the visionary power had receded and nothing more was left — only the nymph of the tree with whom he was to unite in love. She would grant him her love only on condition that he communicated to her all his secrets. He told her all he knew, but still she was unsatisfied. She would fain know how she might hold him prisoner for ever. This secret, too, he had to tell her. It was Merlin's destiny, in fact, to experience as his own personal fate the historic destiny of the power of clairvoyance in mankind. And so it came about that the nymph imprisoned him in the rock, calling as she did so upon the nine spheres, the nine hierarchies, through whose circles the spirit had descended. Here Gawain found him, by whom the narrative is told. Such is the secret of Merlin: he was the one who experienced the tragic destiny of the spirit in mankind as his own personal fate. Yet by this very fact he was elected to become the teacher and guardian of Arthur.

Merlin knew what was going on at any present moment, no matter where upon earth the event was taking place. Through the Arthurian tradition this form of knowing was bequeathed to British history. But the legend with good reason goes on to tell that in the later course of evolution Merlin learned to transform his universal present consciousness into a consciousness of the future. Through the consciousness of things present man attains to nature, whose works and beings he thus learns to love and to revere. He learns to master the forces of the nature-beings, so much so that he grows able to elaborate the whole mineral kingdom, to work it through and through. Yet strong as are the spiritual forces which he applies in so doing, he cannot free himself in this kind of work from being prisoner of matter. His love for the nature-being holds him spell-bound and imprisoned in the world of matter. But there is also a second 'nature' — a nature not yet there in present time, but which man himself can bring to birth as he goes on towards the future.

This 'second nature' is the social world. Original nature was created and enspirited by the divine powers. This second world is being created by man, in whom the divine-spiritual world, having once become flesh in man, comes more and more to realization and to creative activity. Stage by stage in the long course of evolution, the old world of nature — nature from out of which we are born — lost its divine essence. The divine withdrew from the great cosmos, that it might live on in the free and autonomous responsibility of man. When the divine takes leave of nature, nature takes on a character which is indeed still worthy of man's love and reverence, but which will none the less take prisoner the human ego. Moreover, man can only free himself from this imprisonment by social deeds which have their origin in the individual I, in the true human ego.

In the creative development of social structure by mankind, a second nature is, indeed, being brought to birth within the universe. It is as yet only in process of becoming. And in this new world which is arising towards the future, Merlin, too, must find salvation. The moment when the Round Table of King Arthur became a place of loneliness and when the Knights set out upon the quest of the Grail, is the point in evolution whereat man learns courageously and willingly to lose the old clairvoyance which was nature-given but therefore also nature-bound. Man enters bravely upon the intermediate period of quest and search within the world of the physical senses, whereafter he is destined to give birth again to a new clairvoyance. This new clairvoyance, unlike the old, does not unveil the secrets of nature in cosmic Imaginations, but in prophetic pictures no less significant foresees the evolution of the social life. The true quest of the Grail begins only at the point where Merlin dies. It is the quest of the spirit in the crystal cup of matter; it is the seeking of that social love whose coming cannot merely be awaited but will be brought forth by our creative action. This newly awakened love is not the love of antiquity — the love of nature and of the nature-spirits — it is the love within the human kingdom, linking man with man, nay, more, linking whole groups of human beings one with another. Through this alone shall we find the returning way from matter to the stars.

The ancient Norse mythology beheld this path of evolution. It saw the human god hang crucified for nine days long on the cosmic ash-tree, whose ninefold branches are indeed the nine spheres of the cosmos, and it gives the tree in true name: 'Yggdrasil' — ego-bearer. Humanity is crucified upon the tree that bears the ego, and indeed, only by this means attains the turning-point of individualization. But at this turning-point, the ancient gods of nature die. It is the twilight of the gods. One god alone outlives the world-wide downfall, namely the god who himself took human form. By the power of the divine-spiritual Word, which in him underwent humanity, evolution will be guided back to its divine origin, albeit this time in full consciousness and egohood.

Merlin experienced this passage of the divine through matter. And as the legend does not tell us of his eventual release from the spell of matter, we are thus left to feel the more deeply that at this point something is still left unfulfilled — something for us to do.

12. Thomas Aquinas and the Grail

Thomas Aquinas, in the preface to his work on the Epistles of St Paul, spoke in a wonderful way about the Holy Grail. Referring to the Apostle who says of himself, 'Not I, but Christ in me,' Thomas Aquinas writes:

> In considering this chosen vessel, we may look firstly to him who is the Author and Creator of it, who formed it of purest gold and decorated it with rarest diamonds [Thomas Aquinas uses gold to signify the wisdom of Paul and his virtues he calls jewels]; secondly, to the precious liquid wherewith it is filled and which is none other than the divine Name, poured out like fragrant oil — the teaching of Jesus Christ, the teaching the apostle alone desired to give. Thirdly, we may look to the manner in which this vessel is brought to the several nations of the world, by means of epistles and by messengers who are filled with its virtue; and fourthly, to the outpouring of the vessel itself as it goes on for ever and ever through the constant reading of these epistles in the gatherings of the saints. This teaching of the Apostle, carried thus continually farther and farther in time and space, is in reality the teaching of the grace of Jesus Christ. The first nine epistles are addressed to peoples, the following four to leaders in the church, and the last to the Hebrews, among whom Christ had been born; herein is contained the whole order of the mystery. Paul has marked its stages. In the last epistle he considers grace in its source and in its Author and Creator; then he follows it up through the members of the mystical Body: finally he sees it communicated to the whole believing people, so that it flows in all the veins of this Body.

In this passage Thomas Aquinas speaks of the wisdom of

God that lives in Paul who is the vessel in which the Name of God has been brought to the various nations of the world.

In a lecture Rudolf Steiner called Paul 'the great successor of John,' and said that Raphael's *School of Athens* is the school of Paul.★ A significant statement for the light it throws on the continuity of the stream of Christianity. Christ had a disciple whom he loved, one of his own immediate disciples. This was, as Rudolf Steiner has explained, the Lazarus who had been recalled to life by Christ, and who was the writer of the John Gospel. His immediate follower is Paul, the founder of the School of Athens. There is an allusion to the founding of the School of Athens in the Acts of the Apostles, where we read (17:34): 'Howbeit certain men clave unto him [Paul], and believed: among the which was Dionysius the Areopagite, and a woman named Damaris, and others with them.' Speaking of what is contained in the well-known writings of Dionysius the Areopagite, Rudolf Steiner has said that it goes back to the teaching of Paul in the School of Athens; it was, of course, not written down until long afterwards, and not by the original Dionysius but by a later successor. Rudolf Steiner pointed out that the disciples of Dionysius were always named Dionysius after their teacher. The so-called pseudo-Dionysius is thus one who imparted, albeit much later, the genuine Pauline teaching. We shall not enter into an investigation concerning the authenticity of the Pauline Epistles; anyone who knows how to read in them can easily see that their content has its source in the tradition that goes back directly to Christ, John and Paul. And it is because Thomas Aquinas knew this, that he spoke as he did of the Pauline Epistles and their wisdom. The secret of these Epistles of Paul, including the Epistle to the Hebrews, has to be discovered by reading them in reverse order. To understand the words of Thomas Aquinas, we need to begin with the Epistle to the Hebrews. There is opened the fountain of grace, as Thomas Aquinas expresses it. This Epistle closes with the words: 'Grace be with you all. Amen.'

The Epistle to Philemon ends with the words: 'The grace of our Lord Jesus Christ be with your spirit. Amen.'

★ Lecture of May 2, 1912 in *Earthly and Cosmic Man*

The Epistle to Titus ends with the words: 'Grace be with you all. Amen.'

The Second Epistle to Timothy ends: 'Grace be with you. Amen.'

The First Epistle to Timothy ends: 'Grace be with thee. Amen.'

The nine letters to different congregations (continuing in reverse order) end as follows:

'The grace of our Lord Jesus Christ be with you all. Amen.'

'The grace of our Lord Jesus Christ be with you. Amen.'

'Grace be with you. Amen.'

'The grace of our Lord Jesus Christ be with you all. Amen'.

'Grace be with all them that love our Lord Jesus Christ in sincerity. Amen.'

'Brethren, the grace of our Lord Jesus Christ be with your spirit. Amen.'

'The grace of the Lord Jesus Christ, and the love of God, and the communion of the Holy Ghost, be with you all. Amen.'

'The grace of our Lord Jesus Christ be with you. My love be with you all in Christ Jesus. Amen.'

'The grace of our Lord Jesus Christ be with you all. Amen. Now to him that is of power to stablish you according to my gospel, and the preaching of Jesus Christ, according to the revelation of the mystery, which was kept secret since the world began, but now is made manifest, and by the scriptures of the prophets, according to the commandment of the everlasting God, made known to all nations for the obedience of faith: to God only wise, be glory through Jesus Christ for ever. Amen.'

As we read these closing sentences one after the other, taking the Epistles in reverse order, we find Thomas Aquinas justified in what he says about the connection of these Epistles with *grace*.

In these Epistles is contained the secret of the Holy Grail. We discover it when we read them right through backwards. At the very end of the Epistle to the Hebrews (13:20) we find allusion to the 'blood of the ever-lasting covenant,' and there is mention of the city of the living God, the heavenly Jerusalem, where are the angels; and of the assembly and church of the firstborn which are written in heaven (Ch. 12). These words must be brought into connection with the Luke Gospel, where we may catch, as it were, a gentle whisper of the secrets of the Grail. For there it is said that the names of those who are called 'the seventy-two disciples of Christ' are written in heaven (10:20). These seventy-two are the knights of the Holy Grail; they represent the seventy-two peoples of the earth. The temple in which, as the Grail saga relates, seventy-two choirs have been erected for them, is the earth, the body of the Risen One. For the body of the Risen One is the earth, and the temple of his body is the earth. And of those who can behold this, who can behold in the earth the union of the forces of sun and moon — of those who can behold the Grail, it is said: 'Blessed are the eyes which see the things that ye see.' (10:23). In the centre of the Grail temple an altar was erected to the Holy Spirit. The Holy Spirit is the spirit who leads a divided mankind — split up into seventy-two languages — back to the primeval language and speech, back to the divine Word. The Epistle to the Hebrews tells of this Holy Spirit. There it is shown what the Earth was like before the Deed of Christ and what it becomes after the Resurrection. The earth is pictured, to begin with, as a tabernacle; but then it is said (9:11): 'But Christ being come an high priest of good things to come, by a greater and more perfect tabernacle, not made with hands, that is to say, not of *this* building.' These words point to the change that is wrought in the body of Christ — the earth — through the Deed of Christ. Who the high priest really is, in whose place one can in truth only imagine the Christ, is told us in the previous chapter. 'Now of the things which we have spoken, this is the sum: We have such an high priest, who is set on the right hand of the throne of the Majesty in the heavens; a *minister* of the sanctuary, and of the true tabernacle, which the Lord pitched, and not man' (8:1f). Of this minister the Grail saga speaks under the name of Titurel, for Titurel means 'the minister'. This Epistle being addressed to the Hebrews, the communication concerning the Grail is clothed in a form which they can understand.

The Hebrew people are the people who provided the body for the Christ as a physical body. Now they are to learn what the risen body of the Lord is. The physical body which they themselves provided, Christ has changed into the body of the Resurrection. This is what the Hebrews are to understand (7:14–17):

> For it is evident that our Lord sprang out of Juda[h]; of which tribe Moses spake nothing concerning priesthood. And it is yet far more evident: for that after the similitude of Melchisedec there ariseth another priest, who is made, not after the law of a carnal commandment, but after the power of an endless life. For he testifieth, Thou art a priest for ever after the order of Melchisedec.

The order of Melchizedek means that the new tabernacle is the tabernacle of the sun, as the old tabernacle was the tabernacle of the moon. For the body of the old Adam was born of the moon, was born, as is said in the John Gospel, of the will of the flesh, of the will of man. But the body of the new Adam was born of God, not by the power of the moon, not by the force that is inherited from generation to generation, not by the rhythm of the moon that holds sway in embryonal life and growth. The new Adam was born by the power of the sun. Thomas Aquinas knew that, hence his famous sentence: *homo hominem generat ex sol*. This is what the Christ brought to pass. He carried the power of the sun into the power of the moon. Christ unites sun and moon in the earth, and whoever can behold the union of sun and moon in the earth, beholds the Holy Grail. The union will indeed only be fulfilled in the future; but Christ has by his sacrificial Deed given a turn to world-evolution that shall lead to that event. Therefore is it said in the Epistle to the Hebrews (2:5): 'the world to come, whereof we speak'. This Epistle tells of the great and mighty change that is wrought in man and in the world by the Deed of Christ, which is the source and fountain of all grace. And so we read (1:10–12):

> And, Thou, Lord, in the beginning hast laid the foundation of the earth; and the heavens are the

works of thine hands; they shall perish; but thou
remainest; and they all shall wax old as doth a
garment; and as a vesture shalt thou fold them up,
and they shall be changed: but thou art the same,
and thy years shall not fail.

All this is the revelation not of a man but of the Risen One
himself, who has become the teacher of John and of Paul.
John — the Lazarus who has been resurrected from the
dead — has in him the resurrection power of Christ, and
Paul has been converted by the Risen One. And so the
School of Athens is the School of the risen Christ. This is
indicated in the opening words of the Epistle to the Hebrews:
'God, who at sundry times and in divers manners spake in
time past unto the fathers by the prophets, hath in these last
days spoken unto us by his Son, whom he hath appointed
heir of all things, by whom also he made the worlds.'

It would obviously be necessary to study each single verse
of the Epistle from this point of view. In a short essay like
this it cannot be done, but if anyone follows the guidance
of Thomas Aquinas and makes a study of all the Pauline
Epistles in the manner that we have briefly sketched for the
Epistle to the Hebrews, he will find that the source and
fountain of grace — Christ risen in the body — is indeed his
teacher. In the Chapters 1 and 2 of the Epistle to the Hebrews, mention is made of the hierarchies and of their relation
to the Christ and to man. It is said: 'What is man, that thou
art mindful of him? or the son of man that thou visitest him?
Thou madest him a little lower than the angels . . . But he
who was made a little lower than the angels — we see that
it is Jesus, crowned through the suffering of death. . . .'*
The author of the Epistle to the Hebrews would say to us:
Christ has descended from the consciousness of the Logos
through the spheres of the angels down to human existence.
He has humbled himself and abased himself, but we read
(2:5f): The world to come, whereof we speak, hath God not
put in subjection unto the angels, but — so he means —
unto Christ — We must therefore look for the Name of
Christ — the true Name of Christ — high above the sphere

* The English translation has been slightly altered.

of the lower angels. The author of the Epistle says (2:12): 'I will declare thy name unto my brethren'; and it is in reference to these words that Thomas Aquinas points out how one may contemplate the 'precious liquid' wherewith the precious vessel is filled, and which is none other than the divine Name. The secret of this Name is contained in the four previous Epistles to the four leaders of the Church. The Epistle of Paul to Philemon is a letter of introduction. Onesimus is commended to Philemon. This Onesimus Paul calls his son, whom he has begotten in his bonds. It is clear that we have here to do with a figurative mode of speech. A spiritual event is described; it is a sacred gift of the spirit that Paul has bestowed upon Onesimus. Before he had received it, as is indicated in verse 11, Onesimus would have been 'unprofitable' to Philemon, but now he can be of great profit to him, wherefore Paul sends him. This epistle is thus a *man*. Paul sends, not a message, but a messenger. He speaks of him in verse 12 in a deeply significant way. He says Onesimus is his own heart (Revised Standard Version). We miss the point altogether if we interpret what is said in this epistle as though Philemon had a good-for-nothing servant whom Paul converted after he had run away from Philemon, and whom he is now sending back with this letter. That is nonsense. One would not say of such a servant: 'He is my own heart, I have begotten him'. In verse 17, Paul goes so far as to say: 'If thou count me therefore a partner, receive him as myself.' And the verses that follow, where again one could easily misinterpret — they too are to be taken in a spiritual sense. It is a special kind of discipleship that is here suggested.

In the next epistle (in reverse order), the Letter to Titus, he speaks no longer merely of a discipleship, but of the 'washing of regeneration, and renewing of the Holy Ghost' (3:5). In the second Epistle of Paul to Timothy he addresses Timothy and calls him a soldier of Jesus Christ (2:3). He says that he remembers Timothy without ceasing in his prayers night and day (1:3). In the first Epistle he speaks of the master or teacher, no longer of the disciple, nor of one who has undergone the washing of regeneration, nor of the soldier of Christ; he goes beyond all these and speaks of those who desire to be 'masters of the law' (1Tim.1:7).

There is a gradual advance in these epistles. And the mastership consists in this, that he who attains it learns to know the Name of the Lord. For this, he must of course prepare his soul. Paul speaks of this preparation of soul in the picture of the widow, where he says in the First Epistle to Timothy (5:5): 'Now she that is a widow indeed [he means the soul of man], and desolate, trusteth in God, and continueth in supplications and prayers night and day'. Such a widow is the soul of Paul himself, for he spoke of his relation to Timothy in this way, that he had him in remembrance night and day. He gives a warning not to take any such widow under threescore years (5:9). The Grail saga gives the very same indication when it says a man must ride sixty miles through the wood to come to the Grail mountain. Rudolf Steiner once told me that these sixty miles are sixty years of life. Whoever acquits himself thus comes to the 'mystery of faith in a pure conscience' (3:9). The whole is summed up in the words: 'Now the end of the commandment is charity out of a pure heart, and of a good conscience, and of faith unfeigned' (1:5).

But whither, we needs must ask, does this way lead? What does man find by following this path? He finds him 'who only hath immortality, dwelling in the light which no man can approach unto; whom no man hath seen nor can see' (1 Tim. 6:16). It is thus required of man to take the path leading to something no man can see. No less is required than to take the path that leads to the supersensible. Therefore is it said (3:16): 'Without controversy great is the mystery of godliness: God was manifest in the flesh, justified in the Spirit, seen of angels, preached unto the Gentiles, believed on in the world'. Faith is there for those who cannot see. It is thus by the angels alone that a full knowledge of the Name of the Lord can be attained; to men it can only be preached. But Christ, as is said in the passages quoted above, stands higher than the angels, and this is expressed in the words: 'He is the Lord.'

And so the Name of Christ is the divine name, the name of his glory. That is the message of these four epistles. Their theme is that he alone finds the Christ in his glory who lifts himself to the stage of mastership where he becomes like unto the angels. Such a one was Thomas Aquinas, who for this reason went by the name of Doctor Angelicus. In the nine previous epistles we are shown how the stream of grace is guided to the various peoples, to each one in its own special manner. Here again it is always the Lord Jesus Christ, the *Kyrios*, of whom Paul speaks. The whole secret of the divine hierarchies and of Christ's relation to them is contained in these epistles. It is impossible to make mention here of all the passages that bear on this; they can be found by reading the epistles, though one will need to make use of the original Greek as well as the translation. To take one example. In the Epistle to the Ephesians (3:3–6) the words occur:

> How that by revelation he made known unto me
> the mystery; (as I wrote afore in few words,
> whereby, when ye read, ye may understand my
> knowledge in the mystery of Christ) which in other
> ages was not made known unto the sons of men, as
> it is now revealed unto his holy apostles and
> prophets by the Spirit; that the Gentiles should be
> fellowheirs, and of the same body, and partakers
> of his promise in Christ by the gospel.

What do these words mean? They signify that since Paul has received the mystery of Christ and of his place in the hierarchies, therefore the Gentiles can also find access now to Christ. For the gods of the Gentiles are the hierarchies. And he to whom the mystery of the hierarchies has been revealed — he is the Apostle of the Gentiles. Therefore he says:

> Unto me, who am less than the least of all saints, is
> this grace given, that I should preach among the
> Gentiles the unsearchable riches of Christ; and to
> make all men see what is the fellowship of the
> mystery, which from the beginning of the world
> hath been hid in God, who created all things by
> Jesus Christ: to the intent that now unto the
> principalities and powers [these are names of the
> hierarchies] in heavenly places might be known by
> the church the manifold wisdom of God.
> (Eph. 3:8–10).

Thomas Aquinas is indeed right when he says that Paul has made clear the whole ordering of the mystery of the divine Name and has marked its stages. The word *gradalis* that he uses means 'gradually,' 'stage by stage,' hence the word Grail. The mystery of these stages and of this Name is at the same time the mystery of the Holy Grail. The descent of Christ from the heights of divine wisdom through the hierarchies of the angels to human existence — that is the very kernel of the teaching of the School of Athens and also of the history of the Holy — 'gradually' descending and ascending — Grail.

13. The Polarity between Parzival and Gawan

In the period before the eighth century Europe was still covered by forests inhabited by a wild population. It was a bloodthirsty time. Men were still hunters and cults embraced bloody sacrifices. Small groups would often embark on tours of pillage. Yet at certain times it became apparent that their appetite for plunder suddenly seemed to wane. They put their heads together, intimated secrets to one another and remained at home in their forest quarters. What made these people behave in such a peculiar fashion?

Somewhere between the trees they had heard the clatter of horses' hooves and had seen the glint of armour. That was a sign for them to stay at home. The Arthurian knight-hood, which was present all over western Europe at the time, enjoyed great respect, although little is known of it except what has been passed down in the legends. The task of the knights to rid the land of pillaging riff-raff went on for several centuries. They rode out singly or in groups seeking adventure and imposing order with an iron fist wherever they went and always they returned to the court of King Arthur who with no fixed residence, was constantly on the move. But a kind of network of communication existed by which the knights on the one hand knew where Arthur was, and Arthur on the other knew of the where-abouts of his knights.

On certain occasions the knights would meet and relate their adventures. They called themselves 'Knights of the Sword'. The 'Knights of the Sword' were still subject in some degree to the old ties of blood and passion but had raised them to the level of chivalry. Such a knight, as described by Wolfram von Eschenbach, is Duke Orilus de Lalander, the husband of the Lady Jeschute. His armour is covered with images of dragons inlaid in gold. His shield depicts a dragon; another dragon rears up on his helmet.

Anyone who fights with Orilus, says Wolfram, must also fight the hundred dragons on his armour. Orilus represents that old blood bond in a human form, as it were. We meet the same dragon that appears on Orilus' shield at the tent of his sister, the Lady Cunneware of Lalant. 'To one side of the King's ring above a brook which took its rise there, yet on the level ground, stood Cunneware's pavilion, and above it it seemed as though a Dragon were holding half of the entire button of the tent in its claws! The Dragon was tethered to four guy-ropes as if it were alive and on the wing, carrying the pavilion off into the upper air!'*

This culture had lasted a long time. The name of King Arthur and the name of his father, Utepandragun (Dragon Head), provide images for two forces. Arthur means bear, as a ninth century writer, Nennius, reports. The Bear, a constellation in the northern sky, represents forces coming from the north, while southern forces of the blood and the passions are expressed in the dragon. When Orilus became an Arthurian knight, the knight of the dragon served the bear. The tamed dragon in the service of the bear fought against the wild dragon as the Arthurian knights imposed bloody order on bloodthirsty chaos. Goethe rightly adds a third image to the picture of the 'bear' and the 'dragon' in his poem 'Die Geheimnisse' ('The Secrets'). There is indeed a third stream which became active in western Europe from the eighth or ninth centuries onward. It finds its historical expression in the legend of the Holy Grail. Although it became effective at about Charlemagne's time it did not surface until about 1180. The Grail stream is also connected with the forces of the blood; the Grail holds inwardly transformed blood, blood purified of desire, the same pure blood that flowed from the cross on Golgotha and which Joseph of Arimathea collected in the vessel used by Christ at the Last Supper, with his disciples. The vessel itself was made from a stone which fell from Lucifer's crown when he was cast down to earth and angels carried the Grail westwards through the heavens.

* This and following quotations are from Wolfram, *Parzival*, Penguin edition. (p. 146).

There it floated until Titurel built a temple for it. This temple has seventy-two choirs. The number seventy-two is encountered whenever expression is to be given to the idea that a large number are working individually for the same end. Consider the genesis of the Septuagint, or the sending out of the seventy, respectively seventy-two, disciples of Christ. The work of the knights of the Holy Grail is characterized by the harmony resulting from a concord of wisdom and feeling acquired by each single person. Goethe demonstrates this in his poem *'Die Geheimnisse'*. Lessing indicates the same in his play *Nathan der Weise (Nathan the Wise)*. In the first introductory chapter of *Parzival*, which deals with Gahmuret and Belacane, Wolfram shows how Parzival's father, Gahmuret, ignores both racial and religious prejudices. The Christianity of the Grail is tolerant. Christ died for all mankind, black or white, Christian or heathen. The heathen Feirefiz also comes to the Grail. Every religion contains an element of truth for each is a single representation of something belonging to all mankind. The Grail knights seek this all-encompassing element. They know that there is only one truth and they want to serve it. But the one truth has many aspects. there is only one Christ but he shows the comprehensive nature of his being in many ways in different religions. The one *harmonizing* element in the many is the 'Holy Spirit', the 'spirit of truth'. The disciples spoke in *many tongues* when the Holy Spirit alighted on them at Whitsun, but they spoke of the *same being*. *Lucifer*, who caused the confusion of the tongues in Babylon, is the opponent of the Grail. The *one word*, the cosmic Word, the Logos, stands in contrast to the *many languages*. 'Knights of the Word' the Grail knights called themselves.

Historically, this Grail stream was established during the eighth and ninth centuries, the time when Charlemagne had added the 'filioque' to the Creed against the will of the Pope. Although Charlemagne did this on purely political grounds, his addition does contain a truth. It is this truth which was preserved by the Grail stream. Charlemagne used this truth in opposition to the Pope to transfer to his own person certain rights and claims to power which had belonged to Byzantium, thus bringing about the schism between East and West. It was Charlemagne's sword, not the Papacy, which caused the schism. But a deeper truth lies at the base of these outer political events, including the ecclesiastical political events, which we must at least mention. The historical impulses of East and West are different in the most profound sense. The Holy Spirit proceeds both from the Father and from the Son. The Holy Spirit proceeds from the Father in the Baptism in the River Jordan when the Father God speaks from on high: 'This is my beloved son, in whom I am well pleased'. The dove, the Holy Spirit, descends bearing the host from the sun to the vessel which has been prepared to receive it; the Logos becomes incarnated. The Holy Spirit proceeds from the Son in the events surrounding Whitsun. After his appearance in the Ascension to the disciples and many others, Christ sends the comforter, the Holy Spirit, at Whitsun, and therein the Holy Spirit proceeds from the Son. So both are true. But the East, which perceives the divine incarnation in man as a profound problem, uses the Baptism in the Jordan as its starting point whereas the West is faced with the problem of reconciling the unity in the diversity. The West provides the historical continuation of Whitsun.

That, to touch on it only briefly, is where the real difference in the historical development of East and West lies. Or to put it another way, the East tends towards the experience of *nature* filled with spirit while the West tends towards the experience of the individual *human being* filled with spirit.

The Arthurian knights, then, embody a North-South problem because of their link with bear and dragon. The Grail knights, on the other hand, were oriented in a West-East or East-West direction. The Grail comes from the Orient, travels to the West, journeys back to the East. It is borne westwards by angels, it travels eastwards again to the priest-king John. Mankind experiences both polarities, East-West and North-South, as cosmic forces which exercise a formative influence from those spatial points interwoven with the course of history.

Having seen the spiritual dimension of space and cosmic forces at work in history, the individual's spiritual path leads us to see gradual, step-by-step progress through time.

Gradatim, gradalis, the path leads to the Grail, the word indicates that. Not for nothing is the Grail a vessel in which the foods are arranged in a progression of steps one above the other. There are three stages to the soul's development: *simpleness, doubt* and *bliss*. These words are only valid translations if we remember that they are technical terms. The path to the Grail leads through these three; it is the path through life. As children we are simple. We allow ourselves to be driven by our physical development. Fichte mocks those who refuse to leave that simple state throughout their lives when he writes: '. . . let kind nature rule over them and at the right moment give them rain and sunshine, extra sustenance and free flow of the humours as well as — clever thoughts.'* That is not the way to find the Grail. All physical ties, all attributes derived from birth — race, confession, etc. — deny access to the Grail. That is all part of being simple. Those who want to find the Grail have to leave their sleeping selves, the flow of the humours, behind.

But when we overcome our simple nature, moving beyond the shelter of maternal guidance, when we learn not to follow the counsel of Gurnemanz but to leave behind what we were given by birth and education, *doubt* sets in. The soul then says: 'If I break away from family, race, confession (I was born into all of them), if I break away from my education, what is left? I fall prey to doubt.' The soul experiences the *second* stage in its life. It has to struggle to acquire the knowledge of the Grail, of a spiritual world with *one truth* as the source of the many confessions, religions, ideologies. All of them are legitimate aspects, single perceptives of the one truth. Which aspect is revealed to us depends on the body we inhabit, on the environment we are born into. But we do not experience truth itself in our physical body, because the body is the cause of our one-sidedness. Consequently the soul says: 'I have to liberate myself from physical one-sidedness, I have to seek the spirit, the *one* truth, *outside* the body, not in the body but in the psyche: in *bliss*.' Everyone experiences this *bliss* in death. Everyone who has sought it in life has a vision of the Grail's

* *The Vocation of the Scholar*, Preface.

secret in death. All are united in the spirit with Condwir-amurs, the eternal feminine in the human being.

Goethe knew that this path through death could also be pursued in life, that a person could transcend his body in life: while you fail to take this step of dying and becoming, you are but a sorry guest on the dark earth. What is the power which can liberate us from the body in *life*? It is *love*. Through love we learn to experience the other being united with ourselves, we become free of the ties of the physical self. Condwiramurs is the being who brings love to human beings (*conduire amour*).

Parzival cannot reach the castle of the Grail until Condwir-amurs has given him for three nights that which liberates him from the body and the poet makes very clear that this is not the love born of desire (which ties us so firmly to the body). Parzival then leaves Condwiramurs to seek his mother. What is he seeking? He seeks 'Heartache',* for that is his mother. In seeking Herzeloyde he finds the Grail: 'When the human heart wakens from the *simpleness* of physical existence and begins to *doubt*, the human soul begins to contract painfully into itself.' Wolfram says: 'The soul will rue it'. The courageous and resolute mind feels both pain and pleasure in the struggle against the pain. Wolfram says: 'Shame and honour clash' as in the bewitched bird, the magpie, which seems to be half *dove* and half *raven*. But someone who is under such a spell (Feirefiz for example) can still live in hope of achieving *bliss* if both elements really do live within him: Divine realms and deepest chasm. The *unfaithful* man's soul is pitch-black and he will wear black eternally as well. But the man of 'faithful' thoughts, whose thinking is morally strong, adheres to the whiteness of the dove. Such a subtle simile will hardly be thought of by people who have not shaken off their simpleness.

That is a free and extended, yet faithful, rendering of the words with which Wolfram introduces his Parzival. They subtly point to the three stages, to the Grail and its adversary:

If vacillation dwell with the heart the soul will rue

* Herzeloyde (Herzeleide), the name of Parzival's mother, means 'heartache' in German.

it. Shame and honour clash where the courage of
a steadfast man is motley like the magpie. But such
a man may yet make merry, for Heaven and Hell
have equal part in him. Infidelity's friend is black all
over and takes on a murky hue, while the man of
loyal temper holds to the white. This winged
comparison is too swift for unripe wits. They lack
the power to grasp it. (p. 15).

Who is the real adversary of the Grail. It is Clinschor
(Klingsor, Kli-nso-or is the tool of Lucifer) ruler of Kalot
enbolot (Caltabellotta) in Sicily. Clinschor is a Norman duke
of whom very little is known historically and who originally
resided in Capua. He formed an alliance with Iblis★ (Iblis is
the Muslim form of Lucifer). Iblis, the wife of King Ibert, is
described by Wolfram as the woman whose lover Clinschor
illegitimately becomes. The jealous king responds by castrat-
ing Clinschor. The power of Lucifer appears here as the
power which fights against the forces of physical procreation. The cosmic expression of the forces of procreation
and sustenance is the moon. For example, the embryo
develops in accordance with the moon cycles, and our first
nourishment, milk, is also dependent on this cycle. The
moon is the cosmic image of the Grail vessel. *Gangandi greidi*,
food for the way, is the name given to the Grail vessel in
the Nordic version of the Grail legend. The powers which
serve the metabolic processes of nourishment and procreation are high spiritual powers but human beings can
misuse them by giving them to Lucifer through passion,
through lust; these powers can also be taken away but the
seeker of the Grail must *transform* them. The Grail knights
wish to spiritualize love. What that means is indicated by
Wolfram in Parzival's attitude to Condwiramurs. Clinschor,
on the other hand, is robbed of these powers. The nature of
pure love can be learnt from the sun which freely gives its
vitalizing strength and demands nothing in return. Grail love
endeavours to be similarly altruistic, only wanting to give.
The plant grows towards this love in purity and without
desire. As Schiller says:

★ Compare Steiner, *Mysteries of the East*, lecture of Feb 7, 1913.

192

If you seek the highest, the greatest,
Let the plant teach you.

Act intentionally where it has no will, that's the point!
Wolfram depicts two seekers after the Grail in his epic,
Parzival and Gawan. Parzival is to reach his goal through
compassion, Gawan, through *love*. Parzival is guided to the
Grail castle after he has received Condwiramurs' love.
Gawan reaches Schastel marveile after he has shown compassion to the wounded Sir Urjans. By this means Parzival
reaches compassion through love and Gawan love through
compassion. Parzival becomes the Grail king and Gawan the
master of Schastel marveile. Parzival and Gawan are images
of one another, their destinies reflect their opposite paths.

When Parzival sees three drops of blood in the snow, he
enters a curious state. He acts without any awareness of his
actions. He fights and remembers nothing afterwards.
Gawan recognizes that Parzival has been overcome by love.
The sight of white and red rekindles in Parzival a memory
of Condwiramurs' colours. Gawan covers the drops of blood
with a cloth and frees Parzival from the spell. But from that
moment onward Gawan becomes the master of events and
Parzival seems to follow him as if spellbound. He always
remains in the background of the action. This is the second
stage of his path of development. He has been gripped by
doubt. In conversation with Gawan he is overcome by
doubt. He says: 'Alas, what is God?' (VI, p. 172) and thereupon he renounces his service to God. Parzival remains in
the grip of doubt until he prays to God again five and a half
years later (IX, p. 231).

The so-called Gawan episode takes place in this interven-
ing period (in the five years). Many people believe that it
could be omitted but that is not so. On the contrary, the
link between Parzival and Gawan is a very important one.
In the seventh chapter ('Gawan and Obilot') Parzival is present in the background from the beginning. Gawan and
Parzival are members of opposing armies. But by a happy
coincidence they do not meet in combat. Gawan possesses
two horses, one a Grail steed, Gringuljete, and another one,
Ingliart. Ingliart escapes and becomes Parzival's horse. So
Parzival is riding on Gawan's horse during his period of

doubt. Parzival loses this horse, Ingliart, in combat against a knight of the Grail whose horse he mounts in its place. As soon as he does so his doubts disappear. Folding his hands in prayer prevents him from holding the reins. He prays that God may guide the horse. The horse carries Parzival to Trevrizent.

But while Parzival is still riding Gawan's horse, Gawan takes on Parzival's tasks. King Vergulaht, the brother of the lovely Antikonie, has been vanquished by Parzival. He is ordered by Parzival to seek the Grail and serve Condwiramurs. But Vergulaht transfers his tasks to Gawan when the latter becomes his prisoner. Gawan is suspected of having dishonoured Vergulaht's sister, Antikonie. This is false, but Gawan is released only on condition that he assume Vergulaht's tasks. So Parzival is riding Gawan's horse and *doubts* while Gawan undertakes Parzival's tasks and is *defamed*. At first he is described as a merchant, then as a forger. Furthermore, he is accused of the murder of Kingrimursel. All of this is untrue. Defamation is similar to doubt in that it means being doubted by others rather than feeling doubt oneself. Gawan's destiny is always the opposite of Parzival's destiny and the two are intimately linked, in consequence. Parzival experiences all of Gawan's adventures and *vice versa*. But Parzival remains in the background while Gawan is the central figure. For example, Gawan has an experience equivalent to the meeting with Sigune. He comes upon a woman with a wounded knight resting on her lap. Lischois Gwelljus has wounded him as Orilus slew Schionatulander. The parallels can be found everywhere. Thus both win for themselves a garland from the tree of Gramoflanz. But there is little detail as to how Parzival won his. Parzival comes into combat with Gawan who thinks Parzival is Gramoflanz and Parzival, who has not recognized Gawan either, vanquishes him. From that point onward Parzival resumes the central role in events. Both Parzival and Gawan are mounted on Grail steeds in their combat — something which is emphasized by the poet. Now Parzival vanquishes Gramoflanz for Gawan. Parzival thereby renders Gawan a service in return for the latter's having released him from the spell of the three drops of blood. Only after Parzival and Gawan have settled their debt to one another in this way does Parzival meet his brother Feirefiz, who from then on becomes Parzival's main protagonist. Feirefiz comes to the Grail because Parzival selects him to be his companion. It might be held that Feirefiz won the Grail more easily than Parzival, who had to fight for it. But the Grail cannot be won by combat — the poet expressly says so. It is a gift. A certain constellation is required to receive it. That is why Wolfram speaks of 'Kyot, who sent us the authentic tale' (XVI, p. 410). This Kyot knows that the secret of the stellar script cannot be revealed until 'doubt' has been vanquished. Hence Wolfram's words (IX, p. 232): 'Kyot asked me to conceal it because his source forbade him to mention it till the story itself reached that point expressly where it *has* to be spoken of.'

He speaks of it precisely at the point in the story where Parzival appeals to God for guidance:

> All human kind are affected by the revolutions of
> the planets. With his own eyes the heathen
> Flegetanis saw — and he spoke of it reverentially —
> hidden secrets in the constellations. He declared
> there was a thing called the Grail, whose name he
> read in the stars without more ado. (IX, p. 232)*

Rudolf Steiner has drawn attention to the importance of recognizing that Flegetantis' book was an astronomical one. Indeed, the name Flegetantis is interpreted as meaning someone with a knowledge of the stars. He was an astrologer. Kyot then turned the astronomical elements into a narrative when he discovered records in Anjou which corresponded to those elements. Wolfram mentions 'faithfulness' immediately in the beginning lines. No one finds the Grail without it. Titurel the Younger associates specific virtues with the planets. 'Faithfulness' is a gift of Saturn, it says.† No one finds the Grail without the power of Saturn. In Wolfram, Trevrizent says (IX, p. 249): 'God Himself will not abandon you, I counsel you in His name. Now tell me, did you see the Lance at the Castle Munsalvæsche? We knew from the

* Compare Steiner, *Christ and the Spiritual World*, lecture of Jan 1, 1914.
† See Scharfenberg, *Jüngerer Titurel*, stanza 2754, 4.

wound and the summer snow that the planet Saturn had returned to its mark.'

Thus Saturn in a certain aspect brings snow; but why this direct proximity of 'lance' and 'Saturn'? Wolfram explains elsewhere (VI, p. 147): 'A heavy fall of snow had descended on him during the night. Yet according to what I heard it was not the time for snow. All that was ever told of Arthur, the man of the merry month of May, happened at Whitsun or at blossom-time in Spring.' This is the exceptional snow of Saturn in which Parzival sees the three drops of blood. A 'lance' appears once again. Here it is the lance of Sir Taurian. Elsewhere (IX, p. 235) Wolfram recounts that Parzival had without conscious intention taken a painted lance with him when he left Trevrizent's hermitage. Then we are told how he jousts twice with this lance, again without any awareness of what he is doing, and how Gawan has to tell him afterwards what has occurred. Gawan finds him in this strange state of absent-mindedness, staring at the drops of blood. Sir Taurian himself 'forgot' the lance and left it with Trevrizent. Are we not led to believe that the lance represents a force which leads human beings to act without knowing what they are doing? Are we not led to think that the lance represents forces which work to the same unconscious extent as destiny itself? When Parzival prays again for the first time after five-and-a-half years of doubt he gives free reign to his horse and allows it to guide him; in other words, he abandons himself to destiny. He is acting on the basis of the forces of destiny again. I am convinced that Saturn and lance represent forces which drive human beings to act unconsciously. When Parzival enters the Grail castle *consciously* the lance is *missing* (XVI).*

Saturn and lance reveal the divine calling. Divine consciousness, divine leadership take the place of human consciousness. If human consciousness rises to the highest level, to divine consciousness, the human being consciously makes the lance a part of himself, consciously incorporates

---

* The relationship between spear (lance) and blood is unmistakable. The lance 'bleeds'. The drops of 'blood' lie on the Saturn-snow. Spear or lance indicate forces which work subconsciously in the blood. Compare Steiner, *The Effects of Spiritual Development*, lecture of March 25, 1913.

the strength of Saturn into himself; he becomes the Grail king. He is then ruler of a kingdom which encompasses the realm of the planets and stretches from the moon to Saturn. When Cundrie tells Parzival that he has been chosen as the Grail king (XV, p. 388) she also defines his kingdom. She names the seven planets and says: 'All that the planets embrace within their orbits, whatever they shed their light on, marks the scope of what it is for you to attain and achieve.' And adds: 'Greed alone can deny you your portion.' He is no longer spellbound by the sight of the red drops of blood. No Gawan has power over Parzival any longer. Freed from physical constraints, he ascends to his kingdom. What great gift does he receive? ' "My dear lord," Cundrie answered, "one may may go as your companion. Choose him." ' (XV, p. 388). Parzival chooses as his companion the man who is black and white like the magpie. After all, he has learned to call *him* brother as well. We see, then, the wonderful depiction of human development in Wolfram's Parzival. We are shown two kingdoms, the Grail kingdom and the kingdom of Schastel marveile. Those who strive for the Grail have to develop their cognitive powers in a way which adds the power of the word — Inspiration — to the visions of the Grail — Imagination. Otherwise they cannot partake of the highest: Intuition. If we strive for Schastel marveile we are working from forces of the will and our path is the direct opposite of the path which leads to the Grail. Those who approach the Grail castle must ask questions. Those who approach Schastel marveile are told they must not ask, that brings misfortune. The Grail steed carries Parzival to the Grail castle because it carries him to Trevrizent. One cannot ride into Schastel marveile, horses must be left behind at the gate. The merchant on the gate has to look after them. The will is active in the agility of the Lit marveile. One can learn to know this Lit marveile by investigating the sources of our experience, by trying to comprehend classes of concepts as something real; Goethe's archetypal plant is one example. Then we no longer have *fixed* concepts but *activate* our thinking through the will; we shall see the metamorphosis of objects. That is when we enter the generic world.* Gawan has to pass through this world. The image of the fight with the lion shows how the soul must fight in order to preserve its 'self' when it enters the generic world, when it becomes involved in adventures with the Lit marveile. Parzival is faced with the opposite situation. Compassion should lead him beyond his own person into the other self. The polarity of the paths of Gawan and Parzival could be demonstrated to the last detail, and if we take the two of them together we see the full human being: the path of the will and the path of knowledge and their interaction. Once human beings have reached a certain stage on the inner path, they have to remember their fellow human beings. After all, it is not possible to be the guardian of the holy stone without remembering one's fellow man. This characteristic is also wonderfully represented in *The Chymical Wedding of Christian Rosenkreuz*. There the souls are weighed. The modest Rosicrucian brother weighs more than all the other presumptuous people put together. He weighs more than all the weights which may be added and which in this context represent the seven liberal arts. His surplus weight benefits others. He is permitted to take some brothers with him. The relationship between Parzival and Feirefiz is similar. Feirefiz represents our fellow human being whom we must not forget even if he is partially black and not white all over. We have to take him with us. All who search for the Grail should remember that no Grail knight can achieve salvation as long as there is even one fellow human being who is still excluded.

* See Stein, *Die moderne naturwissenschaftliche Vorstellungsart,* p. 30.

14. Tristan and Isolde against the Background of Greek Mythology

The legend of Tristan and Isolde is a picture of the soul as it reaches the experience of the lonely 'I', and in seeking access to a higher being must establish a link with other individual souls. A Greek legend forms the basis of the tale. It tells of a beautiful woman with golden hair; the hair is important. A swallow appears carrying in its beak a golden hair which it presents to King Mark. On seeing it he says: 'If only I could find this woman.' A knight, Tristan, comes forward: 'I will undertake to find her for you.' He sets out to find the woman with the golden hair, succeeds in his quest and wins her — not for himself but for the King. The subsequent tragedy provides the material for the tales of Tristan and Isolde. Tristan has great musical talent, he is a master of the voice and harp and so is enabled to win this woman. He can win her because he is an Apollonian singer. Tristan possesses a lyre called in German literature the swallow. This appears in other works besides Wagner's. The thirteenth chapter of Wolfram von Eschenbach's *Parzival*, for example, refers to it. Not much attention is generally paid to the fact that it is just this lyre which helps Tristan to find Isolde. The Parzival epic provides more detail. When Parzival's friend Gawan entered Klingsor's castle, he had to leave his horse with a shopkeeper who possessed all kinds of precious objects, including the lyre. After vanquishing Klingsor and undergoing many adventures, he conquered the castle and the lyre with it. Gawan is depicted as a friend of Tristan in the Tristan legend. We may therefore assume that Tristan's lyre comes from Klingsor's castle. It is the swallow which acts as intermediary between Mark and Isolde. We have thus established the link between the legends of Gawan, Parzival and Tristan. What kind of a woman, we may ask, can be won by Orphic song? In the Gudrun legend Hilde, whom we meet under her Valkyrian name, is won by song, indicating that if human beings develop the inner faculties which make the soul resound, they acquire the possibility of ascending to this higher state within themselves.

The motifs of the legend recur throughout history. The motif of the swallow can be traced as far back as the Egyptian Book of the Dead, which contains many depictions of the path of the striving human soul. In one section, Spell 86, a vignette of a swallow is followed by a narrative which, notwithstanding its temporal distance from the Tristan legend, casts a light on the area we are concerned with. To begin with there are some words to accompany the dead man, who is to ascend to higher regions: 'May his soul turn into a swallow.' Then the dead man himself speaks: 'I am a swallow, I have become pure.' From this we can see clearly what was in the mind of the Germanic poet when he described the swallow: a human being who possessed sufficient musicality could fly, could give his soul impetus to approach the divine. Tristan must be described as a musical person whose soul can make its way by means of the musical elements it contains. He was, of course, of particular interest to Wagner since his striving for higher things takes place through music.

There are several ways to transcend the commonplace; painting, for example, or sculpture. There is, however, a chapter of German literary history where the *images* before our soul are not important but where it is *music* which is closest to the theme. I will use Gottfried von Strassburg's account. He writes in a melodic style and is deeply affected by the musical element in Tristan. Gottfried has endowed Tristan with some of the memories which were alive in his own soul. In wondrous lines he recounts the childhood and youth of Tristan, who was not idle for a moment and knew many languages even as child. He possessed linguistic and musical talents to an unusual degree and familiarized himself with musicality of every kind — language, song, stringed music. Once he was taken on board a ship to examine the wares and was kidnapped by foreign merchants in the hope that his outstanding qualities and eloquence would be of service to them. The kidnapping takes Tristan to foreign countries where his adventures begin. His music places every achievement within his reach. He grows up and hears King Mark command that the wonderful woman whom he longs for be sought. Mark himself could win nothing more than a hair from the sunlike woman. The means by which Tristan approaches Isolde is his wonderful song. These descriptions, including those of the landscape, are particularly charming. Through his music Tristan manages to land on the foreign shore, reaches the royal court and becomes Isolde's music teacher. His whole way is smoothed by his eloquence and musicality. But Tristan, who is completely devoted to melodious sound and who has managed to approach the wonderful being with the magnificently glistening hair, is only able to do so because his body is afflicted by a mortal wound.

Every human being who strives for the highest has such a wound. (Amfortas for example). Tristan's wound is a special one. How did he receive it? Mark, at whose court Tristan lived, has lost the independence of his realm and ignominiously has to pay tribute to a foreign king — the king at whose court Isolde lives. The lower world has to pay tribute to the higher. It must either pay the tribute or liberate itself through battle. Morold, a mighty hero, comes to the court of King Mark to demand the tribute. What does it consist of? Every third child who reaches the age of fifteen falls prey as tribute to the demands of Morold for the King of Ireland. Why at fifteen? We in the modern age could put it this way: when human beings reach puberty they have to pay a tribute. That happens to every third person approximately. But if musical forces are strongly active human beings can be released from payment of the tribute.

This subject matter is not Germanic in origin but deals with issues relevant to all mankind. They occur in the Greek legends as well. The Cretan king is obliged to pay tribute to the Minotaur. The Minotaur has the right to devour a certain number of youths and maidens. The Greeks tell of Theseus the hero who was victorious over the Minotaur and freed the young people. Theseus, with Ariadne's assistance, does not achieve victory through music, through a poetic deed, but through the intellect. Ariadne gives him the golden thread which leads through the labyrinth of the thought processes, the thread of logical thinking. Greek culture therefore overcame the Minotaur through the intellect, which is born when human beings reach the age of fifteen. The Germanic peoples experienced this crisis in a different way from the Greeks. It is exceedingly interesting to note how in the Germanic legend the lyre, the musical element, is juxtaposed with the golden thread of logical thinking in the Greek saga. The Germanic and Greek souls have both to overcome the same problem.

Tristan counsels King Mark to refuse to pay the tribute. Then, says King Mark, he will have to do battle with Morold. Tristan fights and is victorious, but is grievously wounded. Morold says to him: 'My sword was poisoned. Although I have to die myself, I will reveal the power which can heal your wound. Only my sister, Isolde, can help you. If you find the path to Isolde, then, even though she is related to me, you will have done everything to secure your victory.' Tristan faces a difficult task. He has to work his way into the presence of Isolde not only for Mark's sake but also for his own salvation. Indeed, he has to approach her twice; the first time to be healed, the second time to win her for the King — the cause of the whole tragedy. He succeeds, for the lyre it is that brings him the opportunities.

The motif of healing is also a Greek one. It appears for the first time in the legend of Paris. These are not speculative academic constructions; Gottfried himself says he wants to make such a connection. That is of great importance. Gottfried was highly cultured and had a good knowledge of Greek. He uses Greek mythology with great expertise. We need not, therefore, introduce any foreign elements into his poetic work.

The figure corresponding to Tristan in ancient Greece is Paris, who abducted Helen. This Greek Paris did not live at home as Tristan did when he was young. Paris was rejected by his parents because they were really afraid of him. He grew up on a wonderful river which flows past the city of Troy. There he lived innocently and well with a shepherd. He also became acquainted with a wonderful being, the nymph Oenone, daughter of the god of the river, the equivalent of the Germanic Isolde. The river has not only one, but two remarkable names. Homer says that mortals call it Scamandros and the gods called it Xanthus. In one of Plato's dialogues the philosopher Cratylus comments that Homer still knew that each thing has two names.* Homer was still able to differentiate between the divine and the mortal in the human soul; what might be called the Valkyrie in contrast to Peter or John. Xanthus and Scamandros have the same meaning. The words mean yellow or gold. The Greek Isolde is therefore the being who can be found on the golden river. The Greek version of the story throws light on the Tristan legend.

One day, innocently and happily married to the nymph of the golden river, without yet having lost the divine element in the human soul, Paris stood on the bank of the river when Hermes, god of commerce and cunning, approached him. He carried a golden apple in his hand, the famous apple of discord which caused the Trojan wars and much else. He gave it to Paris, pointed to the three goddesses accompanying him — Hera, Athene and Aphrodite — and said: 'Look at these three goddesses, choose one of them and give this apple to her.' Everyone has to make such a choice in his soul. Everyone encounters worldly power (Hera), wisdom (Athene) and beauty (Aphrodite). Every human 'I' encounters the forces of the will, the source of power; of thinking, leading to wisdom; and of feeling for the golden radiance of beauty. Everyone decides differently. The modern answer would probably be: I want to devote myself to all three. Paris does not give that answer; he was Greek and art ruled supreme for him. It was self-evident, therefore, that he should give the apple to the goddess of beauty. The two spurned goddesses became angry and later, during the Trojan wars when Paris had won Helen, they sided with the Greeks whom they supported against the Trojans. Thus these wars are about more than the struggle for a beautiful woman; they show the split in the human soul, the struggles of the 'I' with the three soul forces in human nature. The decision which Paris made at that time brought this major conflict to mankind.

* Plato, *Cratylus*, Ch. ii.

The decision takes effect on Paris's — or Tristan's — soul. He has a remarkable experience. Aphrodite has shown her gratitude by helping him win Helen. But possession of Helen has a double import, one side of which is not always obvious. By winning the earthly woman, Paris lost the nymph, the higher element in the human soul. That sealed his fate. He, too, must take part in the wars and is wounded in battle. Helen is unable to heal him, only Oenone can do that. On his departure the nymph had prophesied that she would hurry to his aid but would arrive too late because he had gone so far away from her. This prophecy comes true. Paris is killed by a poisoned arrow from the hero Philoctetes. After he has collapsed, Oenone arrives, receives his soul in death and ascends heavenwards with him, fulfilling her Valkyrian destiny. What was the poison? It came from the nine-headed serpent, the Hydra of Lerna which Heracles vanquished by destroying with a firebrand each severed head, so that it could not grow again. This serpent is the counter-image of the nine muses. These represent the higher elements of the soul and the serpent is their physical reflection. It is called scientific thinking. Scientific thinking cannot be held in low esteem, but the truth is that this serpent contains a curious poison. If, at the age of fifteen when, with puberty, the intellect is awakening, human beings have access only to scientific thinking, they are mortally poisoned. Only in death can their higher being be reunited with them. But if they can approach the poison with the power of the muses, if they can purify it, the serpent is transformed, the desires and passions turn into something quite different. In such a case passion serves to uplift Tristan.

These old tales, then, deal with problems which are still relevant. The legend of Tristan gives us the answer to an important contemporary question: how are young people of fourteen and fifteen years of age to be educated? The answer has to be: if true artistic sentiment is added to the necessary intellectuality they can be helped to pass safely through this crisis point and the threat posed by the apple of discord can be neutralized. Many possible sources of conflict are transformed and become Apollonian in nature. These old, ever new problems have relevance for contemporary mankind.

Many people put the following interpretation on the legend of Tristan: when Tristan wins Isolde for King Mark but secretly unites with her in love, this is a glorification of adultery. The meaning is, however, that human beings should join, should unite with the divine in their souls. That is of supreme importance. Human beings must not say: let others be moral first and *then* I will follow them. 'The others first, then I' would be false altruism. Human beings commit a sin against the real purpose of world evolution if they hand their higher mission over to someone else. Is it actually possible to give one's Valkyrie to someone else? Certainly. A typical example of this is Wallenstein. This brilliant man had fully understood the requirements of his time and he granted his army a religious freedom which existed nowhere else. Yet he was fighting on the side of the Counter-Reformation. He should have told himself: 'The age of tolerance has arrived. I want to use this army to fight for the progress of mankind.' But he vacillated. He was unable to carry out his mission; he remained true to the Emperor and not to his Valkyrie; he sold his Valkyrie to someone else. Many such cases occur in history and legend. Siegfried wins the Valkyrie and gives her to Gunther. Tristan wins Isolde and gives her to Mark. That is one and the same process. Tristan finally summons up the courage to stand by his own being, his true mission. Friedrich Ranke tried to promote this point of view in his academic work.★ All of Gottfried's symbolism has to be seen from this higher standpoint. When, we may ask, do human beings experience this powerful meeting with the forces of the soul, with Paris's three goddesses? They come towards it when destiny calls them to approach their eternal self. But they can also sleep through this encounter; indeed, they can die before it occurs.

The whole of the second part of Goethe's *Faust* is an elaboration of this theme of mankind. Helen can be found there; Oenone — in the form of Gretchen — can also be found there. Salvation can only take place in the ascent to

★ Ranke speaks of a 'celebration of love which has entered the realm of religious devotion, a religion of love of astonishing boldness' (*Die Allegorie der Minnegrotte*, p. 16).

heaven. In *Faust*, the three goddesses take the form of the Mothers, to whom Faust descends. A variation in *Faust* is the interpretation of the love-potion; it is brewed in the witches' kitchen and drags human beings down. The love-potion in Tristan is of a different kind. It does not tie the human soul to what is base but to the ascendant, the divine. The potion which Brunhild gives Siegfried in the Edda so that he does not forget her is the same.

The Tristan legend can be interpreted in two ways, superficially as adultery, on the other hand, as a reuniting of the human being with his higher self. Only the second interpretation makes sense. The first cannot explain the final chapter of Tristan as written by Gottfried's successors.* In this Tristan secretly unites with Isolde. Fearing King Mark's jealousy, he flees to a distant country where he marries a second Isolde, Isolde of the White Hands. This may cause some surprise. The explanation is that the poet borrows from Greek legend. Isolde of the White Hands is Helen; the real Isolde is Oenone, the divine element which human beings lose if they unite with the baser element in human nature.

However, the asceticism which medieval monks endeavoured to attain is not the ideal to be promoted. For there are, there have to be, certain forces in human beings which press them to join with Isolde of the White Hands. But they must not lose the true Isolde as a result. The serpent turns into the dove if human beings can succeed in living their physical existence without losing the real Isolde. The dove does not hover in some cloud-cuckoo-land; it is the powerful being which hovers above the Grail, the being which penetrates and transforms matter. The question is, how can the higher and the lower elements in human nature permeate one another to create the full human being? There was good reason for the rise of a worldly brotherhood in the Middle Ages to accompany the monastic life.†

The Tristan legend recounts further that Tristan possessed

* The two most important men to have continued his fragment are Ulrich von Türheim and Heinrich von Freiberg.

† The fraternity of the Rosicrucians, whose outward work began in the mid thirteenth century, springs to mind. Compare Steiner, *The Spiritual Guidance*, pp. 47ff.

an unusual suit of armour (lines 4930ff). This suit of armour is possessed by everyone who rightly follows his life's path. The human being possesses a body which can cause some discomfort. But if he finds Isolde he possesses something more, which becomes active even at a physical level; the body becomes changed, even to its outward appearance. This outwardly visible transformation is described by the poet as Tristan's wonderful armour. (Parzival's armour is the same). And the armour holds yet another secret: Tristan's suit was forged by Vulcan. The prophetess Cassandra decorated his gown. In other words, Vulcan forged the body with the forces of the soul and as a result the powers of a Cassandra were able to reside in it. We are not shown an unworldly ideal but an ideal physical form which is prepared by the soul. Medieval literature comments: 'The human soul has different colours. In some it is the colour of gold, in others rose-coloured, green or blue. All nuances of colour exist.' One need not be clairvoyant to recognize this. Everyone can observe this wonderful play of colours in the human soul. There is something wrong when people use artificial colour. The cheeks can be tinted by the soul.* Vulcan's wonderful knowledge provided the means to practise such artistry of the soul, which can be physically observed. We should re-learn this artistry of the soul. When teaching children one may observe their faces go red and then white; their imagination has been fed. Or they may show a hue of green, a sign that they have been badly taught. The human being who is married to Isolde gives expression to the soul and the spirit in the very artistry of the colours.

The poet knew all this. He tells of the little dog called Petitcreiu, a small creature. Properly translated it means Microcosm. Petitcreiu is the gift which unites Tristan and Isolde. It is meant to signify that the soul is expressed in the colours of the skin. The colours of this animal were indescribably beautiful. It was many-coloured but all the colours merged in 'peach-blossom' in the eye of the beholder. The colours of the human complexion change with every emotion in the soul! The great secret of *inkarnat*, the

* Compare Chapter 8.

flesh tint, is revealed here. The word indicates that the soul is incarnated in the body. We will go one step further: here is nothing other than the philospher's stone. The human body consists of carbon, and the transformation of carbon, which takes on many different colours, finally leads to the creation of the diamond. That is the secret of the medieval alchemists. The soul, the spiritual human being shines from the physical human being through the skin, in those who acquire the bride of the soul.

15. Tristan and Isolde and an Understanding of Minstrel Poetry

In *Tristan and Isolde*, Richard Wagner has given spiritual guidance which enables us to illumine the realm of the 'night' with the clear consciousness of day. He makes us realize that whoever wishes to escape from the illusion of the day-consciousness which appears to separate man from man as by an abyss, and desires to find the bridge leading over from one ego to another, must be able to wed the uniting power of the night-consciousness to the clarity of day-consciousness. When this is achieved, man recognizes that love is an instrument of knowledge. 'Love,' says Rudolf Steiner, 'is the experience of another in one's own soul.' Love overcomes the boundaries existing between one 'I' and another, between soul and soul — boundaries into which the day-consciousness deludes us. Love awakens the spiritual world in the midst of everyday life. Wagner expresses it thus:

TRISTAN: So should we die
    that ne'er again
    our souls might suffer
    parting's pain, —
    that unawakened,
    unforbidden,
    for reach of name
    too deeply hidden,
    our beings we might blend
    in love without an end.★

Such union is granted by the night-consciousness. The day-consciousness isolates men. Wagner speaks of the day as spiteful and false:

ISOLDE: The Day in whom
    all falsehood stirs —

or,

★ Transl. A. Forman

ISOLDE: Was it aught but the Day
    that in him lied
    when the sea he crossed
    to beseech a bride
    for Mark, and in selfsame breath
    to devote his Dearest to death?
Night alone liberates consciousness from its fetters:
    TRISTAN: But hallow'd we now
    had become to the Night;
    The day with its hate
    and its hungry spite
    could keep us perhaps apart.

Or:

    O hail to the potion!
    Hail to the spell!
    Hail to the wonder
    it wrought so well!
    Through the door of death
    that backward rolled
    it let me, no longer
    in dreams behold,
    but clear to waking sight,
    the wonder realm of Night.

Tristan and Isolde are seeking the night-consciousness. They drink what they believe to be a draught of death. For only in death do they hope to find consummate union, such as is not to be found in life. Yet, can it not be that in the world of day-consciousness, too, the ego awakens in contact with another ego, preserving its own being even while merging in the other, clasping the other 'I' within itself and becoming one with it? Can the love-draught in earthly life achieve the same as the death-draught for the realm of night?

This is the deep question of minstrel poetry. It is the minstrel's sorrow that the day robs him of the gift which the night grants — the gift of *fellowship*. This sentiment forms the basis of a whole group of minstrel poems — the 'day songs.' In a 'day song' by Walther von der Vogelweide a lady laments: 'Evil betide thee, Day, that with my own belovéd one thou wilt not let me stay.'

What does the day steal from us? It steals our *Valkyrie*,

our higher soul, the night-consciousness. The love union of two human beings is the reflection in the earthly sphere of the union of the human being with the divine, with the Eternal Feminine, by whom the soul is borne 'upwards and on.'

For this reason the minstrel distinguishes sublime love from lower love. Sublime love knows that the lower love is only a picture, whereas sublime love is a reality.

Sublime love was once sacred to Isis, the deity of the night. Rudolf Steiner indicated how the Isis cult, coming from Egypt and handed down by the Arabs, became the cult of the Madonna when it reached the soil of Spain and France. Then it was secularized and became minstrel poetry. This minstrel poetry is the Isis cult, Christianized and secularized. 'Isis cult,' however, is only the name for an experience which is slumbering and can awaken in every human soul. The fact that such a course was taken by minstrel poetry has been proved by the research of Konrad Burdach and Friedrich Ranke.

In Isis the Greeks beheld the All as experienced by the ego: 'I am the All, which was, is and shall be.' The ego, experienced in thinking, feeling and willing, is only an earthly, human counterpart of Isis. In thinking we live in the past, in feeling in the present, and in will in the future. In the 'I am' we embrace and hold the three.

What, then, is the night-consciousness? It is the union of the human soul with its past, present and future. In the night-consciousness we actually *are* what we shall one day *become*. This was experienced by our forefathers as the 'Valkyrie.' The man who finds his Valkyrie and who is united with her learns to recognize what bears him forward. Through births and deaths the Valkyrie is faithful to us. And when we betray her, when we forget the eternal within us, we in our turn are *not* forgotten by the eternal. In death the hero is united with the Valkyrie.

This was realized to the full by *Jordan*, the author of the modern setting of the Siegfried Saga. He describes it as follows:*

* The original is written in a mixed metre, with a predominance of the anapaest.

With a mighty bound through the sparkling flame
she mounts the saddle of Grani and upwards leaps
with him on the broad-tow'ring pyre. Into the heart
of her steed she plunges her sword and, as he lies
dying, still proudly neighing, she thrusts Balmung*
into her bosom, pressing the belated kiss of the
redeemed Valkyrie on the lips of the Beloved. As
she expires she cries with loud voice: 'Now,
Siegfried, we are united for ever.'

Siegfried, however, found his Valkyrie during his life on earth. Thus it is, when man becomes conscious of his mission. But the Valkyrie can also be lost. When this happens, great conflicts break loose among men. Laments over the destruction of nations resound then from the lips of the bards. For the destiny of *peoples* is dependent upon whether *individuals* recognize their task.

Siegfried, however, yielded Brunhild to the weakling Gunther. Tristan gave up Isolde to Mark. Thereupon strife and tragedy break into a flame.

How can a man give his own Valkyrie to another? History gives us an answer. Wallenstein, too, was one who gained his Valkyrie but ceded her to another and was destined to perish in consequence. He had recognized the dominating idea of his time which Schiller expresses in *Don Carlos* in the following words: 'Your Majesty, grant us freedom of thought.' This was the task of the seventeenth century: Liberty in religion, liberty of creed, freedom of thought; liberty of the individual in all matters of conscience. Wallenstein granted this to his armies. He asked no questions about any man's creed or faith, he looked only for efficiency. But this army that enjoyed liberty of thought was at the same time serving another, an inferior spirit. It served the Counter-Reformation. Wallenstein did not betray his sovereign. The host he led was held together by the power of his own being, not by that of the sovereign's name.

History relates many similar cases. In the destinies of the peoples many Siegfried Sagas are described. But men have grown weary with suffering and venture no more to create

* Siegfried's sword.

212

living mythology. We, however, must once again, and in clear consciousness, find our way to a living, spirit-filled history, because tradition handed down by the blood is unable to receive the intuitions that can fire the will to new impulses and deeds. For this reason we shall, in this article, speak of Tristan and also of Isolde, for the Spirit of our time vigilantly watches to see whether seeking souls will quicken the element that creates fellowship in the body of the people — the fellowship that is based on the discovery and recognition of the aims set by each *individual* who has found *himself*.

The story of Tristan's journey to bring Isolde to King Mark has also been handed down in the following form: One day a swallow brought a golden hair to the court of King Mark. On seeing it, the King said: 'Who will find for me the woman to whom this hair belongs?' Tristan sprang forward, saying that he would find her.

What, then, is this swallow? It is Tristan's harp. 'Swallow' was its name. His friend Gawain, the companion of Parsifal, had given it to him. Gawain had bought this harp with his wares at the gateway of Châtel-merveille, when he had become lord of Châtel-merveille, lord of Klingsor's magic castle. Whoever conquers Klingsor finds this harp. Moreover, it can and should be found, even to-day. Whoever finds it can likewise find his Valkyrie.

Wolfram von Eschenbach mentions this harp (Ch. 13).

> The swallow which as costly harp
> In England [Engel-land] is well known.

This is the swallow. But originally it came from Egypt. The Egyptians spoke of the swallow as a bird of the soul. In the Book of the Dead we read (Chapter 86):

> If this chapter be known (by the dead) he shall come
> forth by day, he shall not be turned back at any
> gate in the underworld, and he shall make his
> transformation into a swallow regularly and
> continually.

The dead man says:

> I am a swallow, I am a swallow . . . I have passed
> on to judgment . . . and I have come forth worthy
> at the gate of Neb-er-tcher. I am pure at the great

213

place of the passage of souls, I have done away
with my sins, I have put away mine offences, and I
have destroyed the evil which appertained into my
members on earth . . . I have gained the mastery
over my footsteps before the God of Light.

Tristan is such a swallow, a man resurrected from the dead.
He is a messenger of the golden, resounding light, a Sun-
harper.

As Horant wins Hilde, so, too, Tristan wins Isolde
through the music of his harp. A Sun-harper tames the
animal nature and thereby gains the divine Hilde, the
Valkyrie.

This is portrayed in the *Gudrunlied* and also in the myth
of Orpheus. Even in our days it still holds good: 'Tame the
beast and the Valkyrie will descend to thee.' This is why we
read in the *Gudrunlied*:*

He began the song of Amalie, that Christian man
hath never learned before or since, except he hath
heard it on unknown seas.

There where the sea is tossing and roaring, when the waves
of the soul tower high but the innermost being remains
calm — there the soul learns to sing melodies which are
chanted by the water-spirits who have power to tame all
that is of an animal nature.

The beasts of the wood left off feeding, the worms
in the grass, and the fishes that swim in the water
lay still to listen. Horant made good use of his skill.
None wearied of his songs. . . . All that heard
Horant yearned towards him.

Thus sings the Gudrun bard. We have also the song of
Apollonius Rhodius, the bard of the Argonauts:

The fish, enamour'd of the strains divine,
Rose from the depths, exulting on the brine,
Of various form and size, the finny droves
Obedient follow where the vessel moves.
As flocks unnumber'd, when the shepherd leads,
Satiate with food, forsake the dewy meads.
He steps before them till their cotes they gain,

---

* *Gudrun* translated by Margaret Armour, pp. 48–49.

His shrilly pipe resounds an artless strain
Of rustic sweetness: with resistless charm
Thy music, Orpheus, led the scaly swarm.

Orpheus is here the player. But Tristan, too, is a master of this art. In the Tristan poem of Gottfried von Strassburg we find the following passage:

While turning his mind ardently to the learning of
books and the art of speech, he devoted,
nevertheless, many an hour to all manner of music.
Whatever the hour of day, he gave his care and
diligence to stringed instruments of every kind, until
his skill had mastered them all. Never did a single
hour find him idle.

But however pleasing his demeanour, however
dexterous his playing — one other skill Tristan
possessed that outshone all others: so vast a number
of languages he understood and spoke that those
who may have travelled far and wide, could never
have encountered such excellency of speech.

Thus the young Tristan won all hearts, and he finally won Isolde. For in speech and song there lives man's conquering egohood, his 'I' that masters the lower nature. Nature herself reminds us of this, for at the age of puberty the human voice breaks. This is a solemn admonition. In future the soul will have to attain by struggle what has hitherto been granted her in 'innocence.' To the external element of music must now be added the inner music, the harmony that is born in spite of the dissonances of the soul. Man is *himself* the harp on which he must play if Isolde is to bestow her grace upon him. When Tristan came to Isolde he was sorely wounded. It was a festering wound which Isolde alone could heal.

Who wounded Tristan? Tristan lived in Cornwall at the court of King Mark. It is beautiful country. A never-ending play of colour sweeps over sea and sky. The surf rushes into the bays and hollows out the cliffs. High above, half hidden, stands Tintagel, with King Arthur's castle. The climate is mild and people call this district the 'English Italy'. The shape of the peninsula itself is reminiscent of that of Italy. The Scilly Isles are like an English Sicily. It is the home of a world of ancient lore and legend, similar in many respects to that of Italy. Here in the North are Merlin and Arthur; in the South: Virgil the Magician, and Klingsor. Such is Tintagel in the heart of this northern English Italy — the home of the Tristan saga. But Morolt, Isolde's near relative, comes from Ireland. There are two Isoldes: mother and daughter. Morolt is brother of the elder Isolde. Isolde the younger is brought by Tristan to King Mark. This Morolt is a figure actually to be found in history. But here, in the saga, he becomes a symbol of human faculties and forces. He plays a kind of Minotaur role. He demands tribute from the King of Ireland. Every third child who has attained the age of fifteen is claimed by him. The mention of the age of fifteen in the saga is not without meaning. At this age the human being falls a prey to the Minotaur if a Theseus does not come to rescue him. The liberator here is Tristan. He desires to fight Morolt, notwithstanding his youth. On no account shall Morolt receive the tribute. Tristan is victorious in this contest. But he is wounded by the poisoned weapon of Morolt, who in the throes of death says prophetically: 'None can heal this wound save my sister Isolde.' Isolde, and later on, Isolde the younger, possess the skill to heal wounds of this particular nature. Tristan has the power to win the favour of Isolde by his music. Without this music he could never have been healed.

It is interesting as well as instructive to compare Theseus and Tristan. For there we perceive the difference in the character of souls faced with the task of solving the same problem at different stages of evolution. Tristan must avail himself of music, whereas Theseus makes use of Ariadne's thread which Rudolf Steiner, in his book, *Christianity as Mystical Fact*, describes as being the thread of logical thought. Only logic can lead the human being out of the labyrinth of problems into which he enters at his fourteenth or fifteenth year. The Greek took refuge in the realm of philosophy when besieged by the Minotaur. But he knew that all logic was prepared for by Orpheus. Tristan is at the stage of Orpheus.

When the human being reaches the age of puberty, his intellect awakens. He wishes to give expression to his *own* judgment. He will be capable of this if his soul has absorbed some of this inner music without which no liberation can be wrought. Herein Tristan is well equipped. Nevertheless he is wounded. After he is healed he returns home in order to fetch Isolde on his second journey. The fact that before this journey Tristan fights and conquers a dragon indicates the issue all the more clearly. *The dragon is within every human being.*

Even from the outline given here it can be seen how many Greek elements are woven into the Tristan saga. Nor have they all been mentioned so far. Tristan is in the same position as Paris who stole Helen and was thus the cause of the Trojan war. Reference to the Greek legend is essential because without it we shall never be able to understand why Tristan who with his secret love for Isolde lives at King Mark's court, after his flight finds another woman and ultimately weds her. She is Iseult Blanche-Main. It is difficult to understand this. How could Tristan, who was capable of so sublime a love, ultimately find satisfaction in his union with Iseult Blanche-Main? But none the less this episode which forms the conclusion of the poem is deeply connected with the whole of it and is by no means an appendix of later date.

But let us first think of Paris. Paris lives on the banks of the golden river which, as Plato tells us in the Dialogue of *Cratylos*, was called 'Skamandros' by men, but 'Xanthos' by the gods. Both names point to the Golden Fleece. Herein lives Oenone, the nymph. Paris is wedded to her. One day, Hermes, the messenger of the gods, appears. He brings three goddesses to Paris. Hera promises Paris strength. Pallas Athene promises wisdom, Aphrodite promises beauty. Paris, as a representative of the Greek civilization, decides in favour of beauty. Aphrodite procures for him the most beautiful of all women: Helen. This sets the Trojan war alight. The marriage with Helen results in the loss of Oenone. Man loses his Valkyrie when he turns wholly to the earthly. Whoever wished to keep the Valkyrie must have chosen the goddesses and Hermes as well. But Paris had chosen Helen. Then Oenone utters her prophecy: — Paris, being wounded, will have to wrestle with death. None but she will be able to succour him. But she will arrive too late at his couch of pain. In death only will they both — man and deity — be united again. And thus events take their course.

This, too, is represented by the end of the Tristan legend. Iseult Blanche-Main is Tristan's Helen; Isolde, his Oenone. The dying Tristan sends a ship to Isolde. He is wounded. She must come to heal him. She does come, but too late. Tristan is lying on the shore, waiting for the ship. Should it bring Isolde it will have white sails. But if she refuses to come its sails will be black. Tristan buries his head in the lap of Iseult Blanche-Main. Presently he asks: 'Dost thou see the ship?' She replies: 'Yea, I see it.' She perceives the white sail. But sorrow grips her. Tristan asks: 'Has the ship a white sail or a black?' He is too weak to lift his head to see for himself. Iseult lies and says: 'The sail is black.' When Tristan hears this he sinks back and dies. At this moment the true Isolde folds him in her arms.

The motif of the white and the black sails, too, has its origin in the Theseus saga.

The sagas are eternal. The problems are eternal. But each epoch solves them differently. We must have the courage to find our own solution. Shall we unite ourselves to the earthly or to the Valkyrie? The signs of the times say: *to both. Penetrate the things of earth with the Spirit. Be true to the earth but true, too, to the Spirit. This is the demand of our age.* For we must not dream. Ours must be a generation equipped for the stress and sorrow of the time but filled, too, with assurance that the Spirit is our guide. How we can draw strength for new deeds from these sagas of antiquity — this is the purport of such studies.

16. The Seven Liberal Arts and the Twelve Philosophies

To illustrate medieval perceptions and feelings, I would like to tell of a knight who after a long life of adventure and campaigning finally sought refuge in a mountainous region, where he lived the life of a hermit. In his youth his friends used to describe this knight, whom I will call 'the old man', as 'quick action', but as time passed he had acquired a calm wisdom through communion with nature. We find him in his hermitage, set back from the road which the merchants use when they travel this part of the country, in a wood by a small lake. He lives beneath a rock with a protective overhang and requires little to satisfy his needs. Long ago he exchanged his glittering armour for a brown hairshirt such as monks wear. But he is no monk. The flash of his eyes still shows his worldly status. He lives in self-imposed isolation, preparing himself for world-wide activity in a future life. Occasionally he speaks about what moves his soul, but infrequently and never to anyone who is unworthy.

One day, a youth came to the old man to take rest on a long journey. The youth asked many questions to which the old man responded.* The old man said: 'Look, the grass grows and the flowers in the grass are blossoming. But you overlook many things if you stop there and seek no further explanation of what you see. If you want to understand reality you have to learn to see through the appearances which provide such a spectacle for the eyes. Something makes the grass grow. To discover what it is, you have to pass from the observation of external appearances to interior listening. If you pay close attention, you will recognize that

---

* The 'old man' and the 'youth' are based on the figures of Trevrizent in Wolfram's *Parzival*, and Schionatulander in Albrecht von Schafenberg's *Jüngerer Titurel*.

the act of remembering an observation is a listening process. A wonderful musicality in things will one day be revealed to you if you live with this thought and repeatedly pass from observation to inner listening. The whole of the plant world will resound. The cup opening upward will be transformed into the sound of trumpets. All growth will then resound with music. And as you learn to listen to nature even more deeply you will learn that the resonance of growth and development is an echo. The real music resounds in the cosmos. The sun and the stars resound; you hear the music of the planets and understand how they are calling the plants. Every opening blossom is a little sun. Every plant twining its way upwards a planetary revolution. Look at a tree: its whole being resounds. The sound of the tonic rumbles muffled in the solid trunk. The interval of a second resounds where the tree first divides, where it first branches out. And so it goes on. But most plants finish with the interval of the fifth. If you want to find a sixth or seventh you have to listen to the sounds which occur when the blossoms open delicately and the insects carry the pollen away to other plants. The new seed is the octave.

'The whole cosmos is music and I listen to it year after year without ever tiring of it. Nothing in the cosmos which is repeated is ever quite the same. So every year, every century has its own music.'

'That is wonderful,' the youth said. 'Allow me to be your pupil and to learn from you.'

'I cannot teach you anything,' the old man replied. 'Your soul is much richer than mine. But I can teach you who your teachers are.'

'And who are my teachers?' the youth asked in surprise.

'The cosmos itself,' the old man told him. 'The only reason you met me was to recognize the poverty of the people of my century. You will enrich them. But look, a bluebell. Observe it closely. Do you see its blue mantle? Protectively it is wrapped around a small yellow light within. This flower is an image of the soul. It, too, carries the light of the spirit within. It must never be extinguished. A blue mantle surrounds this light to prevent it from being extinguished. You also wore such a mantle before your mother conceived you. Keep it in your consciousness.'

The old man also had a good relationship with animals. No animal was afraid of him. They trusted him and did not run away when he approached. And if they were ill or wounded they came to him to be healed. The old man knew which herbs healed which injuries and he also knew the proper time to pick the herbs. The healing properties of one might be brought out by the waxing moon when the sap rises like the tide; another would gain its strength through its fiery, aromatic properties with a waning moon when the sap was held back like the tide at ebb.

The young knight learned all this with the feeling that it was something he had known before. On one occasion he dreamed about the old man; he, the youth, was old and the old man was young. He saw himself as the teacher and the old man his pupil.

The more he experienced these things, the more of a riddle they became. One day he asked the old man, who seemed to be in a communicative mood: 'Tell me, how do you know so much?'

'Nature has taught me,' the old man said, 'its great textbook is inexhaustible.'

'No,' cried the youth, 'you are hiding something. You also know the subjects taught in our Schools. You are more than a hermit, you have learnt more in the past.'

The old man said: 'Now I know that the hour of parting has come. I will tell you who your teachers are because they were mine as well. But once you have heard it you will leave. And rightly so. You only met me to go on and discover other things. So listen:

'Dialectic is taught in the Schools. No one knows who taught this subject first. But I will tell you: it is none other than the moon.* Observe it as it traverses the sky. It does

---

* The seven liberals arts are not listed here in their 'classical' sequence. According to *De nuptiis philologiae et mercurii* by Martianus Capella, a widely known textbook in the Middle Ages, the sequence was: grammar, dialectic, rhetoric, geometry, arithmetic, astronomy, *harmonia* (music). Compare also Karl Heyer's 'Martianus Capella' pp. 32ff. In the present case the sequence is determined by the planetary spheres which the soul traverses after death.

not look at anything from one side only. It looks at everything from all sides. Do likewise. Do not think you know everything and can therefore rest. No, look alertly around you. Everything will look different tomorrow. Furthermore, learn from the moon. Observe how it has reduced its fullness since yesterday. It consumes itself as it revolves. Learn that lesson and you will understand when I say that the moon was my teacher. Happy the man who can subsume his own opinion in the art of dialectic and learn something better. Happy the man who makes his own light disappear, like the moon, in order to receive and reflect illumination from the more exalted sun. Let the moon teach you reflection. Then your knowledge will continue to wax after it has first waned. Are you not aware of the words of John, who baptized Jesus? He said: "He must increase while I must decrease." He was a master of dialectic, as you can see from his words. He also gained his wisdom from the moon. The moon is a good teacher. None but Gabriel, who endows the moon with its soul, has ever taught dialectic.'

The young knight sat in silence beside the old man. The moon slowly made its way through the branches of the giant trees in the forest.

Thereupon the youth said to the old man: 'So dialectic is selflessness?'

'Yes,' the old man said, 'that is it. You see, we become completely unselfish after death. When the soul leaves the body it hankers after material things for a while but then gradually overcomes its craving for material things as it passes through the moon sphere and expands.* It learns to

* The sequence of the planetary spheres as the 'sites' where the soul resides after death is described by Steiner in *Between Death and Rebirth*. Readers should note the transposition of the names of Mercury and Venus which occurred during the transition to the modern age and to which Rudolf Steiner often makes reference. In these lectures he expressly draws attention to the connection between his description and the content of *Theosophy:* 'These reflections can show us that the presentation given in the book *Theosophy* — in rather different words and from a different point of view — contains what has been described as the cosmic aspect in the lectures given this winter. You need only be reminded that in the one case the account is given from the point of view of the soul, and in the other from that of the great cosmic traditions, and you will find that the two descriptions are in complete harmony.' (Lecture of April 1, 1913, (p. 168). The parallels are:
  Moon-sphere and kamaloca region, i.e. the regions from the 'burning desires' to 'attraction and repulsion'

give up the one-sidedness which it adopted during life as a man or a woman born in a particular place. The incidentals of birth are left behind.'

The youth said: 'So learning, science, is the path of death and the real scholars are those who die in life! Speak, old wise man.'

The old man answered: 'It is as you say — in the spirit I once heard a soul speak who was close to me and who had recently passed through the gateway of death:

My "I" has learnt to see.
Death, which you still fear,
Reveals in bright illumination
The most wonderful visions.
Observe the quiet
Magnitude, the absolute
Wonderment and vision
(No longer building)
Of spiritual power.
Creator of the body!
Intense, banished
From physical form,
I rest
To spur you on.
In life learn from the dead!

To achieve objectivity in life, to forsake one's own perspective: that is dialectic!'

The youth then asked: 'Now, old man, reveal your knowledge of the whole progression to me. What can be learnt from Mercury?'

'Mercury is the sphere,' the old man said, 'in which the soul discards pictorial vision, separating itself from ordinary images. The only thing it can take into that sphere is non-pictorial thinking. If you want to live in this sphere you can

---

Mercury-sphere and region of the 'soul-light'
Venus-sphere and region of the 'active soul-force'
Sun-sphere and region of the 'soul-life'
Mars-sphere and region of the 'archetypes of the physical world'
Jupiter-sphere and region of the 'archetypes of life'
Saturn-sphere and region of the 'archetypes of whatever is of the nature of the soul'

The terms of the soul are from Steiner, *Theosophy*, Chapter III.

do so through numbers. If you say: one apple, one pear, the apple or the pear are images in your mind. But if you say one, two, three you inhabit a non-pictorial world. Mercury or Hermes has always been the teacher of arithmetic to all the peoples. The Greeks called him the god of merchants because these have to deal with figures. We, however, call him Raphael, the angel of healing. The art of healing is a secret arithmetic. Physicians always deal with the number three. Know, then, that every number has its secret:

> One is the first, undivided entity
> Two is the contrast of polarities
> Three is the harmony between the poles
> Four reveals what is hidden
> Five is the number of decision
> Six the number of love
> Seven determines the totality of time
> Eight is the number of justice
> Nine is the number of the divine order
> Ten is the number of the human being.

'The Saviour was the third between the two tempters. The one tempter always wants too much, the other too little. The golden mean lies between too much and too little. On the golden path, foolhardiness is too much, cowardice is too little, courage is the golden mean. There are four realms of nature: mineral, plant, animal and human. There are also four elements: fire, air, earth and water. The *Quinta Essentia* is hidden. It is the true nature of light. In the physical world you can only see illuminated matter. In thinking, light itself is revealed to you: enlightenment, the flash of inspiration. Five is the dividing line. I taught you that when we spoke about the plant. A tree propagates, or not, if its seeds fall on stony ground. Events can go in either direction.

'The number six belongs to the bees. They use it to build their combs. Here love is impersonal, devoted completely to the service of the whole. Seven is seen in the rainbow, the week. Eight is twice four: Divine and earthly justice. Nine is the divine choirs and ten represents human beings, for they are the tenth hierarchy.

'But I meant to speak about the number three, because medicine is based on it. There is no sickness which does not originate in the soul. No sin — no sickness. No sickness without consciousness. That is why plants are not sick in a real sense; they themselves do not cause the illness. So our soul condition, which lies at the root of illness, is the first thing. The second is our physical illness. The third thing is external to us. Mineral, plant or whatever else: the medicine which is recombined with the human being. I say recombined because there is nothing in physical nature which has not previously been part of human beings in world evolution. Human beings were born first and everything else separated from them. A time will come when human beings will reabsorb everything they have expelled. But that will happen only in the distant future when all matter has again become spirit. The physician anticipates this development. That is why the third element in medicine is the spirit. The patient spiritualizes the substances by taking the medicine. Therefore medicine rests on this threefold progression: soul, body, spirit. The spirit is the healing element. That is why we use the term "holy" or "healing" spirit.

'Medicine, then, is also learnt from Mercury. Mercury spiritualizes the earth. The moon will reunite with the earth in future. Then birth and death will cease. Mercury will take the position closest to the earth and everything will be filled with spirit. Actually, physicians are always fighting an element of greed in the soul [which was not quite eradicated in the moon sphere] and they heal this soul element, which affects the body, with the spirit of Mercury. That is why physicians are arithmeticians. They work only with the one number: the three.'

The youth said: 'It must be good to be a physician, working with the forces of healing.'

'One can only become a physician,' the old man said, 'through love. Love is the spiritualizing power.'

'And what does Venus teach us?' the youth asked.

The old man became sad when the youth asked this and said: 'Hardly anyone has any notion of Venus. Only people who purify their will, who no longer carry any desire into this sphere, have proper access to it. All selfish thirst for action has to be extinguished here. One who succeeds in that recognizes what real will is: music, nothing but music. The musical element is the essence of objectified will. That is why Eros must be left behind if one would see the Lady Venus naked and experience the most beautiful music in existence. No one has ever learnt music except from Venus. She changes the voice of human beings as they mature on earth. Anyone whose song is noble and pure also has to be selfless and loyal. Treachery and betrayal do not go with the noble art of singing.'

The youth resolved to become a noble minstrel. He would journey through the woods with his lute and make the people noble and good. And then perhaps, at a castle he would find the woman destined for him. But he wanted only someone who loved the stars. That is how he would recognize her.

The old man said: 'The sun shines on things visible while light itself remains behind the world of the senses. Michael, the sun prince, remains hidden behind physical phenomena as does light, but without him world evolution would have no meaning. Understand the meaning which rests hidden behind what is as clear as the sun and you will have learnt the cosmic script of Michael, and will become a student in the art of grammar. First you must learn to discover the letters. Every butterfly wing, the wing of every tiny ladybird will show you the letters of the cosmic script. All the mysterious symbols which are engraved on crystals and stones are his script. There is no butterfly wing on which the stars have not recorded their script. For the stars inscribe the flow of time into the things of this world. And Michael, the sun prince, rules the progress of time.'

When the youth heard this, he felt the urge for action; he wanted to become the defender of justice. 'Master, I want to become a grammarian,' he declared, 'I want to engrave a letter myself of the cosmic script with my life.'

'You will,' the old man said, 'because you are destined to do so and your ardour will enable you to fulfil your vocation. Know, then, that the most wonderful character is the bodily form. You will learn to engrave the form of your future body when you pass after death through the region of the sun to approach the sphere of Mars. Mars is filled with activity. In its sphere you learn to draw the lines for future development. It is the teacher of geometry. But it does not teach tedious geometry; the lines it draws have to be conquered. Great generals are geometricians in the heavenly realms before they descend to do their deeds on earth.'

The old man became filled with enthusiasm. He seemed to know more about this region than about the others. But the youth had not heard everything. He sat there pensively and said: 'Love is stronger than hate, isn't it!'

'It is so indeed,' the old man answered.

'What does the soul experience in sleep?' the youth asked. 'What does it see when it learns to carry the light of consciousness into the darkness?'

'It sees how the soul itself works to restore the body,' the old man said.

'Is the soul then in heaven among the stars?' the youth asked.

'It is. It builds the body according to the archetypes in the stars. When your body lies asleep,' the old man said, 'the soul weaves golden threads from ganglion to ganglion. It draws triangles and all kinds of shapes from the star-pattern.'

'So that is geometry,' the youth said, 'and Mars is its teacher?'

'Of course,' the old man replied. 'You build in the blood according to the archetype of these patterns.'

'God, then, is always engaged in geometry,' the youth said. 'Now teach me the art of Jupiter. I have learnt to create forms which can serve living things. But where does life stream into these forms?'

'That happens in the realm of Jupiter,' the old man said. 'On earth you are only aware of life in the form of thinking.* Thinking, and thus life, have their home in the sphere of Jupiter. It is the origin of life.'

'But which is the art,' the youth cried, 'Teach me the *art* of Jupiter.'

'That is the art of speech,' the old man said, 'for rhetoric is the art of infusing the forms of Samael with life through the power of Zachariel. Mars forms the word in the air but Jupiter fills it with life. Zachariel, the spirit of Jupiter, teaches

---

* The reference is to abstract, dead thinking tied to the brain, and to living super-sensible thinking, respectively.

you to enliven your words so that joy and well-being stream from them.'

'Now there is only one sphere left,' the old man continued. 'It is the furthest one, Saturn. It is Oriphiel who embraces everything and forms its boundary. This is the sphere where the soul turns round after death. In the region of Mars the soul has refashioned the body to the form it should take in the next life. In the region of Jupiter it has prepared the new life which vitalizes the created form. Now, in the sphere of Saturn, it ensouls its creation. In its descent to earth the soul will become filled with spirit and form a new ego-consciousness. Then it chooses the time and place of its birth in anticipation of its descent. At that point the soul learns the art of astronomy.

The soul descends to earth at greater or lesser speed, depending on the characteristics of the human being, and his next form will vary accordingly. Finally, the way passes through the moon sphere again. The soul enters its embryonic life while it is still in the moon sphere. That is why everything before birth takes place in moon rhythms. In the moon sphere it has to become one-sided again while it descends. It enters a particular family, a particular nation. In future it will have to surmount all that once more as a dialectician.'

'I thank you,' the youth said. 'You have taught me much because you have brought me true tidings of the seven arts that liberate the soul and the spirit from the body, which otherwise happens only in death. In life I learn to die and in death to live. The seven Liberal Arts are one path.'*

'Go on your way,' the old man said. 'God will be with you.'

But the youth stood still. 'You spoke nothing of the fixed stars.'

'Every soul finds those itself,' the old man said, 'if it searches. It is different for everyone. Go on your way and you will find what lies in store for you.'

---

* In the Middle Ages they were divided into two groups: the *Trivium* (grammar, rhetoric, dialectic) and the *Quadrivium* (geometry, arithmetic, astronomy, music).

The youth went on his way. Faithfully he reflected on what he had learnt but he was dissatisfied. He was aware that this teaching was nothing new for him. At some point he had meditated on it in an earlier life on earth. The old man had (then) been his pupil. Now the old man had returned to him what once he had received. But he would have to continue the search. Should he go to a School? Pursue his education with the Arabs? Should he ponder in solitude?

He made a peculiar decision. He would hesitate for a short while only and would follow the voice of destiny when it next spoke. And destiny called. He met a young girl, almost a child still and felt that she could teach him more than the old man. Her love would lead him forward. But she was too young. So he joined a knight as his squire. He would have had to wait in any case. And so he travelled into the world.

The knight whom he served was called Gahmuret. He journeyed to the orient and had many adventures. Finally, he died a heroic death far from home. The youth brought the blood-stained shroud back to Gahmuret's wife, Herzeleide. There he found again his beloved.*

But his fate was sad. Sad and yet beautiful. He went into the woods with Sigune. His eyes had been opened a long time ago and he could see into the spiritual world. He taught his companion. Thereupon she said: 'My Schionatulander, I cannot give you my love until I, too, can read the script of the stars which the old man did not reveal to you, since everyone must read it for himself.'

'My love,' Schionatulander said, 'I will do everything for you.' He hunted the heavens and caught a dog. She wanted to read the constellation of the dog, by which Socrates had sworn: Yes, by the dog! Ancient epochs appeared to them and the two of them looked into the flow of history. They read of a long love story between two souls who found one

* The reference is to Sigune.

another, who accompanied one another from life to life in steadfast faithfulness. If you want to know this story you must catch the dog. The story is written on its collar in colourful jewels. Every jewel is a virtue and every pearl a tear. If you read the story on the collar you will tarry a long while. But Schionatulander died. Chasing the dog, he came upon Orilus who had unjustly taken Parzival's land. On this day he was lying in wait for Parzival to kill him. A whole epoch of history would have been destroyed if he had been successful. But Parzival did not appear. Schionatulander came, hunting the stellar script, fulfilling his destiny. Orilus killed Schionatulander. Sigune came too late; she was unable to protect her loved one. There she sat, her beloved in her arms. Then Parzival arrived. Sigune is merely the name the narrator gives her; in reality she is called Elisabeth. Schionatulander had said to her in parting: 'May the holy Elisabeth, Christ's aunt, protect you.' He said that because her name was Elisabeth.

History relates nothing of these events and the Grail legend reports only the ending. But this is a true story of how the Middle Ages felt and thought.

Schionatulander and Elisabeth-Sigune lived for individual love which alone opens the vista into the heaven of the fixed stars. For like the stars, love is eternally steadfast. Those who carry love from one life to the next read the writing in the stars. The others must turn round at Saturn. Those who carry individual love up to the fixed stars meet again, initiated, in a future life. Schionatulander and Sigune carry the wisdom of the planets into those elevated realms always transforming wisdom into love.

Anthroposophy is the philosophy of love. Anyone who sees it as one view of the world among many knows nothing of its true nature. Like love it is all-embracing. It results from reading in the stars and it subsumes all possible conceptions of the world of which each legitimate one is accorded its sphere of influence. Thus the fixed stars will themselves bring us the wisdom which has passed through love.

Essentially, there are twelve philosophies.* Any others are intermediate stages as the compass has only a specific number of designated points in space because the others are found between them. Together, twelve ways of looking at the world provide a comprehensive view. Each is an individual perspective. Each is legitimate but also incomplete and needs to be supplemented by the others. They represent twelve stages of selflessness, twelve philosophies. One conception of the world which has no knowledge of the 'I' transcending itself, which withdraws into itself like a crab, is materialism. Matter, in the sense that materialism uses the term, does not exist in reality. Materialism is not objective. It is in the same position as the sense of touch. That is not objective either. For when I touch matter, the skin and flesh of my finger are pushed back at the point where I touch it. What I really experience is my finger being pushed back; a piece of finger which is normally rounded outwards is not there. I infer something where my finger is not: matter. Matter is only inferred from our sense of touch. The conception of the world which builds on the sense of touch, materialism, infers an object. It never comes anywhere near a real object. It lacks the selflessness which leads to the outside world. The Crab shutting itself off in its shell, the symbol of the missing outside world, is the symbol of materialism.

The complete counter-image to this way of experiencing the world is the view represented spiritually by the constellation of the Twins. This is selfless, to such a degree that it has no subject. It observes its own being, its own 'I', from the outside. Pythagoras was the representative of this conception of the world. Many people are puzzled by it; indeed, fail to understand it, as it assumes complete selflessness. Pythagoras received it from Zarathos, a renowned teacher at the time of the captivity of the Jews in Babylon. This

* The following remarks on the twelve philosophies are based on Rudolf Steiner's lectures *Human and Cosmic Thought*. The connection made here by W. J. Stein between the twelve philosophical directions and the twelve senses is not made systematically and explicitly by Rudolf Steiner in this cycle. Rudolf Steiner schematically links the senses and the constellations of the zodiac from two different standpoints. For example, Aries is assigned to the ego-sense in one instance and Gemini is assigned to it in the other. Compare *Beiträge zur Rudolf Steiner Gesamtausgabe*, Summer 1971, No. 34.

revived Zarathustrian teaching from Persia taught that the 'I' should be observed from the outside, immersed in the other, the alien 'I', in love. Consequently the soul stands beside its own being like a twin. How is the 'I' perceived from the outside? As a number, is Pythagoras' answer. Perhaps this is puzzling but it can be explained. Because if I ignore the inner being of the other person he becomes merely a number.

When a general says 'three men into the trenches', men who might have to die, they are three bodies to the general. To the mother who loses them they are three fully-rounded individuals. An entity observed from the outside becomes a number.

> Love finally resolves the riddle because it is able
> to provide a real solution to the mystery of numbers.
> Numbers are existence observed from the outside.
> And fusion of separate existences is love.
> Observed from the outside: cold calculation.
> O mystery of numbers! The converse side of warm
>   love — all-embracing!
> And the master of love teaches the secret of divine
>   numbers!

Thus spoke Pythagoras in Babylon on receiving the Zarathustrian philosophy which stands under the selfless sign of the Twins.

The remaining ten ways of looking at the world are situated between these two as transitional stages between objectless and subject-less wisdom.

A conception of the world proceeding from the sign of the Lion is formed by the force whereby we experience the health and well-being of our body, and feel alive. Our sense of life enables us to experience the blood forming the body as it streams from the heart (once pictured as the Lion). We experience a section of the outside world but we are still part of that outside world. This was John Locke's philosophy. It presents a passive view of thinking.* We become observers.

---

* 'All that is in a man's power, I think, is only to mind and observe what the ideas are that take their turns in his understanding . . .' John Locke, *An Essay Concerning Human Understanding*, (Book II, Chapter XIV).

Locke teaches that we can only observe the ideas imprinted on the blank page of our soul. His conception is formed on the basis of the passivity with which the senses register the world. Sensualism is a good term for this philosophy.

Berkeley's philosophy is selfless to a greater degree. He denies matter, and this has not yet been refuted. The only reason his philosophy is irrefutable is that his standpoint is one of the twelve legitimate ones. He is a phenomenalist. He regards every phenomenon, be it the result of the external senses, or of inner ideas, as a constituent element of the world. His philosophy is constructed on the basis of the sense through which we perceive the movement of our own limbs. We know where our arm is when we move it. This type of perception is cognition of the outside world which, however, is no longer completely passive. We perceive our own actions with our body, with that section of the world which is us. This idea, expanded into a philosophical system, is Berkeley's philosophy.* So-called matter is the consequence of our thinking activity. We encounter our action as if it is the outside world. Every philosophy is a faculty which has expanded into a way of perceiving the world. Materialism: the philosophy of the sense of touch; sensualism: the philosophy of the sense of life; phenomenalism: the philosophy of the sense of movement.

The sense of balance leads us to observe that section of the world which is still ourselves but which interacts with the cosmic forces of three-dimensional space. The philosophy which corresponds to this sense sees objects as existing independently in space (realism). It is the philosophy of daily life — while Virgo, secluded from the world, is the sign of phenomenalism, which is forced to deny physical matter.

The Scorpion with its sting completely destroys this seclusion. The sense of smell inhales external substance. That is what smell is. It perceives the actions of matter within us. This philosophy studies the dynamics at work in everything and was embraced by Nietzsche in his late period. Rudolf

---

* Berkeley's classical formulation of phenomenalism is that 'esse is percipi'. See George Berkeley, *A Treatise Concerning the Principles of Human Knowledge*, Part I, 3.

Steiner called this philosophy, which thinks with a sledge-hammer, dynamism. It is only legitimate as a single-per-spective philosophy. Nietzsche's writing clearly demon-strates that he philosophizes with his sense of smell. He speaks of the scent, of the sense of smell which he develops for spiritual things.

The sense of taste experiences the penetration of substance into the body itself but also the processing of matter through our own being. We dissolve what we taste. It is a completely internal experience. We experience the nature of the subst-ance entirely subjectively. This experience, expanded into a philosophy, gives us Leibniz's conception of the world: monadology. The monads have no windows, he says. Here it is the ego which struggles with the world. Sagittarius was the name given to this ego-force, this directed power of the will, which still has to find the outside, the target, and is still enclosed in the monad. This peculiar philosophy, which could not be refuted either, is also legitimate. Differential calculus, the study of small, discrete entities, is its progeny.

The eye presents us with a spiritual conception of the world. It observes the world in the rainbow, arranged by number; similarly Dionysius the Areopagite, the pupil of St Paul, sees the world ordered into hierarchies which represent beings ordered by number. The eye is a selfless mediator. It only has an experience of itself when it is unwell, as with a cataract. In all other cases it experiences the world. It has access to the surface of things. Consequently this philosophy comprehends that beings exist outside the monad of the ego but it experiences them from outside as numbers. Capricorn is the sign of this philosophy which leaves its shell (spiritism).

Objects are penetrated by the sense of warmth, for warmth does not gather on the surface as does the sense of sight. The inner aspect of things is revealed in the warmth which penetrates them. The sign of Aquarius is the sign of such cosmic interaction. Jakob Böhme embraced this philosophy. He saw the brotherhood of the ensouled cosmos. St Francis of Assisi experienced the same (pneumatology).

The ear listens to the inner vibration of things. The par-ticular inner qualities are revealed to the selflessly listening ear. Those who expand this sense into a philosophy recognizing the soul element, are adherents of psychism. Johann Gottlieb Fichte had this experience; he described the action of the 'I' (philosophy of identity). Pisces, actually a symbol of the feet, is the sign of hearing because the soul rests on hearing. If we faint we are still able to hear even when all the other senses are rendered useless. Hearing represents those things which support the soul, it represents the soul's last contact with the earth.

Aries, the Lamb, represents the bearer of inner meaning; the lamb who carries the sin of the world. Similarly the word, which speeds through the air, carries meaning. The sense of sound by which we understand language and understand the meaning of words 'stands in Aries'. We hear the words with our ears. As the word contains the inner meaning so the image contains the archetype. That is Plato's philosophy, idealism, a high and selfless philosophy which has many fine things to say about language. A study of the dialogue *Cratylus*, where Plato describes Cratylus his teacher, reveals how the latter, the teacher of Ephesus, proclaims mysteries of the Logos, of the Word.

Taurus is the symbol of retrospective thinking. The head of the Bull is looking backwards in all the old depictions. It symbolizes the sense of thinking, the ability to take up a thought which someone else has produced. Expanded into a philosophy it is the world-view of Moses who proclaims the Law — thinking as manifest power. That is why Michelangelo depicts him with bull's horns (rationalism).

The final, highest sense is the sense which perceives another 'I'. This intuitive cognition allows us to look back at our own being as if it were a number, to embrace the other lovingly.

We have become acquainted, then, with the round table at which every legitimate philosophy has its place, at which none is excluded. Anthroposophy is that schooling of the soul which learns to know all of them, to sit at table with each one; but then to give each one up again selflessly in order to do justice to all of them.

Anthroposophy is the schooling of the soul which teaches us to make ourselves selfless at all times to such a degree that we can live with everyone. *Anthropos* in Greek is the human being, and Sophia is wisdom, but a wisdom which is experienced in its all-embracing nature and which thus turns to love. Anthroposophy is a high ideal, it is a schooling which will teach us to love all mankind.

Bibliography

Berkeley, George, *A Treatise Concerning the Principles of Human Knowledge*.
Eschenbach, *see* Wolfram von Eschenbach.
Fichte, J. G., *The Vocation of the Scholar*.
Geiger, Lazarus, *Human Language and Reason*.
Gottfried von Strassburg, *Tristan*, Penguin Classics 1960
Gundrun, trans. Margaret Armour, Everyman.
Heyer, Karl, 'Martianus Capella und die sieben freie Künste,' in *Vom genius des Mittelalters*, Kressbronn 1960.
Hoditz, Arthur Count Polzer-, *see* Polzer-Hoditz.
Kiesewetter, Carl, *Die Geheimwissenschaften*, Schwarzenburg 1977.
Kirchweger, Anton Joseph, *Anulus Platoni*, (also called *Aurea Catena Homeri*), Berlin 1921.
Locke, John, *An Essay Concerning Human Understanding*.
Malory, Sir Thomas, *Le Morte d'Arthur*. Ed. H. Oscar Sommer, 3 vols., London 1889–91.
——, Penguin Classics 1986.
Markham, C. R., *Richard III — his Life and Character Reviewed in the Light of Recent Research*, London 1906.
Marshall, Alfred, *Economics for Industry*, London 1929.
Neilson, George, *Huchown of the Awle Ryale* by Sir Hew of Eglinton, Glasgow 1902.
Polzer-Hoditz, Arthur Count, *Kaiser Karl — Aus der Geheimmappe seines Kabinettschefs*. Zürich 1929.
——, *The Emperor Karl*, London 1930.
Ranke, Friedrich, *Die Allegorie der Minnegrotte*, Berlin 1925.
Robertson, Richard, *The ancient Order Society and Unitie of Prince Arthur and his Knightly Armory of the Round Table*, printed John Wolf, London 1583.
Scharfenberg, Albrecht von, *Jüngerer Titurel*.
Schröer, Karl Julius, *Geschichte der deutschen Literatur*, Pest 1853.
Shore, W. T. *King Arthur and the Round Table at Winchester*, 1902.
Stein, Walter Johannes, *The British — their Psychology and Destiny*, New Knowledge, East Grinstead 1958.
——, *Die moderne naturwissenschaftliche Vorstellungsart und die Weltanschauung Goethes wie sie Rudolf Steiner vertritt*. (The mode of thought of modern science and the world-conception of Goethe as represented by Rudolf Steiner), 2 ed. Stuttgart 1921. (3 ed. Dornach 1985).
——, *The Ninth Century*, Temple Lodge, London 1989.
——, *Weltgeschichte im Lichte des heiligen Grals*, Stuttgart 1977.
Steiner, Rudolf, *Between Death and Rebirth*, Steiner Press, London 1975.
——, *Christ and the Spiritual World. The Search for the Holy Grail*, Steiner Press, London 1963.
——, *Earthly and Cosmic Man*, Steiner Press, London 1948.
——, *The Effects of Spiritual Development*, Steiner Press, London 1978.
——, 'Goethes *Faust* vom Geisteswissenschaftlichen Standpunkt,' in *Geisteswissenschaftliche Erläuterungen zu Goethes Faust*, (GA 272) Dornach 1981.

——, *The Gospel of Luke*, Steiner Press, London 1975.
——, *Human and Cosmic Thought*, Steiner Press, London 1967.
——, *Karmic Relationships*, Vol. 2, Steiner Press, London 1974.
——, *Knowledge of the Higher Worlds. How is it Achieved?* Steiner Press, London 1976.
——, *The Mysteries of the East and of Christianity*, Steiner Press, London 1972.
——, *An Occult Physiology*, Steiner Press, London 1951.
——, *Occult Science, an Outline*, Steiner Press, London 1969.
——, *The Philosophy of Freedom*, Steiner Press, London 1964.
——, *The Philosophy of Spiritual Activity*, Steinerbooks, New York 1980.
——, *The Spiritual Guidance of Man and Humanity*, Anthroposophic Press, New York 1970.
——, *Theosophy*, Steiner Press, London 1970.
Stöhr, Adolf, *Heraclitus*, Strache, Vienna, Leipzig, Prague 1920.
Strassburg, *see* Gottfried von Strassburg.
Tautz, Johannes, *W. J. Stein, Eine Biographie*, Goetheanum, Dornach 1989. Now in an English translation published by Temple Lodge Press, London 1990.
Valentinus, Basilius, *Basilii Valentini Chymische Schriften, alle, soviel deren vorhanden sind*, Republished Gerstenberg Verlag 1976.
——, 'A Practick Treatise together with the XII Keys and Appendix of the Great Stone of the Ancient Philosophers' in *The Last Will and Testament of Basil Valentine*, London 1670.
Waitz, Georg, *Jahrbücher der Deutschen Geschichte, König Heinrich I*, Leipzig 1885.
Wolfram von Eschenbach, *Parzival*, Penguin Classics.
Wueleker, R. P., *Die Arthursage in der englischen Literatur*, 1895.

Sources

1. **Memoirs**
First published in three parts in *The Present Age* under the title 'Reminiscences of life as an aid to the understanding of our time'. London 1936, Vol 1, No. 8, pp. 8–27; No. 9, pp. 6–26; No. 11, pp. 52–64.

2. **Historical Periods and the Fate of the Nations**
First published in *The Present Age*, London 1936, Vol 1, No. 4, pp. 5–11.

3. **England and the Foundation of Commercial Towns**
First published in *The Present Age*, London 1936, Vol 1, No. 3, pp. 5–13.

4. **Portugal as the Preparer of the British Mission**
First published in *The Present Age*, London 1936, Vol 1, No. 6, pp. 5–14.

5. **The Immortality of Nations Revealed in Myth and Legend**
First published in *The Present Age*, London 1936, Vol 1, No. 5, pp. 12–24.

6. **Is King Arthur a Historical Character?**
First published in *The Present Age*, London 1936, Vol 1, No. 2 pp. 5–11.

7. **King Arthur and the Problem of East and West**
First published in *Anthroposophical Movement*, London 1932, Vol 9, No. 2, pp. 9–12; No. 3, pp. 20–21.

8. **The Revival of the Arthurian Legend in the Fifteenth Century**
First published in the journal *Korrespondenz der anthroposophischen Arbeitsgemeinschaft*, Stuttgart 1934, Vol. 4, No. 3, pp. 6–10. Translated by Christian and Ingrid von Arnim.

9. **Basilius Valentinus in the Context of Arthurian Legend**
First published in the journal *Korrespondenz der anthroposophischen Arbeitsgemeinschaft*, Stuttgart 1935, Vol. 4, No. 5, pp. 5–14. Translated by Christian and Ingrid von Arnim.

10. **The Hare in Myth and Alchemy**
The manuscript was found in Stein's estate with the German title 'The Easter hare book for parents'. Probably written in England after 1940. Translated by Donald Maclean.

11. **The Death of Merlin**
First published in *The Present Age*, London 1936, Vol. 1, No. 7, pp. 10–16.

12. **Thomas Aquinas and the Grail**
First published in *Die Drei*, Stuttgart 1926, Vol. 6, No. 6, pp. 648–56. First published in English in *Anthroposophy*, London 1932, Vol. 7, No. 2, pp. 166–77.

13. **The Polarity between Parzival and Gawan**
First published under the title 'Betrachtungen über Wolfram von Eschenbachs Parzival' in *Die Drei*, Stuttgart 1924, Vol. 4, No. 5, pp. 355–68. Translated by Christian and Ingrid von Arnim.

14. Tristan and Isolde against the Background of Greek Mythology
This lecture was the third in a series delivered in Stuttgart probably at the beginning of the 1930s. Found in W. J. Stein's estate. Translated by Christian and Ingrid von Arnim.

15. Tristan and Isolde and an Understanding of Minstrel Poetry
First published in *Anthroposophical Movement*, London 1934, Vol. 11, No. 8, pp. 59–64.

16. The Seven Liberal Arts and the Twelve Philosophies
It was Ita Wegman's wish that this possibly incomplete typescript (found in W. J. Stein's estate) of a lecture delivered in Glastonbury in 1932, should be printed in *Natura*. Translated by Christian and Ingrid von Arnim.